THE EVERLASTING SPELL

by the same author

FANNY BRAWNE

RACHEL

THÉOPHILE GAUTIER: HIS LIFE AND TIMES

SARAH BERNHARDT

THE DISASTROUS MARRIAGE

MY DEAREST UNCLE

THE PRE-EMINENT VICTORIAN

KEATS

From a copy of the life-mask at Keats House

JOANNA RICHARDSON

THE EVERLASTING SPELL

A Study of Keats and his Friends

I am certain he has some spell that attaches
them to him, or else he has fortunately
met with a set of friends that I did not
believe could be found in the world.
FANNY BRAWNE to FANNY KEATS,
September 18th, 1820

JONATHAN CAPE
THIRTY BEDFORD SQUARE LONDON

FIRST PUBLISHED 1963

PRINTED IN GREAT BRITAIN
BY EBENEZER BAYLIS AND SON LIMITED
THE TRINITY PRESS, WORCESTER, AND LONDON
ON PAPER MADE BY JOHN DICKINSON AND CO. LTD
BOUND BY A. W. BAIN AND CO. LTD, LONDON

A.S.

CONTENTS

5

CONTENTS

Part Five

CHARLES BROWN THE EMIGRANT

ILLUSTRATIONS

ILLUSTRATIONS

8

For
Edmund Blunden

INTRODUCTION

ON April 9th, 1818, Keats wrote: 'I could not live without the love of my friends.' Since his brother George sailed for America only two months later, since his brother Tom died six months after that, and since his only sister, Fanny, was virtually imprisoned by her guardian, Richard Abbey, at Walthamstow, he was given little chance of enjoying family affection. He knew romance and friendship, briefly, with Fanny Brawne; for the rest, he truly depended on his friends. And, but for that incurable philistine, Mr Abbey, everyone within the charmed Keats circle gave him immediate, devoted friendship. 'I am certain he has some spell that attaches them to him,' Fanny Brawne would tell his sister, 'or else he has met with a set of friends that I did not believe could be found in the world.'

Keats was the last person, as she knew, 'to exert himself to gain people's friendship'. He despised petty social conventions, superficial acquaintance-ship, 'where all the evening's amusement consists in saying your good health *your* good health, and YOUR good health – and (O I beg your pardon) your's Miss —.' He was incapable of cultivating those who might serve a purpose. He could only be himself: translucently sincere. But no man has shown deeper sympathy with his friends: he could enter the mind of each of them, just as he could share the life of the sparrow pecking on the gravel. He could be solemn, witty, scholarly and flippant, bawdy and sensitive, gentle and tough. He also radiated, quite unconsciously, a personal magic that held his friends in fee. 'If you knew him,' wrote his publisher, 'you would also feel that strange personal Interest in all that concerns him.' The magic that enthralled John Taylor keeps its power today.

This book is, briefly, an account of Keats and his friends, and of their effect on one another. I have begun with a detailed study of Keats and the 'capital friend' who stood only next in importance to Fanny Brawne. One of the greatest blessings given to Keats was, undoubtedly, his friendship with Charles Brown. It was the stolid, vigorous Brown who gave him domestic security, drank with him in health and nursed him in his illness; it was Brown who encouraged his writing, and copied and preserved it. It was the devoted Brown who, after Keats had died, suggested his memorial, wrote his biography, exhibited pictures of him, published his poetry, gave the first lecture on him, and vigilantly guarded his fame. Six years after Brown had died, Richard Monckton Milnes revealed Keats to the English-speaking world; but Milnes would not have published the *Life, Letters and Literary Remains of John Keats*, in 1848, had Brown not given him his papers, and entrusted him with the task.

Brown chose wisely when he chose the future Lord Houghton to introduce the life and work of Keats; but Milnes's work contained many errors and notable omissions, and he could not discuss the central inspiration of Keats's life while Fanny Brawne, Mrs Lindon, was still alive. She died in 1865, having proved to those who knew her an entire devotion to Keats and his fame. She had guarded his letters carefully, well aware of their importance. In 1878, when her husband, too, had died, and her children had given their help and sanction, Harry Buxton Forman published the *Letters of John Keats to Fanny Brawne*. Henceforward, no one could ignore the passion that had shaped the most creative years of Keats's life. The publication of these letters was the last landmark in Keats studies until, at last, in 1937, the letters of Fanny Brawne to the poet's sister were published, and Fanny Brawne was finally justified.

Lord Houghton and Mr Forman were, in their own ways, friends of Keats; so was Charles Wentworth Dilke, who, like Charles Brown, deserves a full-length portrait. It is the true companion to Brown's, for to their early friendship we owe the very building of Wentworth Place. Dilke's literary companionship, his genial family life, the affection of his relatives, meant much to Keats; and, after Keats had died, Dilke showed his practical devotion by solving the financial problems of Fanny Brawne as well as those of the poet's family. He helped Monckton Milnes, he publicized Keats in his *Athenaeum*, and he bequeathed his devotion – though none of his understanding or scholarship – to his favourite grandson.

Sir Charles Dilke inherited a superb collection of Keatsiana – he added to it largely – but his adamant prejudice, his personal tragedy did devastating harm to the understanding of Keats and his circle.

Much about Keats may be explained by the characters of his friends. A thousand personal chances helped to shape the poet's life, and they have helped to guide the course of his fame. The love of Keats has itself inspired strange extremes of behaviour. It has reflected weakness and militant affection, prejudice and enlightenment; it has generated rivalry and bitterness as well as poetry. But Keats, who could not live without the love of his friends, has always made himself indispensable. He remains the most endearing, the most human of English poets. Keats is always real to us, and that to a degree that no other poet has achieved. He touches not only the intellect but the heart. Keats is always magically personal. And that same 'strange personal Interest' that touched his publisher, nearly a century and a half ago, the 'spell' that Fanny Brawne herself acknowledged, has led me to write this book.

I should like to record my gratitude to the many people who have helped me with my research: especially Professor Edmund Blunden, and the late Professor Hyder E. Rollins, whose monumental edition of the letters and papers of the Keats circle has been my constant guide. I am indebted to the librarians of Fulham, Lambeth, Plymouth, St Marylebone, St Pancras and Westminster, the Director of the Victoria Art Gallery and Municipal Library, Bath, the West Sussex County Librarian and the County Archivists of Hampshire and Middlesex, and the Clerk of the Devon County Council. I owe my thanks to *The Hampshire Chronicle*, the Headmaster of Shrewsbury, the High Master, St Paul's School, the Head-master, Westminster School, the Clerk to the Old Etonian Association, the Secretary, the Law Society, and the Secretary, General Council of the Bar. I am grateful to the Trustees of the British Museum for permission to quote from the Dilke and Leigh Hunt papers; and to the Keeper of Western Manuscripts at the Bodleian Library, Oxford, for permission to use the Finch papers. I must express my gratitude to the Chief Librarian of Hampstead, and to the Hampstead Public Libraries and Keats House Committee, for letting me quote material in Keats House and the Keats Memorial Library. I should like to thank the Oxford University Press for permission to use passages from *Some Letters and Miscellanea of Charles Brown*, edited by the late Maurice Buxton Forman, and the Harvard University Press for letting me use excerpts from *The Keats Circle: Letters and Papers*, edited by the late Professor Hyder E. Rollins. I owe much to the late Ethel, Lady Dilke, who allowed me to consult the Dilke papers in her possession; to Sir John Dilke and Mr Christopher Dilke, for making inquiries among their family; to Mrs H. C. Brooke Taylor, and Mr Michael Brooke Taylor, collateral descendants of John Taylor, who gave me the freedom of their family papers; to Mr R. A. Walker and Mr Anthony Walker, collateral descendants of Charles Brown. I am particu-larly glad to record my gratitude to Brown's granddaughter, the late Mrs Osborne: indeed, to our global correspondence (for, like Brown, she lived in New Zealand) and to her enthusiasm I owe much of this book.

J.R.

Hampstead,
January 1963

BOOK ONE

CHARLES BROWN

PART ONE

Prologue to Friendship

I

THE YOUTH OF WALTER HAZLEBOURN

ON the fourteenth of April, 1787, when early flowers enhanced the Lambeth fields, and children gathered herbs round the big lonely house in Gray's Walk, Jane Brown, wife of William, gave birth to her sixth son. Charles (for so he was christened in the parish church, on August 25th) had virtues to inherit: the natural generosity of his Welsh mother, the stolid perseverance of his father, who had come from Scotland – with a bible, they said, as his only property – and had safely established himself as a broker. And if there were further need to explain why the new-born child became, in the course of years, a citizen of the world, one might point to his Flemish grandfather, Le Brun, the Huguenot weaver, who had long since settled in Scotland to escape religious persecution.[1]

Charles was among the youngest in a large and affectionate family; but in eighteenth-century Lambeth his childhood was not sheltered. His father was often away; his eldest brother, John Armitage, was a London merchant; another brother, Henry, sailed the tropics as a midshipman; and so it fell to Charles, as a boy, to carry a blunderbuss and take his turn at defending the house from burglars. There was room for courage: once the thieves were boring a hole in the door to pick the lock before they were stopped.

His education may be inferred from his autobiographical novel, *Walter Hazlebourn*: his mother would not send him to a public school, while his father wanted to give him wide practical knowledge. As a compromise, Charles was sent to a small school run by a clergyman, and a second school where – goes tradition – he met Charles Wentworth Dilke. Dilke was the son of an Admiralty clerk[2] who was working at Portsmouth with Dickens's father.

* * *

The pedigree of the Dilkes of Maxstoke, penned in Dilke senior's hand, stretches back to Thebotaw, Duke of Slesvic, in the eighth century. The brother of the heir of Maxstoke, Fisher Dilke, from whom he descended, had married Sybil Wentworth, sister of one of Cromwell's Councillors of State, and the Dilkes inherited property through her, provided that they assumed her family name. In the seventeenth and eighteenth centuries Fisher Dilke's descendants had duly been Wentworth Dilke or, from time to time, Dilke Wentworth; and in the reign of George II a Wentworth Dilke had been Clerk to the Board of Green Cloth at Kew Palace. His grandson, Charles Wentworth Dilke, was the first of five who would bear this combination of names in succession; and it was this Dilke, a civil servant with many quarterings, who, at Portsmouth, just after his fortieth birthday, on February 17th, 1783, had married a Dorset girl of seventeen. Sarah Blewford[3] bore him two daughters and two sons. Letitia was born on April 4th, 1784; Jane followed on October 24th, 1785, and died in infancy.[4] Charles Wentworth was born on December 8th, 1789 – an appropriate year for the future radical – and William on August 16th, 1796.

The Dilkes had long shown literary tastes: among the family papers[5] is *The Lover's Luck: a Comedy written by Mr T. Dilke*, 1696; and the Admiralty clerk cherished a copy of the Rev. James Dallaway's *Observations on English Architecture*, which he interleaved with his own architectural drawings. He also wrote, and carefully illustrated, a bound manuscript book, 'The Practical Architect', which he dedicated to Henry Flitcroft, Controller of His Majesty's Board of Works. On his retirement this lover of architecture would move, appropriately, to Chichester, live there until his death at eighty-two, and be buried in the cathedral cloisters.

To the young Charles Brown, Dilke senior was a second father; and this solid, civilized family seemed a soothing change from his own. Between him and the young Charles Wentworth, based on a love of literature, and strengthened by Brown's affection for the family, there developed a momentous friendship.

* * *

At school Brown began to study Shakespeare 'without note or comment', and 'in my youth', recalled William Dilke, 'Mr Brown was so kind as to allow me to read under his guidance, and I well remember that both Rousseau and Shakespeare were favourite authors of his, and that he was of opinion that Shakespeare's life ... might be written from his sonnets.'[6] Brown was so versed in the plays that when, in later years, he read Shakespearean criticism, he seemed to enter 'a company whose sole conversation was directed to the merits of a dear friend'.

But in the age of industrial revolution, in a hard, middle-class, competitive world, there was small time for conventional education, and he left school by the age of fourteen for a counting-house and a salary of £40 a year. His parents, encouraged, perhaps, by the success of John Armitage, pointed out that 'no profession could be more honourable than that of a merchant'; and 'nothing', recorded Brown himself, 'would displease my father more than my taking disgust at a mercantile profession. Thus spurred on to industry, I did my best, and succeeded so well that my [brother] resolved to establish a firm in St Petersburg as well as in London.'[7] By the time he was eighteen John Armitage had taken him into partnership, and Brown had crossed the Continent to join him.

'At last,' he wrote of his journey, 'we came to one of the gates of St Petersburg, a high triumphal arch ... We were wheeled up to my [brother's] house, where he received me most cordially, and I found myself again completely installed in the duties of a counting-house ... After the first welcome nothing was talked of, even during my supper, but prices of tallow, hemp, flax, bristles...' There was not much time for him to satisfy his curiosity in this 'wide-streeted, portentous-looking city'.[8]

Yet in *Walter Hazlebourn* one may trace a little more of his experience: in Fidalma Vivaldi, the 'seraph' who abandoned him, one may recognize the remembrance of first love. Miss Kennedy, the original, was the daughter of a governess to the Grand Duke Michael; she deserted Brown for a wealthier English merchant who later died a bankrupt. Years afterwards, she offered to meet her former suitor again, but 'he had suffered too keenly to forget or forgive the injury; and it was his intention to gibbet the lady in a novel'. Brown's intention changed with time. He was always romantic at heart. In the outline of *Walter Hazlebourn*, which he wrote in middle age, he met Fidalma again, in Florence, and left his wife to live with her.

The Russian episode, which gave him the experience of first love, also brought commercial failure. His brother's firm traded chiefly in bristles, and a substitute, fringed whalebone, appeared on the market. Before it was found to be worthless, John Armitage had been ruined. At about the time he came of age, Brown crossed the Baltic home.

* * *

The Russian failure was not the only disaster in his family. Two of his brothers died prematurely; his father drank, and died in an asylum,[9] leaving a considerable fortune. This proved to be a doubtful benefit, for his widow soon found a second husband, Joseph Rennoit Browne,[10] who was intensely disliked by her children. It was months before she discovered that he was secretly dissipating her money; and though she regained control of her property, family life remained so difficult that Brown, in middle age, refused to recall the 'catalogue of dismal particulars'.

* * *

But whatever Brown's domestic disappointments, the interlude at St Petersburg proved to have a certain worth. Late in 1809 he set his hand to *Narensky, or, the Road to Yaroslaf*, a comic opera based on an event in his Russian days. It was accepted for Drury Lane, to be performed there early in 1814.

Narensky brought him the friendship of men of letters and the theatre, whose company would always be his delight. Samuel Arnold, director of the Theatre Royal, had himself written comic opera, and consolidated his career by marrying the Poet Laureate's daughter; to Arnold's knowledge of the stage the eager novice owed much. He was indebted to John Braham for 'unfailing personal civilities', and this, at the height of Braham's career, could have given Brown no small satisfaction. That the leading tenor of the day should, moreover, take the chief part in his opera, was incalculably fortunate for a beginner. Indeed, one can only marvel at the chance which gave Brown such support: for he also enjoyed the 'talents, exertions and kind anxiety' of that consummate actress with the 'divine, plain face': Fanny Kelly, beloved of Charles Lamb. There must have been some expectancy when, on January 11th, 1814, *The Times* announced:

THEATRE-ROYAL, DRURY LANE

THIS EVENING, (1st. time), a new Serio-Comic opera, in 3 acts, to be called NARENSKY or, The Road to Yaroslaf. To which will be added the new grand comic Pantomime, called HARLEQUIN HARPER, or A Jump from Japan!

* * *

From the performers Brown received 'hearty congratulations' on his success; they seem to have been the only felicitations. 'It was received with considerable applause,' *The Times* wrote of *Narensky*, 'through the vocal excellence of BRAHAM and Mrs DICKONS, who were encored in almost every song. We have not room at present for any particular remarks on its faults or its merits.'

Other papers were less restrained: *The Examiner* offered its readers 'the receipt for an Opera ... give directions for a dozen black wigs, twice as many black whiskers ... When you have thus equipped and characterized your hand, a fig for the critic who shall dispute your discrimination.'[11] *The Champion* condemned *Narensky* with malicious glee: 'It would be most unmerciful,' it decided, 'to give a minute detail of the plot ... Almost all the hilarity was confined to the performers, to whom the author had consigned perpetual peals of laughter, under the notion, no doubt, that it was much easier to excite it in others by sympathy than by wit .. Mrs DICKONS danced about the stage with an intention of girlish playfulness not very likely to succeed in a personage of her years and figure.' Nor was Mrs Dickons the only anachronism: 'One spokesman assured us it was summer time, and his assertion was corroborated by the flowers blooming around the cottages, yet Mr OXBERRY came on in a mountebank dress, shivering in a muff.' The unlucky Miss Kelly, wearing an 'epicene sort of fancy jacket', had been 'condemned to degrade herself, her sex, and the stage, by going through a parcel of antics. Oh!' concluded *The Champion*, 'for shame! for shame!'[12]

The libretto of the opera was published, and there appeared a pamphlet, 'Forget Me Not, Favourite Song, sung by Mr Braham in the Comic Opera called Narensky'. Brown himself received £300 and a silver ticket: his free admission for life to Drury Lane. Independent as usual, he declared that he had received far more than the opera was worth, and destroyed every copy of the libretto which he could find.

Narensky was acted only 'about 10 times' and reduced to a mere two acts. Apart from occasional songs, it was worthless bombast. And yet one cannot entirely dismiss it, for it reflects some permanent traits in the author's character: his occasional callousness and sentimentality, his dislike of wealth and cant, his delight in wit and his pleasure in good living:

> The weasel that crept thro' a hole in the wall,
> And stuffed his fur jacket with plenty of grain,
> Was a fool to sneak out till he'd eaten up all,
> 'Twas then time enough to grow slender again.

In the song of Affonassy, the postmaster's servant, one catches a hint of *fay ce que vouldras*. It was an endearing part of Brown's philosophy.

* * *

In 1814, in his middle twenties, Charles Brown was a disillusioned businessman with some knowledge of men of letters and a longing to be of their company. He was established as the agent of his elder brother James, the East India Company's Resident at Kroë, Sumatra.

In May 1815, 'on board the Larkyns, Indiaman', James Brown set sail for England. He had long been mysteriously ill. In his will he left Charles a share of his estates, £10,000, 'and every part of a Landed Estate in the Parish of Lambeth, Surrey, which may devolve on me on the death of my mother'. On October 22nd, despite the ministrations of Robert Bree, an eminent London physician, he died at Osborne's Hotel, Adelphi, at the age of thirty-five. Rumour said he had been slowly poisoned by a native servant.[13]

The enterprise of John Armitage had given Brown commercial experience; the death of James now brought him financial security. It was at this opportune moment that the friend of his schooldays, Charles Wentworth Dilke, whose clerical work at the Navy Pay Office kept him in London, dreamed of building a country cottage which Brown could share. The following month, November 1815, under their joint supervision, the builders started work on a modest house in Hampstead. Dilke adopted his family name, and called it Wentworth Place.

* * *

The part of Hampstead in which it stood was 'delightfully situated near the Heath, and well adapted', wrote Brown, who tried to sell some of his land, 'for the erection of buildings in the cottage style: the ground possesses every convenience, a good road, the stages passing daily'. Wentworth Place, a modest, white-stuccoed block, stood in 'a large-sized garden well stocked with ornamental and useful trees': pear, plum, and apple, and a venerable mulberry. Some years earlier, Dilke had married an engaging Yorkshire girl: Maria, the gay, unpunctual, remarkably pretty daughter of Edward Walker, of the East India Company's Service; and on February 18th, 1810, she had given him an only son, Charley, on whom he openly doted. Maria also encouraged him in his literary ventures; and the clerk at Somerset House was now busy editing *Dodsley's Old Plays*. This sympathetic trio lived 'in a most complete happiness' in the larger half of Wentworth Place; Brown had two parlours, three bedrooms and two kitchens: spacious quarters for a bachelor.

John Armitage[14] had a house near by; but it was not only the thought of his brother which had led Brown to Hampstead. A practical man must have seen the advantages. The village was so celebrated for tonic atmosphere that ailing city-dwellers would ride over every night 'for the benefit of the Air and return to Town every Morning'. In the summer *The Times* published frequent applications for houses. And Hampstead had less mundane virtues: no one who possessed a sense of the picturesque, a touch of the romantic – and Brown had both – could remain unmoved by the green sweep of the hills, the numberless flowers, the fruit trees growing wild and abundantly, the pastoral scenes which Morland had painted, and Leigh Hunt, imprisoned, recorded in poetry.

'Dear Hampstead, revelling in varieties', was the home of Hunt; and when, in 1816, Brown moved into the freshly-painted Wentworth Place, he found himself near the *salon* of English Romanticism. Leigh Hunt was a host of recognized charm. His stubborn radicalism, his enthusiasm for music, his well-informed love of classical, Italian and English literature: there was much about him to win him friends. And so to the Vale of Health there came Thomas Barnes, the editor of *The Times*; Vincent Novello, famed as an organist; and Benjamin Robert Haydon, egocentric, would-be genius, exhibitor at the Royal Academy and triumphant defender of the Elgin Marbles. Hazlitt knew Hunt, and the ineffectual, angelic Shelley would visit him. John Hamilton Reynolds, the young lawyer expected to be a luminary in literature, would come to him for company and encouragement. In this varied, vigorous, cordial society Brown moved with delight, and was recognized as 'one of the most genuine wits now living'.

So life at Hampstead continued in Hunt's cottage, in the garden of Wentworth Place, in the house itself where the capacious cellar, a set of Hogarth engravings, and a thirty-seven volume edition of Shakespeare suggested the inhabitant's affections. It was not, however, in the Vale of Health, or at Wentworth Place, but on the Hampstead Road, late in the summer of 1817, that Brown first met a youth of twenty-one with 'the hazel eyes of a wild gipsy set in the face of a god'.

'In that interview of a minute,' he wrote, 'I inwardly desired his acquaintanceship, if not his friendship.' The 'minutest circumstances' of his first meeting with Keats remained in his memory to the end of his life.

PART TWO

The Friend of Keats

2

WALKS IN THE NORTH, AND WENTWORTH PLACE

KEATS had never known domestic security. The sudden death of his father, the unfortunate second marriage, long illness, and death of his mother, had been followed by the loss of the one surviving relation, his grandmother, who might have given the family a home. As it was, they had been disturbed and scattered: the brothers to Hampstead lodgings and the sister to Walthamstow, where she was virtually imprisoned by her guardian, Richard Abbey. The absence of women from his family helped to embarrass Keats when he met them elsewhere. He was so unassured that people were sometimes surprised to find him the eldest of the family. On one point, however, he had shown unchangeable decision: in the face of Abbey, the uncompromising tea-merchant, who believed in nothing but money and held the family purse-strings, he had recently renounced his medical training for poetry. He was certain of his poetical powers.

Both his insecurity and his decision made the meeting on the Hampstead road the more momentous, for Brown had also had a troubled background, and had renounced a solid profession in favour of literature. In the wise and genial man of thirty, Keats found the companion he needed. In the youth of twenty-one, Brown recognized a friend intensely lovable, whose humour outsoared his own, whose like in wit and depth and delicacy of mind he had never yet encountered. He recognized him as a superior being. 'Every one who met him,' wrote Brown, 'sought for his society.' 'I succeeded in making him come often to my house by never asking him to come oftener; and I let him feel himself at perfect liberty there, chiefly by avoiding to assure him of the fact. We quickly became intimate.'[1]

By the autumn Keats was visiting Brown on successive days for dinner and 'bobbish' conversation, and December found them plodding home together from Drury Lane, where Brown had brandished his silver ticket and Keats had reviewed the pantomime for *The Champion*. On the strength of the silver ticket, a few weeks later, Keats enjoyed 'a spice of Richard III', and by the end of January he was in the habit of copying out his work at Wentworth Place. 'I am a good deal with Dilke and Brown,' he told his brothers, 'we are very thick.' On June 22nd, 1818, having let his house for the summer, Brown left with him on a walking tour of the Lake District and Highlands. At Liverpool they bade farewell to George Keats and his wife, who were sailing for America, and Brown moved, unchangeably, into the position of elder brother.

He was not only the poet's fraternal and 'capital friend': already he saw fit to record the minutiae of his journey: each evening he pulled from his knapsack '1st his paper – 2^{ndly} his pens and last his ink. Now I say,' remarked Keats, 'why not take out his pens first sometimes – But I might as well tell a hen to hold up her head before she drinks instead of afterwards.' Yet Brown's diligent journalism was more than a fad, a habit surviving from early commercial days, more than the instinct to describe his holidays to a friend. Those who knew Keats felt a strange personal interest in all that concerned him; they preserved his letters, copied his poetry, noted the slightest incidents of his life, conscious that they lived with genius. 'And who am I?' asked Brown. 'Not one indeed who can share the transports of his imagination, but an humble plodding man, a commonplace fellow, who had the foresight to carry with him pens and paper, and the wilful industry to write a sketch of all he saw and all he felt.'[2] Brown was more than commonplace: he had the inspiration to understand, even now, that he must be a Boswell.

He also assisted the poet's muse; for as he walked with Keats towards Ballantrae, skirting the wooded hills and craggy mountains, he told him *Guy Mannering* in its native setting.

There was a little spot, close to our pathway, where, without a shadow of doubt, old Meg Merrilies had often boiled her kettle, and, haply, cooked a chicken. It was among fragments of rock, and brambles, and broom, and most tastefully ornamented with a profusion of honeysuckle, wild roses, and fox-glove, all in the very blush and fulness of blossom. While finishing breakfast, and both employed in writing, I could not avoid noticing that Keats's letter was not running in regular prose. He told me he was writing to his little sister, and giving a ballad on old Meg for her amusement. Though he called it too much a trifle to be copied, I soon inserted it in my Journal.

Twenty-two years later, he would recall his 'Walks in the North' for *The Plymouth and Devonport Weekly Journal*. Now, on August 7th, from Inverness, he sent a note to Dilke's nephew, Henry Snook, at Eton:

> Mr Keats will leave me here, and I am full of sorrow about it, he is not well enough to go on; a violent cold and an ulcerated throat make it a matter of prudence that he should go to London in the Packet.[3]

Twelve days later, at Wentworth Place, Maria Dilke recorded: 'John Keats arrived here last night, as brown and as shabby as you can imagine; scarcely any shoes left, his jacket all torn at the back, a fur cap, a great plaid, and his knapsack. I cannot tell what he looked like.'

* * *

Keats returned to find the *Blackwood's* review of *Endymion* (but, wrote his publisher, James Hessey, 'Keats does not seem to care at all about Blackwood, he thinks it so poorly done').[4] He returned to his momentous meeting with Fanny Brawne. It was Brown who had let his house to Mrs Brawne and her children for the summer: Brown who was indirectly responsible for her friendship with the Dilkes, and for her decision to settle again in Hampstead. It was Brown who introduced Keats, now, to her mercurial yet steadfast daughter: to this child of eighteen who would show Keats more constant understanding than any of her numberless detractors. Fanny Brawne entered the life of Keats with exquisite precision, when marriage was in his mind, when he was losing his forced indifference to women, when he was profoundly in need of gaiety and comfort. He loved her irrevocably, and at once. And then, on December 1st, after lingering illness, Tom Keats died of consumption. Keats had lost both his brothers in six months. In that moment of unsurpassed loneliness, he turned to Brown instinctively. Within an hour of Tom's death, Brown invited Keats to live with him.

In mid-December Keats moved from Well Walk to Wentworth Place. He paid £5 a month for his board, and Brown 'always had a running account' with him and noted such expenses as 'Examiners – 2.10.0. Half

Wine and Spirits' bill – 5.9.6. Boot-makers bill – 3.6.6.' But it was never merely a business arrangement: Brown was devoted to Keats, and Keats had assured himself of the daily companionship he needed.

Brown's ebullient social life soon burst upon him. They went with Hunt to Novello's for music, cheese, and 'true Lutheran beer'. Soon afterwards, John and James, the children of John Armitage, scampered into Wentworth Place, and Brown, the model of avuncular affection, bore them off to the menagerie at the Tower to see the lions. In January 1819, he and Keats set off to visit old Mr Dilke at Chichester. 'You will find him a very odd young man,' warned Maria Dilke, introducing the poet, 'but good-tempered, and good-hearted, and very clever indeed.'[5] From Chichester they walked to Bedhampton, to stay with Letitia Dilke, now Mrs John Snook, and 'have a little Religion and politics together almost every evening'. In the intervals they talked farming, ate game, saw a chapel consecrated, and dispatched a flirtatious note to 'charming, dear Mrs Dilke' in Hampstead. 'Nothing worth speaking of happened at either place', Keats told George, in America. 'I [wrote] a little Poem call'd "St Agnes Eve".'

Early in February they were home, and Fidalma's suitor was busy writing Fanny Brawne a valentine. Charles Brown might be unkind to the stupid, plain and middle-aged, but he remained susceptible to the fair, intelligent and young; besides, he prided himself on his versifying: 'In my time I have penned many Valentines,' he confessed in *The New Monthly Magazine*, 'and have been *professionally* consulted on many more … I have in my possession a considerable stock of poems of this sort.'[6]

*   *   *

Brown makes some social appearances in the letters of 1819: he has tea with the Dilkes on Charley Dilke's ninth birthday. ('Dilke makes the most delightful father I ever saw,' Maria reported to Chichester. 'He never allows the boy to see him in a bad temper.'[7]) He gives a party for Burridge Davenport, the dull but kindly merchant from Church Row, 'Miss Barnes Miss Winter with the Children'[8]; he entertains Joseph Severn, the future Gold Medallist of the Royal Academy, and John Cawthorn, bookseller to the Princess of Wales, 'print-virtuoso', and the publisher of *Narensky*.

There were, however, less fortunate entertainments: in April 'the Boys', Brown's nephews, reappeared, on their Easter holidays, and made what Keats described as 'a bit of a racket'. 'I recollect Keats coming down to breakfast', wrote James, plausibly, 'and sitting opposite to me looking very ill and dejected. I have a perfectly clear recollection of his solemn sad eyes and my Uncle pressing him to take a cup of arrowroot.'[9] James also recalled, at the end of the century, that the poet often wrote in a summer-house in the front garden: it was probably a mirage in his memory. Nowhere at Wentworth Place could Keats escape 'the little Browns'. 'They have been a toothache to me', he wrote, when the servant fetched them at last: 'Their little voices are like wasps stings.' But their uncle offered him compensation at a claret feast, and Keats delighted in claret 'to a degree'. The genial Dilke was there, and John Hamilton Reynolds, with 'a laugh that sat as easy on his unpuckered lips as if he were born laughing'; Robert Skynner came, Brown's solicitor, and Mancur,[10] that benevolent and elusive man of letters; John Armitage Brown arrived, still an energetic speculator; and John Martin, epicure and publisher – he had sold Brown's comic opera – and future librarian to the Duke of Bedford. They were company after Brown's own heart, and the eight of them became 'a little tipsy – but pleasantly so'.

* * *

These social occasions punctuated the life of lettered ease which Brown had always wanted to lead. He was absorbed in literature, needing no title-page to identify Marlowe or Ben Jonson, Webster or Dekker, Massinger, Beaumont and Fletcher. To Shakespeare he gave 'affectionate homage, unalloyed admiration', but he did not thoughtlessly accept Shakespeare's work. He could suggest which three-fifths of *Pericles* were not from Shakespeare's pen, and compare *All's Well That Ends Well* with Boccaccio. It is said that he taught Keats all he knew of Ariosto; he would certainly argue with him on the merits of Rousseau; and an informed, provocative companion Keats must have found him.

Little of Brown's own writing at this period is identified, but perhaps it was now that he began to appear in Colburn's *New Monthly Magazine*. His known work, genial, frivolous, and sometimes earthy, includes what he would have called a fairy-tale, an essay in the *genre* in which he believed himself to excel:

Brown and I [so Keats described it] sit opposite one another all day authorizing ... He is at present writing a Story of an old Woman who lived in a forest and to whom the Devil or one [of] his Aid de feus came one night very late and in disguise ... On going he leaves her three pips of eve's apple – and some how she, having liv'd a virgin all her life, begins to repent of it and wishes herself beautiful enough to make all the world and even the other world fall in love with her. So it happens – she sets out from her smoaky Cottage in magnificent apparel; the first city she enters eve[r]y one falls in love with her – from the Prince to the Blacksmith. A young gentleman on his way to the church to be married leaves his unfortunate Bride and follows this nonsuch. A whole regiment of soldiers are smitten at once and follow her. A whole convent of Monks in corpus christi procession join the Soldiers. The Mayor and Corporation follow the same road. Old and young, deaf and dumb – all but the blind are smitten and form an immense concourse of people who – what Brown will do with them I know not. The devil himself falls in love with her flies away with her to a desert place – in consequence of which she lays an infinite number of Eggs. The eggs being hatched from time to time fill the world with many nuisances such as John Knox – George Fox – Johanna Southcote – Gifford ... Brown is going on [Keats added four days later] with the story of his old woman and the Devil – He makes but slow progress – the fact is it is a Libel on the Devil and as that person is Brown's Muse ... how can he expect to write – Either Brown or his muse must turn tale.

And Brown was not above displaying the pangs of authorship; for in the parlour at Hampstead, which could be crossed in two strides, he paced up and down 'a breeding – now at this moment he is being delivered of a couplet – and I dare say will be as well as can be expected. Gracious', added Keats, 'he has twins!'

Even the intricate verse-forms came readily: in April, Brown composed a Spenserian stanza on Keats, Fanny Brawne and her mother, which marked an event in the life at Hampstead. For Dilke, despite his radical views, despite Brown's condemnation of 'the horrid System of fagging at great Schools', had decided to send his son as a day-boy to Westminster. The Dilkes had moved to Great Smith Street to be nearer the school, and, a few days before the stanzas were written, the Brawnes had moved to Wentworth Place. Brown observed the all-absorbing love of Keats with his usual gaiety and some want of tact. Keats retaliated by drawing the happiest Hogarthian portrait of the jovial, stout, be-whiskered *bon vivant*:

He is to weet a melancholy Carle
Thin in the waist, with bushy head of hair
As hath the seeded thistle when in parle
It holds the Zephyr ere it sendeth fair
Its light balloons into the summer air
Therto his beard had not begun to bloom,
No brush had touch'd his chin or razor sheer;
No care had touch['d] his cheek with mortal doom
But new he was and bright as scarf from persian loom.

Ne cared he for wine, or half and half
Ne cared he for fish or flesh or fowl
And sauces held he worthless as the chaff;
He 'sdeign'd the swine herd at the wassail bowl
Ne with lewd ribbalds sat he cheek by jowl
Ne with sly Lemans in the scorner's chair
But after water brooks this Pilgrim's soul
Panted, and all his food was woodland air
Though he would oft times feast on gilliflowers rare.

The slang of cities in no wise he knew
Tipping the wink to him was he[a]then greek
He sipp'd no olden Tom or ruin blue
Or nantz or cherry-brandy drank full meek
By many a damsel hoarse and rouge of cheek
Nor did he know each aged watchman's beat
Nor in obscured purlieus would he seek
For curled Jewesses, with ankles neat
Who as they walk abroad make tinkling with their feet.

The portrait of Brown was one of ten poems sent in Keats's current letter to George: the Brawnes' arrival at Wentworth Place marked the beginning of his most intensely creative period. In April he wrote, among other poems, the Hermes Sonnet, *La Belle Dame Sans Merci*, the sonnet *To Sleep*, and the first of the great Odes, the *Ode to Psyche*; in May he wrote the *Ode on a Grecian Urn*. He seems the incarnation of the poetic spirit, offering in abundance, with humility, even apology, what many accept as his supreme achievement. He composed 'without a shadow of public thought', knowing that he would write even if the labours of each

31

night were to be destroyed next morning; and it was the provident Brown who rescued the scraps of paper and saved the *Ode to a Nightingale*; it was Brown who searched for more of his 'fugitive pieces' and 'rummaged up' and copied his old sonnets. 'He gave me permission to copy any verses he might write, and I fully availed myself of it. He cared so little for them himself, when once his imagination was released, that it required a friend at hand to preserve them.' It was one of the chief blessings given to Keats that the loyal companion of his life made himself the faithful curator of his work.

Brown had considered spending the summer with Keats in Brussels; but – perhaps for financial reasons – he decided instead to follow him to the Isle of Wight. In May he lent him money; indeed, Keats was so unsettled that he considered re-entering his old profession as apothecary or ship's surgeon on an Indiaman. Again Brown showed his vision. He did not express convictions mildly or in theory; he lent Keats a further sum for immediate needs, and persuaded him 'to try the press once more'.

So Keats recorded on June 17th: the date which his adviser pencilled in a virgin notebook.[11] On the first page Brown copied Drayton's tribute to the power of fairy-tales, and beneath it he inscribed his own title: *The Fairies' Triumph*. The tall green ape and dumb, strong-bodied dwarf in the story recall the companions in Keats's impromptu 'When they were come unto the Fairy's court ...'; they also suggest that the author of *Narensky* had not outgrown his affection for melodrama. But *The Fairies' Triumph*, a conventional narrative of the search for a lost princess, a story unfinished in prose and again in verse, is remarkable among fairy-tales as the combined production of Brown and Keats.

Posterity, reading Brown's notebook, watches them at work as, once more, they sit together, 'authorizing'. The errant princes in Brown's tale ignore the fairy warning, and pick the forbidden flower:

In a moment it drooped, it withered, shrunk almost to nothing, then into dust ... neither could find words which might console the other, and they stood there like statues of grief. At length immediately over their heads they heard a most enchanting melody breathed forth; and looking up they saw, perched upon a slender bough, a bird of lovely form, and brilliant plumage, and it gazed down upon them with its dove-like eyes, and warbled its song to cheer them:

Shed no tear, – O shed no tear!
The flower will bloom another year;
Weep no more, – O weep no more!
Young buds sleep in the root's white core;
Dry your eyes, – O dry your eyes!
For I was taught in Paradise
To ease the heart in melodies, –
            Shed no tear!

Over-head – look overhead,
'Mong the blossoms white and red;
Look up, look up – I flutter now
On this flush pomegranate bough;
See me – 'tis this silvery bill
Ever cures the good man's ill.
Shed no tear – O shed no tear!
The flower will bloom another year.
Adieu, – adieu – I fly, adieu!
I vanish in the heaven's blue;
            Adieu, adieu!

Our youths were awakened from their trance of grief by this song, and
having regained their horses, quietly feeding upon the rich pasture,
they proceeded slowly, exchanging but few words, along the road.

It is, perhaps, to Brown's encouragement, to Brown's prosaic setting
that posterity owes this poem; and years later, when Brown himself
'tried the press' with Keats's work, he published *The Fairy Bird's Song* and
followed it with the *Fairy Dirge*: designed, in all probability, for a chapter
of the tale which remained unwritten.

Meanwhile, in the summer of 1819, he abandoned *The Fairies' Triumph*;
and on June 27th Keats left for the Isle of Wight to work intensely on
higher poetry.

3

FRIENDSHIP AND MARRIAGE

B Y July 24th Brown had let his part of Wentworth Place for the summer, and was with him in Shanklin. He found himself one of a party: the delightful but ailing James Rice[1] had been Keats's companion for the last few weeks, and John Martin was there to make up a four for cards. They played 'night and morning' after which the Wentworthians stayed on alone to enjoy a little sketching; and the diligent artist, who had already cut 'a very capital' silhouette of Keats, now turned his hand to landscape: 'The Art of Poetry', Keats explained, 'is not sufficient for us, and if we get on in that as well as we do in painting we shall by next winter crush the Reviews and the Royal Academy. Indeed if Brown would take a little of my advice he would not fail to be the first pallet of his day ... The other day he was sketching Shanklin Church and as I saw how the business was going on, I challenged him to a trial of Skill – he lent me Pencil and Paper – we keep the sketches to contend for the Prize at the Gallery. I will not say whose I think best – but really I do not think Brown's done to the top of the Art.' Brown made amends; one evening, as Keats sat dreaming, he drew his portrait: a delicate, pencilled profile that caught the poet's vision and profundity. Rising above himself, he showed not only care but inspiration.

However, art remained their second occupation. In July, Keats began *Lamia*, and he and Brown collaborated once more, this time in writing *Otho the Great*. Brown provided the plot: a series of betrayals, confessions and violent deaths; and even he remarked that the progress of the tragedy was 'curious'. As he recited the first four acts, Keats clothed them in dialogue, never inquiring about the scene to come; but having heard the incidents which would fill the final act, he suddenly regained discrimination and took the work entirely upon himself. *Otho the Great* remains a strange hybrid. Brown had led Keats back to the adolescent overwriting he had long since condemned; and Keats's potential dramatic achievement must be judged by the fragment of *King Stephen* which, immediately afterwards, and at Brown's suggestion, he wrote alone.

The routine at Shanklin was briefly interrupted while the sturdy Brown

34

'went gadding about the country with his ancient knapsack', and on August 12th they moved to Winchester. Their financial straits were now serious, for Brown, who depended on quarterly and half-yearly 'driblets', had been lending money to Keats for the last three months and was 'not at all flush', while Keats himself, awaiting the repayment of some £230, was threatened with a suit in Chancery and could make no demands of Abbey, who controlled his capital. The only security for the future seemed to be *Otho the Great*, and on the strength of the tragedy he wrote to his publisher, asking for a loan; Brown added his own practical, kindly comment: 'A man of business should have every security in his power, and Keats especially would be uncomfortable at borrowing unless he gave all *in his power*; besides his own name to a Bill he has none to offer but mine, which I readily agree to ... It would be painful to me to have it withheld when it ought to be given.'

Taylor, on holiday, did not reply; Keats sent another letter. Again there was no answer. At last, in September, when they had only shillings left, and lived 'in fear of the Winchester Jail', Taylor's partner, Hessey, sent £30, Brown borrowed a further £30 from a Hampshire friend, and Keats found that an unknown sum awaited him in the Chichester post office. Brown left Keats in Winchester 'to make a trial of solitude', and went to Bedhampton and Chichester 'a-visiting'.

The thought of poetry remained with him as he wandered round the cathedral city, reflecting upon the monuments to great men: Burns's cottage at Dumfries, 'the abode of his unhappiness', and that 'insolent piece of matter-of-fact', Shakespeare's tomb at Stratford. Brown had 'no taste for the miserable ... I never went into Collins' house at the corner of [Chichester] cloisters ... How melancholy it looks! There seems contagion in its very walls and window sashes. Often I stood before it, and before Flaxman's monument to his memory, with as little desire to pass the threshold as to enter his grave ...' He was brought back, suddenly by a letter, to the problems of living poets. Keats, determined to wean himself from Fanny Brawne and from dependence on Brown, had decided not to return to Hampstead.

Brown hastened back to Winchester, knowing, even then, that Keats could never cure himself of love. Keats was inflexible. About October 8th they returned to London, Keats to the lodgings in Westminster which Dilke had found for him, and Brown to Wentworth Place.

It was at this moment of independence that the abandoned suitor of

35

Fidalma, the friend of Jenny Jacobs, the inveterate writer of Valentines, chose to take to himself his housekeeper, Abigail Donohue.

* * *

It is said that he had already married Abigail in Ireland or in London;[2] it is only certain that in October he was living with her. The Donohues in Killarney were active Fenians, and as Abigail was 'something of a firebrand'[3] they had sent her to England to keep her out of trouble. She replaced one of her friends as Brown's housekeeper at Hampstead, and he chose her, their son remarked later, with cynical detachment, 'for her splendid physique, for the sake of the offspring'. She was certainly strong and handsome – 'very pretty', said her mother – with an Irish temper; and a gift for repartee was among her subsidiary charms.

'Suppose, reader (if thou art a parlour-gentleman) that an act of Parliament were to pass, enforcing thee to take Dolly from the kitchen as thy wife. Truly, whatever deserving qualities Dolly might possess, or however good her education might be, we fear thou wouldst not perceive them, partly owing to thine own indignation at so tyrannical a law.'[4] That may be Charles Brown's comment on his marriage. But though he hardly admired his wife, and even her son referred to her as 'a woman of the peasant class', Abigail was not illiterate, and she was probably more than a rustic beauty. Brown respected her enough to marry her, as she insisted, in a Catholic church; and though a Catholic marriage was not then valid in England, he always considered himself to be her husband. Years later, when he was living alone and his son urged him to marry, he answered: 'You forget, I have a wife.'

4

THE OFFICE OF HEAD NURSE

In October 1819, Brown's relationship with Abigail remained of minor importance at Wentworth Place. As he had surmised, the poet's second trial of solitude had failed. Keats was incapable of living in London away from Fanny Brawne. Two days after he settled in College Street, he came to see her; and Fanny, who had suffered throughout the summer from the hard, prosaic criticism of relations, the bitter and uncertain moods of his letters, received him lovingly. Within a week he had decided to return to Hampstead.

He was 'rooted in misery', disturbed by his own lack of money, and by his brother George's recent financial disaster; he probably recognized his indolence and his persistent sore throat as the first signs of consumption, and the very nearness of passion, the return of love, increased his pain. Brown observed him with 'great uneasiness', but 'all that a friend could say, or offer, or urge was not enough to heal his many wounds'. He secretly took laudanum until Brown discovered it and sternly made him promise not to take more. Already, to the affection of an elder brother, the vigilance of a curator, Charles Brown added the 'office of head Nurse'.

And aware, as usual, of the need for constructive advice, he encouraged him to write *The Cap and Bells*. Just as in *Otho the Great* he had given Keats his own bombastic brand of melodrama, so he now suggested a comic fairy-tale in the Spenserian stanza, the style and subject after his own heart. The poem was to be published, so they planned, under the pseudonym of Lucy Vaughan Lloyd, and no doubt it was Brown who gave her an authentic address: China Walk, Lambeth, not far from his birthplace. Keats, who was recasting *Hyperion*, found *The Cap and Bells* pleasant light relief every morning; he wrote it easily, and Brown promptly copied it, on one occasion twelve stanzas before dinner.

But the diligent scribe was more concerned about *Otho the Great*: remembering *Narensky*, he had sent the manuscript to the manager of Drury Lane, and prudently omitted Keats's name, 'so utterly had it become a by-word of reproach in literature'. However, 'we have heard

37

nothing from Elliston', Keats told his brother on November 19th. 'The piece was sent in ... three weeks and more ago. The reason may be that Kean has not return'd, whose opinion Elliston will partly rely on. Brown is still very sanguine.'

Both playwrights had hoped that in the part of Ludolph, Otho's son, Kean would find 'another opportunity to shine'. Indeed, Brown learned, indirectly, that Kean had wanted to play the principal character. But there seems to have been some misunderstanding, for Kean was in America, and Elliston, having agreed to produce the play that season, told Brown that the promise had been mistaken, and that *Otho* would appear the next season if possible, or the season after that. Keats, whose mind was now barren of poetry, depended more than ever on profits from *Otho the Great*, and Brown was determined to make him popular in spite of his detractors; nor, admittedly, did he want to delay his own income. 'I was in hopes of you and Jack being able ... to witness our tragedy,' he explained to Henry Snook, 'but no – at Drury Lane they engaged to play it *next* season and I not liking the delay took it home.'[1]

Early in the new year, when he and Keats had 'patched it up', they sent *Otho the Great* to Covent Garden. Keats had now grown indifferent, and was ready to see Charles Young, 'a ranting, coxcombical tasteless Actor – a Disgust A Nausea', in the part which Kean should have played. To his sister-in-law he wrote: 'I am *not* affraid it will be damn'd in the Garden.' *Otho* was not condemned by an audience: it was 'speedily' returned with a rejection slip in the handwriting of a boy. Brown believed that the manuscript had never been unrolled.

In December 1819, however, the fate of the tragedy lay in the future, and the two dramatists continued their 'old dog trot of Breakfast, dinner (not tea for we have left that off) supper Sleep, Confab, stirring the fire and reading'. On Christmas Day they dined at Great Smith Street, where the conversation turned to fairy-tales, and, fired by the occasion, Brown wagered a beef-steak supper that he could beat Dilke at writing one. Four critics were to decide the contest: Rice and Reynolds, Keats and Thomas Richards (a civil servant and 'a capital appreciator of talent and genius'). But the votes were even, and in January Keats's publisher received an urgent request in Brown's copperplate hand:

> My dear Sir.—Will you have the kindness to settle the contention? You will see [the fairy-tales] are written on two distinct models, – one after the style of *Prince Arthur*, – the other after that of the *comic Faery*

Tales, – the question is – which – and the preference is to be decisively in favour of one of them.

Taylor, recognizing the anxieties of an author, considerately answered by return:

> My dear Sir, – Speedy Injustice is better than Tardy Justice: if I am wrong, therefore, my decision shall have as little of the Sin of Delay in it as possible. There is another Proverb 'When two men ride on Horseback' &c. Now in my Judgment you must be content with the Crupper – (for I know which is your story by the Handwriting).

At eight o'clock on the following Saturday the candidates and critics dined with Dilke; it was Brown, the author of the comic tale, who paid for the 'BEEF-STEAKS AND PUNCH – the food of the "Cockney School" '.

January 1820 was further enlivened by a 'pianoforte hop' at Great Smith Street, parties at Wentworth Place, and a visit from George Keats, who had come from America to settle financial affairs. George left for Louisville on January 28th. Six days later, in bitter weather, Keats returned from London outside the coach, and had the haemorrhage that announced his death.

*   *   *

'Mr Keats fell very ill yesterday week,' wrote Brown to Henry Snook on February 11th, 'and my office of head Nurse has too much employed me to allow of my answering your letter immediately; he is somewhat better but I'm in a very anxious state about him.'

As he sat by Keats's bedside, too disturbed to do creative work, he began to copy his favourite Hogarth heads: their bawdiness and perception had always attracted him, and now they diverted him pleasantly.[2] He copied them in sepia, with his customary diligence, and in March he was still 'progressing mightily'. But Keats, in his highly nervous state, found them 'so damn'd melancholy' that he had 'a psalm-singing nightmare'; he was too weak to rise from his bed, too troubled even to receive a letter. Brown, 'wretchedly depressed', sent to London for Robert Bree, the specialist in respiratory diseases, who had attended his brother; and Dr Bree, who charged four guineas, declared despite all evidence to the contrary that there was 'no organic defect whatever'. In a few days there

were plans for a holiday at Bedhampton, and on March 16th Taylor told
John Clare: 'Keats came to dine with me the Day before yesterday for the
first Time since his Illness.' But Keats again relapsed; and a tired Brown
told Henry Snook on March 24th: 'I have been nurse Night and day to
Mr Keats for 7 weeks – no – only 12 nights [sic]. He will get well by
degrees. This nurseship of mine prevented my writing to you, ... for tho'
I had time enough, he could not endure me to sit down to pen and ink;
even now he has begun to feel quite nervous at the sight of this scrawl
going on.'[3]

Brown's nursing was unusually difficult. Keats hovered between fever
and lassitude, a prey, like all consumptives, to a quickened imagination,
but the victim also of his 'horrid Morbidity of temperament'. Yet during
these first months of 1820 he drew closer to Brown than he had ever been;
and Brown remembered: 'While I waited on him, day and night, his
acceptance of my offices, by a glance of his eye, a motion of his hand,
made me regard my mechanical duty as absolutely nothing compared to
his silent acknowledgement ... It was an innate virtue in him, well nigh
magical.'

At last it seemed as if his health was returning with the spring. He was
well enough to walk with Brown over the Heath: past the gipsy encamp-
ments to Collins's Farm, the little Morland farmhouse where Blake had
stayed, and North End, where the bird-catcher lingered with decoys and
nets, the hedger with his high tanned glove and billhook, and rustic
children played in the lush fields. They wandered down Millfield Lane,
where the primroses glinted in the high banks, and Constable would
come, in time, to paint the big bronze dock-leaves and sere, moss-covered
branches. They made their way through the huddle of disreputable yards
and alleys to Church Row, where the toll-gate barred public traffic, and
the Davenports lived in manorial grandeur. Keats was strong enough to
go to London, indeed the doctor ventured to suggest another Scottish
tour. Keats himself was too well aware of the hardships of the Highlands
to accept the suggestion, and towards the end of April he decided to
go to Kentish Town, while Brown let his house and set off, north,
alone.

It is hard to explain how Brown could go on holiday when Abigail's
child, his own child, was so soon to be born. It is hard to explain how he
could compel Keats to leave Wentworth Place for months when his health
had been perilous and remained uncertain. But Brown did not leave him
without provision: he paid a week's rent in advance at Kentish Town,

and borrowed from Skynner, his lawyer, to lend him £50. And it is certain that, like the doctors, he had no idea of Keats's true condition when, on May 7th, 1820, he sailed with him in the Scottish smack as far as Gravesend.

5

THE GREAT DIVORCER

THE first letter Brown received from Kentish Town was spirited and encouraging: 'I am well enough', Keats had written, 'to extract more pleasure than pain out of the summer'; he might send him some of *The Cap and Bells* as proof of good health. The Dilkes confirmed the best hopes of the traveller, and in June Keats wrote again, vivaciously, assuring Brown of his recovery. Brown continued his journey; and there arrived at Kentish Town 'a letter from Mr Brown, dated Dunvegan Castle, Island of Sky'. The writer was 'very well in health and spirits'. The letter came on July 5th. That day Mary Russell Mitford told Sir William Elford, the artist and politician: 'Poor John Keats is dying of the *Quarterly Review*. This is a sad silly thing; but it is true.'[1]

Keats was unaffected by criticism, but he had now suffered a grave relapse. He had been away from Hampstead for two months, he was spitting blood, he was physically weak, and he was possessed by anguish. He had moved to Leigh Hunt's, in Mortimer Terrace, but Hunt was temperamental, and he could not confide in him; he needed Brown's understanding and reassurance more than ever. In the absence of Brown, as he grieved in the present, and gazed upon the future with apprehension, Keats turned to the past, and magnified it to a tragic size. Accusing Fanny of forgetfulness, indifference, even suggesting that she might be unfaithful, he attacked Brown for the first time in his life: 'When you were in the habit of flirting with Brown, you would have left off, could your heart have felt one half of one pang mine did. Brown is a good sort of Man – he did not know he was doing me to death by inches. I feel the effect of every one of those hours in my side now; and ... though I know his love and friendship for me, though at this moment I should be without pence were it not for his assistance, I will never see or speak to him again until we are both old men, if we are to be.'

'I see nothing but thorns for the future', he wrote again in August. 'Wherever I may be next winter in Italy or nowhere Brown will be living near you with his indecencies ... At any rate I shall indulge myself by never seeing any more Dilke or Brown or any of their Friends. I wish I

42

was either in your arms full of faith or that a Thunderbolt would strike
me.'

Fanny's answer to this letter, the bitterest he had sent her, was brought
to him, by a series of chances, open; the love which he had hidden became
the common gossip of the garrulous Mrs Gisborne and Mrs Hunt. For
several hours Keats wept; then, despite Hunt's entreaties, he returned to
Wentworth Place.

* * *

His physicians[2] had warned him that an English winter might kill him,
and Shelley, told by the Gisbornes of his illness, had invited him to Pisa.
The days were already growing short and cool, and within a month he
must sail. For a moment, to Fanny, the long-awaited marriage seemed
imminent; but she was not yet of age, and Mrs Brawne merely promised
that when Keats returned from Italy he should marry Fanny and live with
them. Secretly she was aware that the promise could not be kept. But
throughout his last weeks in England, she and Fanny nursed him devotedly,
and, though he recognized his condition, Keats felt newly tranquil as he
wrote asking Brown to come to Italy.

Brown himself was tramping on from one post office to another,
vainly awaiting letters. Not until September 9th, at Dunkeld, did he
receive a batch of correspondence, among it the two letters from Wentworth Place. He turned 'undeviatingly homewards'. He reached Dundee
as a smack was about to sail, and the wind was fair. On the night of
September 17th he anchored off Gravesend. Unknown to himself, and to
a passenger on the neighbouring brig, he had moored within hail of the
Maria Crowther. Keats was on board, on his way to Italy.

* * *

So it was Severn who sailed with Keats; and he was not unaware of the
benefits an Italian visit might bring him: in Rome he might work for the
Academy's travelling scholarship, and keep himself while he trained as a
painter. Severn was not entirely disinterested; nor was he wholly suitable.
He was only twenty-one, he had never yet been abroad, and he was much
too highly-strung to be the best companion on such a journey. But Severn
had always recognized Keats as a soul apart; and if, in his own words,
'I obtruded my miniature self on his superior society', that was because
Keats had been a prophet, revealing the hidden glamour of the world,

and teaching him 'the Religion of the Beautiful, the Religion of Joy'. Keats could not be in more admiring, more affectionate charge; it seemed unnecessary to follow him at once, and Brown told the Brawnes he would do so 'in a very few weeks'. 'But I contented myself', he wrote, in his Life of Keats, 'with preparing to follow him very early in the spring, and not return, should he prefer to live [in Italy]. I thought of nothing but his recovery; for all the medical men who attended him were constant in their assertions that his lungs were uninjured; and his mind, I hoped, by change of scene, and renewed strength of body, would become tranquil.' Brown left for Chichester. It seemed that the poet's star was predominant, for the *Maria Crowther*, blown by contrary winds, had put into Portsmouth, and Keats was staying seven miles away, with the Snooks, at Bedhampton. 'Does Bedhampton stand where it did,' Dilke would muse, 'with its little streams running here and there and everywhere, its little picturesque Church, nestling like a bird's nest in its own little wood – and the rookery as of old – and the Mills and their ceaseless music? I rejoice to know that the same kind good people are there, on the hill and under the hill ...'[3] Here, in this most English of landscapes, the most English of poets was spending his last night on English soil.

Brown did not know it at the time; but Keats, unable to go inland in case the brig should sail, was told that Brown was near him.

My dear Brown,
... Land and Sea, weakness and decline are great seperators, but death is the great divorcer for ever.

∗   ∗   ∗

Late in October, Brown returned to Hampstead; on December 1st there came a letter from Naples:

... The persuasion that I shall see her no more will kill me. I cannot q[uit] My dear Brown, I should have had her when I was in health, and I should have remained well. I can bear to die – I cannot bear to leave her. O, God! God! God! ... O that I could be buried near where she lives! I am afraid to write to her – to receive a letter from her – to see her handwriting would be more than I can bear. My dear Brown, what am I to do? Where can I look for consolation or ease? If I had any chance of recovery, this passion would kill me. Indeed through the whole of my illness, both at your house and at Kentish Town, this fever has never ceased wearing me out. When you write to me, which you will do immediately, write to Rome (poste restante) – if she is well and happy put a mark thus +, if — . . .

If I were in better health I should urge your coming to Rome. I fear there is no one can give me any comfort ... My dear Brown, for my sake, be her advocate for ever ...

*   *   *

'Keats' letter to me *I must not show*, – I wish I might,' wrote Brown, 'the showing it would even relieve me, for the thoughts of it quite weigh me down.' The news from Italy came slowly, sometimes at second or third hand: William Haslam, the lawyer, the eager friend,[4] sent on a letter from Severn, comparatively hopeful. Yet even this Brown could not show in its entirety, but read it to the Brawnes, 'skipping & adding' in mistaken kindness. He answered Keats in his old ebullient manner: 'Thank God, you are getting better! ...' 'But I am afraid,' he told Haslam, 'very afraid.'

> My dear Severn [wrote Haslam],
> Your letter from shipboard when under quarantine gave me an extent of anxiety such as my heart hath not known since I parted with Keats at Gravesend. It hung about me intensely for days, and at nights I dreamt of you, but I did not, could not, show it to a soul. I could not bring myself to give occasion to that grief to any man that the perusal had forced on me ... Why have you not kept your diary? I ask you solemnly, for no one thing on earth can give such satisfaction at home as such minute detail as you set out with. If you have discontinued it, in God's name resume it, and send it regularly to me ... Keats must get himself well again, Severn, if but for us. I, for one, cannot afford to lose him. If I know what it is to love, I truly love John Keats.[5]

Brown, also, truly loved him. He continued to feign cheerfulness. Mrs Brawne repressed emotion, Fanny hid her misery in fits of boisterous gaiety. On January 9th Brown heard from Severn: Keats had wanted to kill himself; he was tortured by memory and imagination, and there was little chance of his recovery.

Mrs Brawne was 'greatly agitated'; Fanny bore the news 'with great firmness, mournfully but without affectation'. Brown was distraught. 'Your letter of 17th December arrived here last Tuesday, the 9th. I cannot dwell on the subject of it', he answered Severn. 'Either I am shortly to receive more favourable accounts, or to suffer the bitterest news ... Until this morning it has been utterly out of my power to write ... He is present to me everywhere and at all times – he now seems sitting by my side and looking hard in my face, though I have taken the opportunity of writing this in company, – for I scarcely believe I could do it alone. Much as I have loved him, I never knew how closely he was wound about my heart.'

He sat 'planning schemes of vengeance' on George: for George, on his final visit, had borrowed from Keats, had knowingly left him in debt without prospect of repayment; it was George, he felt, who had helped to make him die of grief. 'Exposure and infamy shall consign him to perpetual exile. I will have no mercy,' wrote Brown. 'The world will cry aloud for the cause of Keats's untimely death, and I will give it.'

Throughout February the tension grew, and he 'eagerly wished & prayed' Keats's suffering at an end; but when, early in March, he heard again from Severn, he 'blundered thro' the letter in a horror' of apprehension.

Dear Severn [wrote Hunt],
... I hear he does not like to be told that he may get better ... If he still cannot bear this, tell him – tell that great poet and noble-hearted man that we shall bear his memory in the most precious part of our hearts, and that the world shall bow their heads to it, as our loves do.[6]

On March 18th Brown sent a note to Keats's publisher. 'It is all over. I leave to you the care of inserting his death in the papers, – word it as *you* please, – you will do it better than I can, – in fact I can't do it.'[7]

46

6

THE CIRCLE BREAKS

Fanny Brawne, distraught, put on a widow's weeds. She was to wear her mourning for six years. Brown mourned 'outwardly as well as inwardly: as for a brother'. Their bereavement was soon disturbed. 'Poor Keats' Death I saw noticed in the Morning Chronicle', wrote James Taylor to his brother, Keats's publisher. 'I wish you wo^d put your best Talent to work to write a Memoir.'[1] Barely a fortnight after the news of the poet's death had come, Taylor asked Severn for help in an official biography. Taylor was genuinely concerned with Keats's fame, and might have produced a competent account, but his venture disunited the Keats circle for the first time. From Brown it roused a burst of righteous and justified anger:

> Immediately on receipt of your letter announcing poor Keats's death [he wrote to Severn], almost in the same newspapers where there was a notice of his death, even before Mrs Brawne's family and myself had got our mourning, in these very newspapers was advertised 'speedily will be published, a biographical memoir of the late John Keats, &c.,' and I, among others, was applied to by Reynolds to collect with all haste, papers, letters, and so on, in order to assist Mr Taylor. This indecent haste over (as it were) the newly covered grave of my dear friend shocked me excessively. I told Mr Taylor it looked as if his friends had been collecting information about his life in expectation of his death. This, indeed, was the fact ... I then came to the conclusion, that Messrs Taylor and Reynolds, who could show such a want of feeling at such a moment, ought not to be confided in by me unreservedly ... I will not consent to be a party in a bookseller's job ... I rejoice you sent *me* the papers, and under the circumstances, I think you will rejoice likewise.[2]

The poet's friends had sunk far beneath their old graciousness.

Henceforward, Taylor's feelings changed towards Brown, and Brown mistrusted Taylor: 'In my opinion Taylor neither comprehended [Keats]

47

THE FRIEND OF KEATS

nor his poetry.' Reynolds seemed to be making trouble between Brown and Keats's publisher, and to be furthering his own ambition: 'Reynolds is the secret spring', Brown insisted. 'It is wished he should shine as the dear friend of poor Keats (at least I suppose so) – when the fact is he was no dear friend to Keats, nor did Keats think him so.' And while angry rumours still buzzed abroad, there came the news that the poet's school-friend, Cowden Clarke, considered writing a brief biography. Brown himself was moved by a deep sense of purpose. 'To give my aid to a thing of so momentous a description as the fame of Keats without being satisfied on every point is more than I can do in duty to the memory of the dearest friend I ever had.' So he told Severn; and Severn, who had sent him the poet's papers, answered with conviction: 'You are the only one to write Keats's memoir.'

There were other affairs to settle. Brown called on Richard Abbey to determine Keats's property. According to the poet's testament, he divided the books among his friends, keeping, in remembrance, Bacon's *Advancement of Learning*, which Keats had known as a boy; he took back *The Anatomy of Melancholy* which he himself had given, its notes recalling the pleasure they had taken in it at Winchester; and he kept the volumes of Beaumont and Fletcher, which Keats had read 'with Great pleasure', two years ago, in his first spring at Wentworth Place. Somewhere among the pages, with splendid prodigality, he had left a fragment of a poem and the first, spontaneous draft of *Bards of Passion*. Now there were other words of his to be remembered: the bitter epitaph he had chosen for his tomb: 'Here lies one whose name was writ in water.' Perhaps it was a reminiscence of Beaumont and Fletcher; more probably Brown recognized it as a phrase from *Henry VIII*, a final remembrance of Shakespeare, whom Keats would have chosen, above all, to sum up his life.

Severn had already designed a monument: a Grecian altar with half-strung lyre upon it; and Taylor felt that on this memorial the brief words of committal should stand alone. Brown believed that Keats's friends should write the epitaph. Yet Hunt, who covered pages with facility, was now unable to offer a few lines. It was Brown himself who suggested a compromise:

This Grave
Contains all that was Mortal
of a
Young English Poet
Who, on his death-bed, in bitter anguish

at the neglect of his countrymen, desired
these words to be engraven on his tomb-stone

HERE LIES ONE WHOSE NAME WAS WRIT IN WATER

Hunt, Richards and Dilke, everyone to whom he showed it, were 'greatly pleased with it'; the words, only slightly altered, may be read on Keats's tomb. And already, towards the close of 1821, with Brown's loving, meticulous help, Severn was working on a happier memorial: a portrait of Keats at Wentworth Place, the likeness of Shakespeare, his 'Presidor', on the wall above him, the summer garden seen through the open window. So Keats, 'like the picture of somebody reading', sits for posterity in his familiar way, leaning his head upon his hand, and scanning the open book upon his knee.

* * *

The last few months, disturbed by the bitter quarrels of friends, bitter as only the quarrels of friends can be, had also been marked by a growing friendship between Brown and Severn. Brown had felt Severn's devotion to Keats as if it were shown to himself; and when Severn, 'ill, out of spirits, and friendless', wrote for his help in solving a personal problem, it seemed like a renewal of his old responsibility.

Severn was afraid that William Hilton, the historical painter – now a Royal Academician[3] – would prevent him from winning the Academy's scholarship. He prepared to submit his picture, *The Death of Alcibiades*, in September, and suddenly learned that the closing date for entries was August 10th; he sent the picture at once, unfinished, but it went astray, and on August 13th Brown was still 'busying himself from house to house about it'. 'Over and over again,' wrote Brown, with kindly wisdom, 'have I to Keats and others lamented your reliance on a band of Academicians, in preference to the pursuit of the art on your own account ... Think of this, my dear Severn ... Do not let hopes destroy your happiness.'

* * *

He himself was still pursuing the literary art. Many poems and articles, in which one knows his hand or seems to trace it, were appearing in *The New Monthly Magazine*.[4]

Darkness! I love thee, for thou art the birth
Of infant thought; and though thy hue be sad
And thy dusk form in sombre garment clad,
Still are there in thee worlds of dreamy mirth ...

The sonnet *On Darkness* holds a reminiscence. Sometimes there echoes a
rollicking song which would have gratified Keats and Mancur at a claret
feast; and Keats himself would have relished the essay 'On Affectation in
Portraiture':

There are several eras, or rather schools, in affectation. The first is
the Lely, or wig-and-armour. [Next] the lady, or cherry-and-parrot,
... the Reynolds, or lamb-and-shepherdess; the Jervas, or wig, or
night-cap and bedroom; the Kneller, or wry-wigged; the Romney,
or white-cap; the modern, or the most superlative affectation; but
this we shall leave untouched for some future paper.

The subject proved too tempting to be delayed; and the article, which
gave full rein to Brown's facility, ended with a salvo worthy of *Blackwood's*:

To say truly, this is the age of affectation. A man will not write his
apology to his tailor, unless you allow him to sit in the attitude of the
latest portrait of Lord Byron; or sing a manly English song without
mincing it Tuscanly; or wear his shirt-collar, unless it hangs by his
cheeks like a white greyhound's ears, or comb his hair, unless it be
with the Milton division running up the middle ... In truth, the
wholesome manliness of England is gone or going ... It is a starch-
collared, man-stayed, French-dancing, Italian-squalling, sightseeing,
splendour-loving, over-excited and sated age.

* * *

Despite his disdain of the 'Tuscanly' and 'Italian-squalling', the claims
of Italy were often in Brown's mind. Keats himself had urged him to go
there; now Keats was dead, but Brown thought of moving to Italy as a
citizen of the world. Late in the summer of 1821 Valentine Llanos, 'lean,
silent, dusky and literary', arrived from Rome; he had spoken to the poet
three days before he died, and by the end of September, through Fanny

Brawne's introduction, he had met Fanny Keats, his future wife, at Walthamstow. As the memorable year drew to its close, there came William Ewing, the sculptor, who had shown constant kindness to Keats in Rome, and now bore an introduction from Severn. Brown showed him Severn's miniature of the poet, and, for a moment, as they returned it to its owner, Ewing – 'so fluttered and confused that I could make nothing of him' – found himself face to face with Fanny Brawne. Twice Brown invited him to dine; and Ewing found him 'very friendly' and 'very kind'. Late in October the prospect of Italy came yet nearer:

HAMPSTEAD. – To be LET, on LEASE, a small COTTAGE, pleasantly situate, containing 2 parlours, 3 bedrooms, and 2 kitchens; together with a large sized garden, well stocked with ornamental and useful trees; terms £50 per annum; fixtures to be taken at a valuation. Apply (if by letter, post paid) to W.S., Wentworth-place, Down-shire-hill, Hampstead.[5]

In mid-November, while the house remained unlet, and it seemed that Brown would be kept in England till the spring, Leigh Hunt and his wife and six children left for Pisa, and he 'thought it a melancholy sight to see the whole of the family stuffed into a Hackney Coach, in search of a more favourable climate and more favourable friends'. The friends were Byron and Shelley, with whom Hunt – who had so often suffered for bold publications – was to produce a new magazine, *The Liberal*; with splendid bravado the three of them, and others, were to contribute their 'liberalities in the shape of Poetry, Essays, Tales, Translations, and other amenities, of which kings themselves might read and profit'.

Of the innermost Keats circle, only the Brawnes and Brown now remained in Hampstead. The village was populated by the past.[6] It was to Italy, to the warm south which Keats himself had sought, and known too late, to the society of Shelley, Hunt and Severn, that Brown longed, increasingly, to go: 'I will lay me down in the sun at Pisa.'

* * *

November brought, to Brown's delight, a triumph for Severn; his *Alcibiades* was found in a battered tin case in the Royal Academy, and Hilton took the lead in securing the scholarship for him. But it was now Brown's turn to be anxious: his life with Abigail had always been stormy, and now that they were living apart, she insisted on taking charge of their son. However small his affection for Abby, Brown doted on Carlino, and he could hardly content himself 'with imagining how good a father I should be, if circumstances permitted it'. As 1822 advanced, the problem grew more acute: Abby changed her mind and wanted to give Carlino back to him; Mrs Dilke asked to look after the child, and Thomas Richards offered to bring him up, with his own children, at Providence Place, near Vauxhall Gardens. Brown would have liked to see Carlino with the Richards family; yet as late as March he still could not decide on the long separation.

But the Chancery suit by which Shelley had been deprived of his children was fresh in memory, and finally set the seal on his resolve. It seemed just possible that the vacillating Abby might gain legal custody of her child. He decided to take Carlino to Italy.

There remained one link with Hampstead to be broken. On June 18th he signed the final agreement transferring his part of Wentworth Place to old Mr Dilke of Chichester. Firmly, as Dilke witnessed it, Charles Brown sealed the assignment, impressing the scarlet wax with a Tassie head of Shakespeare. The gesture must have pleased the watching shade of Keats.

PART THREE

Italian Interlude

7

THE SUN AT PISA

Less than a year after Keats had left for Italy, Brown and Carlino set out on their journey. Brown bought a carriage at Calais – to be sold across the frontier – and on they drove to Chambéry, and on, through a shady winding lane, under walnut and chestnut trees, to pay tribute to the memory of Rousseau; then on again, through the waveless plain of Lombardy, to Milan.

And there Brown met a strange young peer of twenty-two, who was travelling as Mr Tupper and earned his 'very great sympathy'. Lord Charles Murray, the son of the Duke of Atholl, had escaped, he told Brown, from a lunatic asylum and worked his passage to northern Italy; but in Milan he was warned that there was a penalty for using an alias, and he was now to leave Lombardy. His story seemed the sadder as Brown believed him to be sane. In the Italian August, with this 'noble and philanthropic' youth who was to die in the Greek War of Independence,[1] Brown drove on to Genoa, and spent four 'abominable' days in the Leghorn felucca, 'favoured with a storm and contrary winds', before, at last, he landed at Lerici. Only a few weeks earlier, in sight of the same shore, Shelley had been drowned. From Lerici, Brown, Carlino and Lord Charles took a carriage to Pisa, which they reached on August 31st.

There was someone of long acquaintance to welcome Brown to Pisa: the harassed, impractical Hunt, with his difficult wife and his swarming brood of noisy children; and Hunt presented Brown to the author of *Don Juan*. 'Mr Brown, in spite of his vow, has made an acquaintance with Lord Byron', Fanny Brawne announced to Keats's sister. It was not the only occasion on which Brown meant to show his disapproval of an injustice to Keats; but his qualms were soon satisfied. He learned that when Byron had heard of Keats's death, he had ordered all comments on him to be struck from his work. 'And this, foolish soul that I am,' wrote Brown, 'quite satisfied me, together with his eulogium on *Hyperion*.' Indeed, he decided that he liked Byron 'very much'; and the unorthodox peer, who appreciated his radical sympathies, his wit and delight in good living, took a liking to Brown, and did him some small service. It was the only occasion on which Charles Brown, against all his principles, uttered the words 'My Lord', and 'Lord Byron noticed it at once by a quick glance of his eye.'² Soon afterwards the Hunts and Byron moved to Genoa. And there, imbibing Italian wine and Italian sunshine, Byron asked Hunt, with a sneer, for the meaning of 'a beaker full of the warm South'.

* * *

Brown, alone in Pisa, revelled in Italian life; and, independent as ever, he announced to Richards that the Tuscan government was the best in Europe: 'As for the Tuscans themselves, as far as I am acquainted with them, I like them, all in all, better than the English – you need not start, for I am more a Citizen of the World than an Englishman.'

Yet despite the verve in his letter, his insistence on the pleasures of Tuscany, he had not cut his English friends from his thoughts; and there was one tie with England of which he was constantly reminded: Severn was designing and redesigning the gravestone for Keats. He disliked Brown's suggested inscription, and proposed another with a half-strung lyre, and oak and myrtle. Early in 1823, the stone was still not set, though it was nearly two years since Keats had died. Severn now asked Brown to consider a memorial in England.

Brown showed both devotion and discretion. The English Press continued to scoff at Keats's work and jest about the weakling 'snuff'd out by an article'. 'His fame is not sufficiently general', Brown answered Severn: 'A monument to his memory might even retard it, and it might provoke ill-nature, and (shall I say it?) ridicule ... In prudence we ought to wait awhile. Ten years hence, to my mind, is time enough. You, in your affection for him, think nothing can be done too much. Alas! I, knowing the wretched literary world, think otherwise.'

And so they continued to vie in affection; Severn refused contributions from strangers towards the Roman memorial; he was even unwilling to let Brown pay his share. Resolutely, Brown demanded his rights, refusing to give Severn 'all the pleasure'.

8

THE FLORENTINE CIRCLE

By mid-June, leaving Carlino with the Pisan *padrona*, the 'capital friend' of Keats was in Florence with Severn, 'a quite perfect fellow'. Severn, who considered him his closest friend, gladly gave him the reins of the household, and under his sensible management they enjoyed the comforts of home. Towards the end of the month, Carlino arrived on a visit, and in a delicate miniature Severn preserved a likeness of the blue-eyed, golden-haired child who so resembled Abby, the child whose humour and intelligence recalled those of Charles Brown. Abby often expressed the hope that her son would die in childhood and escape eternal damnation: she put her foot through Carlino's portrait, which Brown had loyally sent her, but the boy himself felt no lack of affection.

The Florentine circle, in this summer of 1823, was famous and diverting: it included Shelley's Edward Trelawny, great, glowing, and rich in romance; and Byron, preparing to fight for 'the poor Greeks'. Severn promptly 'made two small pictures of them, they were one and all delighted',[1] and Brown declared he had never seen portraits done with such speed and style. There came a full-blooded artist from Yorkshire, William Etty, and it was Brown's fortune to know that slightly sinister figure who flits round Romantic literature: the Reverend Colonel Finch. Robert Finch, in the style of Shelley's cousin, Thomas Medwin, was an unscrupulous nomad with influential friends and a taste for gossip. Once a poor curate at Hampstead, he had married a wealthy wife and he now lived stylishly on the Continent, usurping the title of colonel and patronizing the arts; he was in time to make his mark when Mary Shelley published his wild account of the last days of Keats. With this notorious character and Mrs Finch (who, said her husband, had 'virtue, prudence, affection, good-sense, extensive learning, refin'd taste, vivid imagination, and complete accomplishments'), with Mrs Finch's sister (the talented Miss Thompson), Severn, and a servant, Brown set out for Vallombrosa one August morning; 'for of course, Brown', Dilke had said, when they were discussing Milton, 'you will make a point of visiting Vallombrosa'. Throughout the summer, the energetic traveller flitted round Italy.

August found him on the wing for Venice, where he half expected to come face to face with Shylock on the Rialto, and the sultry days passed in coffee-houses, perhaps in Venetian *salons* where the *tiene appartamento* continued until the small hours of morning. Nearly every day he translated Italian literature; and in the gondolas and watermen, the Palazzo Bartanzo where the anchorage poles were still topped with Byron's coronet, he was not slow to see a subject for his brush. He was also – and he described it typically – turning domestic experience to account: 'Severn is astonished at my right down English dinners. He, & Messrs Etty and Evans, dined yesterday with me on a boiled leg of mutton, caper sauce, and carrots. What d'ye think of that? and all admirably cooked, I assure you. 'Twas I that scraped carrots and cut capers, and mine was all the praise.'[2]

* * *

Early in October he and Severn returned to Florence, where Mrs Hunt now bore yet another baby at her bosom. The joy of meeting Severn again after three years, the 'prodigious' chat about English friends, almost compensated Hunt for Byron's ill-treatment. Byron, who had been partly responsible for Hunt's journey to Italy, who had given him financial assistance and the copyright of *The Vision of Judgment* for *The Liberal*, had also publicly criticized the magazine, shown his dislike of Marianne and the children, and sailed for Greece without bidding Hunt farewell. When Brown heard the full account of his behaviour, any lingering regard for Byron vanished. A few months later, when Byron died in the marshes of Missolonghi, Brown pronounced a harsh final judgment: 'Talk of Lord Byron as a poet ad libitum, but as a man you had better be silent. There is more truth in those unfeeling sentiments of his "Don Juan" than the world believes, – all the heartlessness, the faith in the badness of mankind, and the anger shown towards goodness, were parts and parcels of the author's self.'

Brown and Severn spent three days in Florence; they left accompanied by a problem child of eleven: John Hunt, who was 'plainly too much both for father and mother to manage'. Leigh Hunt had recited a startling list of the boy's deficiencies; 'and now, Mr Brown,' he had ended, 'take him or leave him.' Carlino's father was convinced of John's good nature and talents, he privately admired his rebelliousness. So it was that a small boy, 'most anxious to earn a good character', and taking inadequate luggage in his hurry, set out for Rome in the first week of October with Severn and a strict but genial tutor.

And so it was that, nearly three years after he had passed through the Lateran Gate with Keats, Severn returned to Rome; he entered it with the other devoted friend whose love of Keats had saved him from oblivion. And Brown, in coming to Rome, had at last fulfilled a wish that Keats had made.

*   *   *

He went to the deserted burial ground where the stone was still not set. He saw the grave from a distance, without emotion, for 'a grave never affects me: the living man was a stranger to it, and it contains only a clod like itself.' But now, continually, on his way through the city, he had to come down the Spanish Steps, or through the Piazza di Spagna, past the high, orange-coloured, shuttered house, past the window of the very room in which Keats had died; and to him it was 'a stronger memorial of his death than his grave ... One single circumstance of his life, brought to mind by a trifle that he loved or hated, affects me always, – but not mournfully, – quite the contrary. I have taught myself to think with pleasure of his having been alive and been my friend, – not with sorrow at his death ... If your eternal sorrowers think it very odd in me, – why, – I'm an odd fellow, you know, and so let the argument end.'

*   *   *

The routine at Rome continued pleasantly, as the two friends of Keats kept house together. ('Mr Brown,' wrote Severn, 'is the acting manager and keeps us young shakers in order.') In a room 'entirely covered' with Severn's paintings, they entertained Ewing, and West, a nephew of the President of the Royal Academy. There came Charles Eastlake, who had just exhibited his first picture, and would in time hold the presidential office; Cook, the Academician, John Gibson who had offered to sculpt the lyre on Keats's tomb, and Richard Westmacott, the sculptor's son. One of the few diverting Englishmen not to be invited was the Reverend Colonel Finch, whose incurable mendacity had now made him the outcast of Roman society. The sentence was severe, and Mrs Finch and Miss Thompson, ostracized through no fault of their own, met Severn in the street and 'inquired after Mr Brown with tears in their eyes'.[3]

Brown himself was too busy to regret Miss Thompson: he was collecting engravings, writing articles for Hunt, contemplating a novel, and an opera libretto for music by Severn's brother; about Christmas time he nursed Severn himself through an attack of jaundice, an act of friendship which called forth a eulogy:

> O! what a good kind man he is! Putting aside his delightful conversation and learning – he has such a fine open and generous heart – that I can never repay the kindness and service he has rendered me – that I advise with him on all subjects – and he always sets me right – he cheers up my spirits when I am melancholy – with his perpetual good nature and ready wit – and when I am ill he nurses me and tells me the cause of it ... I could not have met a more valuable friend – particularly as he is a man of business, he has managed my money affairs and now reduced my expences.[4]

And Brown combined his familiar duties of elder brother, nurse and financial adviser, with those of a tutor: John Hunt, 'after one dire struggle', had obeyed his orders with good grace.

But despite the favourable omens, the triumph was not complete. Brown had offered to keep him half the year. In January, after three months, John left with an adult escort as hastily as he had come. The reason is best given in Brown's words:

Rome, 21st Jany. 1824.

My dear Hunt,

 ... I wrote about John's offer to betray private conversation, and you may tell him, if you think proper, of the consequence. It is true Mr Ewing stopped him before he was allowed to say what it was that Severn had spoken against him, but Mr Ewing perceived, so it now appears, that Severn's obligation was against his own address and manners ... and Mr E. is extremely sensitive on this point ... Now as soon as John had left us, Mr E. made allusions to the subject with Mr Severn, and acted towards him so as to leave little doubt of all the cordiality of their friendship being destroyed ... The great struggle I had in making up my mind to part with John was on your account. You had earnestly hoped, as I had confidently expected, to receive him at the end of six months, from my own hand, a good affectionate boy, and I cannot bear to think of your disappointment. Yet, as I have told you before, – he is better in respect to truth, honesty and cleanliness, and for that amendment he merits your praise.[5]

* *   *

It was evident that Brown himself was incapable of reform. He returned to Florence by the spring, and there, at Maiano, a situation which enchanted him, he took a lease of the little convent of San Baldassare.[6] His study, which had probably housed the relics of the saints, was filled with modern literature, 'not the less Christian', added Hunt, in haste, 'for being a little sceptical'. It was good to discourse of love and wine in the rooms of the Lady Abbess, as Brown entertained the wits of Florence and the beauties of the English colony; and he and Hunt regaled the guests with the irreverent jokes of Sydney Smith until the convent echoed with laughter and cries of 'Oh ma bello! ma bellissimo!'

> There once was a convent of beautiful Nuns,
>   Sing heigh, and their looks were so holy,
> That the pouting and scorn of those pale pretty ones
>   Made the Devil himself melancholy.
>
> Ho, ho! quoth the Devil, but I will not flinch;
>   And his way he by hook or by crook made,
> Till at last he contrived, in the guise of a wench,
>   To be hired in their house for a cook-maid.
>
> Grammercy, sweet maids, could ye ever believe
>   Ye should meet with a snare so bewitching,
> As that he who had offered the apple to Eve
>   Was to cook apple-pies in your kitchen?

Brown's scandalous song, *The Devil and the Nuns*[7] might have been tossed off in anticipation of Maiano.

* * *

'Kirkup, – wicked Man,' wrote Severn, in October, 'stays in Florence from sheer love of it ... It's that Brown – none but a fat man – & one who loves Wine, & has his trowsers cut short – could like Florence.'[8] Brown, it seems, had left San Baldassare, and kept house in the city with Seymour Kirkup, the vivacious artist and Dante scholar. But whatever Severn's comment, they did not lead an entirely Bacchic life. Brown was still a man of business; he now found himself immersed in the problems of *The Examiner*.

Leigh Hunt, a proprietor of the paper, had relied on his brother for money. John had offered him an annuity and payment for his articles, but *The Examiner* did not make much profit, and John had pointed out that Leigh owed him nearly £2,000, and asked him to stop drawing on their account. The financial adviser of Keats and Severn had offered to help Leigh Hunt, and faced 'the most perplexing papers' ever laid before him.

Accounts which should have been duplicates differed in sums and dates, and often debtors and creditors changed columns; there were possibly £800 worth of errors. Brown sent John Hunt his findings, but John's case was not so clear and his son Henry condemned Brown's 'fresh embroilment of the matter'. 'In doing what I conceived my duty,' answered Brown, 'God forbid that I should have embroiled anything ... The words you have addressed to me, written in violence against one of my friends, I should blush to notice.'[9] Henry insisted on Leigh's debts and threatened to charge interest. Leigh wavered on the verge of poverty. 'It would have been better,' Brown told Henry, 'had your uncle endured an ounce of suffering at the first, than thus to be crushed with a ton at last ... Were it possible for me to have a half-hour's conversation with your father and yourself, I am convinced there would be no difficulty in coming to an arrangement.'[10] Transcontinental business was less easily settled. Early in 1825 he was forced to tell John: 'Unless there are certain clauses in that Deed to the contrary, and with penalties attached to them, your brother is still entitled to his due share of the nett profits, and that as long as the Examiner exists.'[11]

Hunt, in desperation, offered to go home as political and theatrical editor of *The Examiner*; and Brown, abandoning the businesslike for the personal and dramatic, sent John a sketch of life at the Villa Morandi which was calculated to touch the least fraternal heart.

The ruin of Leigh Hunt, he wrote, was nearly completed. If he were again cursed with ill health for a month or two, it would be despairing. He lives here, with a wife and seven children, in a foreign country; without a friend but myself ... His house is bare and comfortless; the furniture of the sparest and the shabbiest; there is but one servant, an unskilful drudge, as such a one consents to serve for a pittance; the wife is in fact the servant, struggling against disease, and the children help to perform the duties of the house; the dinner of the family is one dish of the cheapest kind; luxuries, though so cheap in Italy, are there forbidden; they sit over a shivering fire during the bitter cold of an Italian winter ... Thornton, whose abilities promised so much, cannot be sent to school, owing to the expence of three crowns a month, and thus his hopes seem to be blasted, – his schooling stopped on receipt of your letter ... Your brother is fearful of a visitor, – for all are fearful of exposing a poverty-struck dwelling; no one is admitted, and from this cause, but myself ...[12]

One other visitor, however, found a welcome at the villa: Hazlitt, touring the Continent with his new wife. Deliciously he described the moment when he came to the brow of the hill overlooking Florence: an enchanted city, ringed with sparkling villas, bosomed in olive trees. In this glimmering landscape, the friend of both Hunts, the contributor to their *Examiner*, heard the story of the conflict from Charles Brown; their opinions 'perfectly coincided', and Brown asked John for an up-to-date account of the paper's profits.[13] The mention of Hazlitt had the anticipated effect, for John asked Leigh what he wished to be done. 'The general answer to this,' Brown advised him, 'is that you wish for nothing but what is just; and that, after having the entire history of the affair ... before the Arbitrators, you will willingly abide by their award.'[14] John, who once hoped to have Brown on his side, had now quarrelled with him 'in the most unjustifiable manner'.[15] But to Brown it mattered little. Leigh's affairs were suddenly settled from another quarter. Colburn, of *The New Monthly Magazine*, had sent him an enticing offer, and money in advance; and Leigh, whose Italian interlude had been from the first ill-starred, was ready to return to the green and Cockney landscape he sorely missed.

On the Hunts' last evening at the Villa Morandi, Brown and Severn came for a 'proper Bacchanalian parting'. Next morning, dry-eyed, the family took leave of the Valley of Ladies. Leigh found that 'the grave face of Brown was not so easily to be parted with. I was obliged to gulp down a sensation in the throat, such as men cannot very well afford to confess.'

*   *   *

Brown remained the Hunts' business manager. One feels his firmness and astuteness in the accounts he forwarded to England; it was he who arranged for Hunt's belongings to be stored in his friend Landor's villa until he himself could move house and have the furniture valued. In the drought, there was not water enough in the Arno to transport the five packing-cases crammed with miscellaneous contents, and two pieces of furniture gave him particular trouble. He wrote to Hunt in September:

> I must ask you to reconsider the matter of your two favourite sofa's. They will occupy, in space, above two tuns, and the expense of ship carriage to London, with Arno carriage here, will amount to far beyond their worth – at least £5; add to which, the large sofa cannot be taken to pieces ... Landor says there is not the slightest doubt but that it will be smashed on purpose! Even if you forbid it to be sent [he added], I will not permit either of them to pass into unhallowed hands.[16]

Was one of the sofas the sofa-bed on which Shelley had slept the night before he was drowned? Hunt had received it from Mary Shelley, and he sold it to Brown.

* * *

By the middle of October, however, when Brown next wrote to Hunt, the problems of moving sofas seemed trivial. Fidalma's suitor, the friend of Jenny Jacobs, the husband of Abigail Donohue, was once again in love.

> At least I begin to suspect as much for I woke in the middle of last night, and could not go to sleep again for thinking of my dear Euphemia. To be caught at last! Is it not an uncommonly foolish-sensible sort of thing? She has the most beautiful eyes, forehead, nose, mouth, chin, cheeks, neck and all that, and such a figure, such a shape! She is going, (or talks of it,) to teach embroidery in a Convent, the jade! She wants me to marry her, – jade again! ... Yet she is false-hearted on one point, I am sure, for she pretends to be 'tanto innamorata di me!' – this won't do ... I think I've made her a very handsome offer, – to be governess to Charley, or my housekeeper, – whichever title she likes best, – and if neither of these pleases, why I must be her 'amico' in a private way, for I'll have nothing to do with priests, – or I must be unhappy, and cut a weeping willow twig, and hang myself on it. I wonder how it will end.[17]

Alas, he was already married, and Euphemia's principles seem to have come between them. The bill-broker's daughter disappears from record. Soon afterwards Brown moved into his large new house in Florence.

Even when Hunt's furniture arrived, the rooms seemed bare, and the cost of 'curtainising' was outrageous. He sat in his print-hung parlour dashing off 'Italian Chat' for *The New Monthly Magazine*, and inquiring anxiously if Colburn would pay him a guinea a page.

He had some cause for anxiety: Abby must receive her annual allowance, Carlino was living with him, his extensive circle of friends must be entertained, some 'poor fellow' was waiting for a loan, and there were still domestic improvements to make. Mancur, of the claret feast, who was a friend of Colburn's,[18] gave no hint of the fees which his worried contributor would receive, and Hunt was too preoccupied to tell him, for 'Mrs Hunt, who will never have done', had given birth to an eighth child when they reached England. It was in the midst of this confusion, and the continuing feud about *The Examiner*, that Brown received some news which made him 'wild' with pleasure. Dilke was coming to Florence in September. It would be the first time they had met for four years, and together they would go to meet Severn in Rome.

The months before Dilke's arrival did not pass unrecorded. While Brown raged against the stubborn silence of Colburn, he was planning to write for *The Morning Chronicle*, helping an Italian friend, Gianetti, to translate *Macbeth*, and gardening till he was 'quite in a lily dew'. By mid-May his orange- and lemon-blossom gave forth a 'fine rich odour', and 'whenever you want a glass of lemonade', he reminded Hunt, in Hampstead, 'you have merely to step into my garden, pluck a lemon, call for a knife, a tumbler, water, powdered sugar, and "ecco fatto!" – pray don't be ceremonious.'[19] But the guest who most often stepped into his garden was the leonine Walter Savage Landor, who walked over one day from Bellosguardo to ask if there were a portrait of Shelley. 'Landor is anxious to know', Brown told Hunt. 'He begs you will urge Mrs Hunt, in case there should not be one, to make one, either in clay, or in paper, as a profile.'[20] Marianne set to work with her scissors, and dispatched several silhouettes to Italy. The likenesses of the ineffectual angel vanished on the way. It is not known that Charles Brown ever saw Shelley plain, though in Piazza del Duomo, as he slept in Shelley's bed and was waited on by Shelley's Florentine servant, Maddalena, the author of *Adonais* was not forgotten.

It was Maddalena who 'never failed in a Catholic joke' as she served Brown with his *magro*: for the first time since he came to Italy, he admitted that he was unwell. Reluctantly, he left off wine; in May he found himself 'living on bread, butter, cheese, fruit, vegetables, and puddings, and drink-

ing water! So', he emphasized proudly, 'I've turned Bramin!'[21] But there
was brighter news to report: Lord Normanby, counsellor at the Legation –
and novelist in his free moments – had been organizing amateur theatricals.
Lord Blessington and the Apollonian D'Orsay had performed, and the
part-author of *Otho the Great* had watched Lord Dillon 'play one of the
monks in *Bertram*! This gave me', he was forced to confess, 'a horrid pain
in my internals, because decency forbade me the relief of a hearty laugh.'[22]

Brown, who had once refused 'to put his feet under a lord's table',
had quietly come to approve of social distinction. He left his card at Lord
Dillon's house, and Dillon came once a week to Piazza del Duomo, sometimes to read his epic, *The Tyrant of Padua*, and always to enjoy the warming wit and wine of the host. There were other peers and princes whom
Brown must have known: for Landor, who called twice a week at Casa
Pecori, to revel in *sorbetti* and fine conversation, to gaze upon 'the smooth
and glassy Arno' and the no less obvious charms of Lady Blessington,
introduced his admired, flamboyant friend. Brown had a glimpse of the
fabulous Prince Demidoff, who owned gold- and silver-mines, and a
theatrical troupe with which he amused foreign visitors; and sometimes,
at night, he would see the prince who gave Lady Blessington 'the notion
of a man sheathed in a *couvre-pied* of eiderdown': Prince Borghese, too
gross to lie down, would be driven round Florence, dozing, in his carriage.

* * *

At last, in September, a massive Englishman, with an air both genial and
authoritative, an Englishman who looked more than his thirty-six years,
'pushed open the great outer door; rang the bell; said "Good day" in
answer to Maddalena's good-tempered welcoming', and stood warming
himself, impatiently, at the stove. Dilke had arrived. After the first joyous
meeting, Brown described him as 'a grave, fat, comely old gentleman …
Mem.', he added, in haste, 'I'm not so fat as I was, much handsomer than
a twelvemonth ago, and shan't be forty till 14th April next.' Indeed, in his
visitor's eyes he seemed younger than ever. 'Dilke says I'm a boy,' he
recorded, with ill-disguised pleasure, 'and that when I was a boy I was
an old man! God a' mercy! What a monster does he make of me!'[23] The
'uncommonly handsome service of real China' was brought out, Brown
abandoned his Brahmin way of life, and, as Shelley's servant waited on
them, the two friends of Keats outsoared the claret feasts of long ago.

* * *

KEATS
From the pencil drawing by Charles Brown, 1819

CHARLES BROWN
From the bust made by Andrew Wilson in Florence, 1828
now at Keats House

Accompanied by Charley Dilke, an Old Westminster of sixteen,[24] they visited the Landors, and Brown compared the two fathers 'each by the side of his double'. 'No doubt by sympathy,' he remarked, 'they seemed to take a liking for each other'. Dilke who had been so often and so long 'in greek histories and antiquit[i]es', had recognized Landor as a kindred spirit.

Brown dismissed the visit to Rome in a sentence to Leigh Hunt. 'I would not stay at the inn with the Dilkes, but chose to be with my dear Severn.' It was Dilke who recorded the moment when, in almost un-broken silence, he led them to the unweathered stone which now marked Keats's grave. As they stood there, Charley weeping, the stalwart Dilke hardly able to conceal his emotion, Charles Brown turned away to hide his tears.

*　　*　　*

On they went to Naples, to Mola di Gaeta where they read Spenser under the orange trees – Spenser, who had lightened Keats's time 'very much' in his last summer; then they returned to Florence, where Dilke, who 'always felt a cut in the heart at parting from anybody', brought himself to bid farewell for two years to his only son. Charley was to stay with Brown until he went up to Cambridge. And the household in Florence, which Carlino brightened 'like a jewel', was still to be enlarged. On New Year's Day, Seymour Kirkup arrived, triumphantly, with an attractive visitor, and Maria bore the title which Euphemia had refused, that of 'aja del bambino di Signor Carlo Brown'.

As the year continued, Hunt was often in the Signor's mind; for the news of his coming memoirs had reached Italy. Eagerly Brown awaited Hunt's recollections of Keats; but the announcement that he himself would appear among Byron's contemporaries gave him no small disquietude: 'Since you have threatened me, Sir,' he explained to the author, 'I must tell you that every thing, in my favour, coming from you, will give me pleasure; but the pleasure will by no means be increased by passing through a printer's dirty fingers and by being read by ten thousand scoundrels.'

As he heard of Hunt's ventures, his thoughts for a moment played round a partnership which should have gone down in history: 'You have given me an odd dream, a *waking* one. I have supposed that you and I set up the "Companion", – I with the drudgery and what money I could spare, – you with your everlasting talents, – and that we became mightily rich. This of course supposes me in England with fifty other suppositions. Dreaming is mightily pleasant.'

* * *

It was not Brown but Charley Dilke who went back to England, prematurely, that summer. Brown, said Dilke, seemed 'quietly domiciled in Italy for life'.

The comment was not wholly just, for the Signor's household was now disturbed by 'a very fine woman of 40', with a solid income, and, ironically, a title. Brown, virile and assured, had always attracted women; now, himself past forty, less intolerant of their middle age, he was tempted to accept Lady King's suggestion and 'join housekeeping with her'. He discussed his affairs, as usual, with Carlino, and the perspicacious child pointed out the advantages of another income, double Brown's in size. 'Of course,' added Brown, 'the understanding would be, that it was a platonic arrangement, but I doubt if it would continue so, and *that* would not be good for your interests.' He declined the invitation. One can picture him doing so, for his one known likeness[25] was taken at the time. Andrew Wilson – probably introduced by Kirkup or Severn – was a sculptor of judgment and skill; and his bust of Brown, confirming the portrait implied in all the letters, convincingly records the solidity, the shrewdness and independence of Keats's 'capital friend'.

One friendship forced a decision on Brown by the midsummer of this year: he and Kirkup found they could not live together. Brown moved to 1905, Via Maggia, and there could have been no more felicitous choice; he had scarcely taken possession when he discovered it had once been Petrarch's house. It was probably from Via Maggia that, in October, Severn married Elizabeth Montgomerie. Elizabeth was the orphan daughter of General Lord Montgomerie, and the ward of Severn's patron, Lady Westmorland. That 'fiery particle', as he called her, opposed the marriage in the best tradition of melodrama; but the romantic Brown warmly approved of it, and Severn was 'impelled to shape his life anew'. So Severn went; and, early in the new year, came Trelawny; the 'glorious mad fellow' who had sailed with Byron to Greece, whose life made a Gothic novel sound like drawing-room reading. His hand was still scarred, for he had seized Shelley's heart from the fire. This companion, with the appearance of a Cornish pirate, described Brown as 'a huge feeder' and a lethargic bookworm; it was an ungrateful likeness of the gastronome and literary adviser who offered him board and encouraged him to write his autobiography. 'I have been goaded on by others', Trelawny announced to Claire Clairmont, somewhat nervously, in 1829, 'to undertake the writing a History of my life ... seventy printed pages are already done – no one has seen it but Brown and Landor – and they urge me on.' Trelawny's physical prowess was hardly matched by his literary skill, and his education had been so neglected that his memoirs had to be largely rewritten. Brown pointed out the moral to Carlino, and, years afterwards, when Carlino's children grew lazy, the lesson was repeated to them.

* * *

In March 1829, as Trelawny was settling in the Via Maggia, his authorship so fostered by Brown that he planned to write Shelley's life, two more visitors made their appearance: James Cobbett and his sister, the children of the Radical journalist, the agitator for parliamentary reform, the impassioned author of *Rural Rides*. 'Beautiful day,' James noted, as they walked to Bellosguardo, 'the buds of the pear-trees are bursting, and the white thorn is coming out in leaf'; from the hilltop they gazed across the valley of the Arno which was covered with vines and corn and 'besprinkled with white houses as an English grass-plot is with daisies', and Brown remarked that a friend from London had missed the English woods, live hedges and green fields. Had it been Hunt, who loved Hampstead Heath with such abiding affection? 'Give me Tuscany in Middlesex or Berkshire', Hunt had written, 'and the valley of Ladies between Harrow and Jack Straw's Castle.'

The Cobbetts left for Rome, equipped with a tantalizing document given them by an Englishman, 'a housekeeper himself', who was 'about as well informed as it is possible to be'. Brown's account of the cost of living in the late 1820s gives a pleasant suggestion of the household at Via Maggia: 'Best last year's red wine, per bottle, 4d. Turkies (small), each, 2s. House-maid, £4 per annum. Clever man-servant, £16.' And, since there had been a reconciliation, Brown also wrote, in his most clerkly style, to Colonel Finch:

My dear Sir,
    It is little to say that I take on myself the responsibility of introducing to you Miss and Mr Cobbett, Junr., because I am certain you will thank me. To you and me they have an interest, exclusive of

themselves, on account of their father, who has effected more, in a political point of view, than any other man of his age ... They give the lie to the million slanders that the venal press of England has poured forth against him. You will find his son and daughter good and sensible beings, without show, affectation, pretence, or presumption. Miss Cobbett is a greater favourite of mine than I have yet told her.[26]

* * *

The 1820s drew to an end. Severn was 'daughter'd'. Landor, banished from Tuscany by mistake, expostulated with the Grand Duke, had his sentence annulled, and returned to Florence 'roaring with laughter'.[27] Brown took Carlino away from school, maintaining that walks on the Tuscan hills were more useful than books. He believed so strongly in independence that he taught him not to say 'Sir' to anyone; and there were vehement words about Carlino's education: he was brought up, Landor told Crabb Robinson, on the principle of doing what he liked, and he was 'the wickedest boy he had ever known'.

The verdict was not entirely just: Brown believed in discipline. When Carlino sulked, he consulted his watch: 'You have stood in that corner', he said, 'for five minutes to please yourself. Now stand there another five to please me.'[28] Yet Landor spoke with a certain feeling of the boy's misdeeds, for Carlino often played with his four children, and one of their favourite occupations was to slide down the stairs in fruit-baskets; Landor's meditations had been more than once disturbed as the baskets upset and flung their shrieking passengers against his study door.[29] Landor's rage was, however, vain: Jean-Jacques had decreed that nature should guide education, and Charles Brown never failed to take Jean-Jacques to heart.

In 1829, accompanied by his sturdy son, he seldom found a ten-mile walk too long as he strode to Settignano to admire the view, or climbed the castled hill above the deserted Villa Morandi. It was on his explorations that he discovered Arcetri; and less than a year after he had moved into Petrarch's house, he prepared to establish himself in Galileo's, where 'the Dominicans annoyed him, and where Milton visited him'. He set to work, cultivating the owner, 'a spacious lady of sixty ... Don't be jealous of this spacious lady,' he comforted Mrs Hunt, 'I assure you, on my honour, nothing has hitherto passed between her and me in any way improper, – unless it be the money I paid her for a barrel of Certosa wine.'[30]

Another proposition was hatching in his fertile mind. Hunt had turned novelist, booksellers said that novels were profitable, and the friend of Keats, who had written opera and tragedy, verse, translation, essay and criticism, would hardly hesitate to try such a simple *genre*. 'Pray ask Hunt', he requested Marianne, 'if Colburn would *engage* to purchase a novel in two or three vols *to be* written by me ... The scene would be in Florence about three hundred years ago, immediately after the destruction of the republic.'[31]

He would enjoy declaring his opinions through fiction; it was direct personal writing that he disliked. Hunt, in his memoirs, had called him grave. 'I was angry,' Brown objected, 'at your publicly noticing my grave face – my curse. Had I a hump back, would you have called every one's attention to it? I hate the present literary fashion of being personal.'

* * *

Yet Charles Brown has left a pleasant self-portrait, drawn in this year of grace. 'Now I'll put you into a violent passion', he warned Leigh Hunt in London. 'I have been studying Mother Rundell and Father Kitchener, – and the result is this in my store-room; – 200 Tuscan pounds weight, including cherry brandy, of preserves; of sauces, various, two gallons ... Mixed pickle, 2 gallons; pickled wallnuts 3 quarts. I know that, as you read this list, you are stamping your feet and tearing your hair ... Mem. brandy peaches must now be put in practice.'[32] The only fruit he could not eat were apricots, and he assumed Carlino was allergic to them, too. Apricots were banned from the store-room; and Carlino, who enjoyed them, was compelled to have his feasts in secret.[33]

Brown's sociability, like his *gourmandise*, had not altered with the years. Landor frequently entertained his 'good kind' friend at the Villa Gherardesca, his new and handsome house near Fiesole. Here, among the clouds of olive trees, the spires of cypress, and accompanied by Landor's tame leveret, his formidable mastiff, Parigi, or Cincirillo, the cat, they would stroll discussing questions as wide as literature. Occasionally Brown met Mr Nicholson, 'an Irish Gent': with a large family and 'the indiscriminate good nature and hospitality of his countrymen'. He came, in time, to know G. P. R. James, the author of the triumphant *Darnley* and a further sixty novels. He had taken up whist again, and, as usual, with his 'cold-blooded calculation, beat all the table'. Trelawny, who had gone to live with his daughter, Zella Trelawny, might abuse him for 'whisting', but, as the winter drew on, Brown was asked to parties every night, and had to restrict himself to three a week. One regular invitation, however, he accepted: on Sundays he always visited Colonel Wardle.

Gwyllm Lloyd Wardle, now in his sixties, could look back on a varied career: Harrow, Cambridge, the 'ancient British Light Dragoons', gin-distilling, and the House of Commons. As the Member for Okehampton, he had accused the Duke of York and his mistress, Mrs Clarke, of corruption, caused a seven-weeks' debate in Parliament, and proved sufficient indiscretions for the Duke to retire from the post of Commander-in-Chief of the British Army. His speech on political economy had earned him the freedom of the City, even the striking of a Wardle medallion; then, like a meteor, he had fallen from popularity, lost a further action against Mrs Clarke, and found himself forced to lead a farmer's life, 'selling milk about Tonbridge'. Under financial pressure, he had fled to the Continent.

It was an original circle of friends in which Brown moved in 1829.

9

CHARLES BROWN, BIOGRAPHER

At last, as the decade drew to its close, Brown was once more reminded of the pre-eminent figure in his life. He received a letter from Galignani, the Parisian publishers, saying they were about to publish the poems of Keats.

He answered 'in a manner to make them wish for my pen', offering a memoir, mentioning the unpublished manuscripts he guarded. He decided that, whether or not they accepted it, the time had come to write Keats's life. He would correct Hunt's impression of 'a whining, puling boy', resenting his humble origin ('though you and I', he wrote to Dilke, 'would not have cared if Keats had been the hangman's bastard'). He would show them the man he 'dearly loved, and honoured as a superior being'. He would explain the poet's financial distress, expose the malice of the critics, and set him in his place in literature. Uncertain of money though he was, determined though he could be to secure his payment as a journalist, Brown expected to make a loss on his memoir. His life of Keats was, from the first, and in the fullest sense, a work of love. A few days before Christmas, 1829, he wrote to the three people who, besides himself, were most intimately concerned.

*   *   *

He broke a long silence to ask Fanny Brawne if he might publish letters which concerned her, and poems which Keats had addressed to her and he himself had copied. 'It is impossible to me to judge of your feelings, ... but whatever they are, you are certain that I shall obey them. To my mind,' he wrote, 'you ought to consent, as no greater honour can be paid to a woman than to be beloved by such a man as Keats. As his love for you formed so great a part of him, we may be doing him an injustice in being silent on it.' Fanny Brawne received the letter within a week of her mother's tragic death; in her answer, which reflected deep and immediate emotion, she gave him permission to publish all he wanted: *'To your publishing his poems addressed to me I do not see there can be any objection ... if* you think them worthy of him. I entirely agree with you that if his life is to be published, no part ought to be kept back ... It is perhaps the duty of those who loved and valued him best to vindicate him also, and if it can be done, all the friends that time has left him and I above all must be deeply indebted to you.'[1] Fanny Brawne did not, for a moment, show a lack of proportion; her letter fairly measured the love which lasted all her life.

Severn, too, answered eagerly:

> ... I feel that if you can get over my defective writing, and promise me (which I know you will) not to expose it to the public as mine (for I am not a little proud of Keats as my friend) that I can supply you with ample materials ...
>
> I ... shall be proud to make my appearance as the unchanged friend of Keats, loving his memory now he is dead, as I did himself and his works when he was alive, and this is an honour that no one shall share with me, not even the engraver, for I will take up the graver once more and fancy myself inspired to give his resemblance to the world, faulty as it may be, yet done with all my heart and soul.[2]

Severn agreed that the profits from the memoir should be spent in foster-ing Keats's fame, that his friends should raise a Roman monument to his memory: 'Something very handsome' might be made for £200, and already he imagined a bas-relief: 'It is Keats sitting with his half-strung lyre – the three Fates arrest him – one catches his arm – another cuts the thread – and the third pronounces his end ... As his gravestone is so un-worthy,' he explained to Brown, 'and as the spot is so beautiful, I hope you will agree to it.' In his sketch-book he roughly drew the classical figures, Keats in their midst; a design which, alas, was never transferred to stone.

Brown's letter to Dilke, on December 17th, 1829, revived an important question. For the past nine years, since George had sailed for America, Brown had been concerned with the brothers' financial relations; he could not exculpate George from grave injustice to Keats. In 1824 George had sent a long explanation to Dilke, asking him to make a public defence; Dilke had sent a summary to Brown,[3] and 'what you have written', Brown answered, 'has given me pleasure ... No one would rejoice more than myself to find him guiltless of the charge against him; and when I can rejoice on that score, I will make him all the amends in my power.

At present every thing rests on his own assertion, not only in opposition to his brother's, but to Mr Abbey's.'[4]

For more than nine years, however, Brown had believed that George had wronged his brother; for more than nine years, in the opinion of Dilke and of others, Brown had made a cruel and baseless charge. Now, at last, as he prepared to write the poet's life, he opened 'a bundle of papers which belonged to Keats, part in his own handwriting ... They were', he told Severn, 'chiefly letters between Keats and his brothers ... After awhile, as if by an invisible hand, a passage in one of George's own letters was turned towards me, which gave the lie direct to the groundwork of his defence! I then searched further, and found an Acc^t Curr^t of Abbey's; when, by these two documents, I was instantly enabled to prove that every tittle of his defence was false.'[5] He asked Dilke for a verbatim copy of George's letter: 'Be not fearful that I will make a cruel use of the letter from George ... All that I want,' he explained, 'is authority for stating that Keats's generosity, ... diminished his fortune, or rather finished it.'[6]

Dilke did not send a copy of the letter; he still denied that Keats had been left in debt through kindness to George. Brown again bent his brows over George's old defence, putting it under 'keen scrutiny, backed by staunch documents. [I] have no hesitation', he answered, 'in declaring that if that is his defence, and if you believe in it, you have been grossly imposed on.' Point by point he refuted it:

1st. *John was indebted to George* ... Here is a passage from a letter written by [George] to John, on 18th. March 1818: – 'I intend calculating the probable amount *Tom and I are indebted to you.*'

2nd. *John had not one shilling.* – that is, in June 1818. Now I have before me Abbey Cock & Co's Acct. Current with John ... They acknowledge themselves debtors to him on 4 June 1818 for £500.

3rd. *John received £300 from George* before he first went to America. Here I am the principal evidence. Immediately after our leaving George at Manchester, John told me that George had repaid the monies, furnished to him, when under age, with £70 or £80 ... This John did not believe was sufficient, and regretted that George had not kept, as he had expected, a regular account ... Now it is impossible that John could have related this to me

73

within two or three days after having received £300 from him ... John, in all likelihood, was, even at that time, his creditor.

4th. He says that, on his return to America, he arrived with exactly £700. Then, forgetting his arithmetic, in his haste to depreciate Tom's estate and prove that he, a creditor for more than £400, only borrowed of John £170, he makes it out that he could not possibly have left London with more than £440, – unless, indeed, some kind friend there made him a present of £260, and paid his passage!

5th. You make him say Tom's estate, after paying the Doctor's bill, and the funeral expences, was reduced to about £1,600 ... So, Sawrey's bill, (a moderate one, though I forget the amount,) and the Undertakers, (under £28,) amounted to about £400!

6th. George says he left £100 with John, when he went, for the second time, to America. John, after taking leave of him, in town, came to me at Hampstead, pulled out a packet of notes from his pocket, placed them in my hands, and told me that was all George had left him. I counted them instantly; they amounted to £40. He and I then sat down to calculate how much he owed and we found it to be about £60; so he was left by George about £20 in debt.

7th. George says that, on his return from America, he found that John had used £100 of Tom's estate. John told me he had not touched a penny of it, and that George had taken it all, except the £40. John was certainly in the right, as I can pretty well prove.[7]

More than once, as he wrote his account of George's 'crime', Brown was tempted to burn it. But he restrained himself, for it remained the proof of his own right judgment, the explanation of Keats's penury; it was, above all, the proof that Keats had not wrongly accused his brother. Brown felt inclined to use the papers vindictively, but he contented himself with asking Dilke to circulate his letter.

As Keats had recognized, years ago, Dilke felt he had no character unless he had made up his mind about everything. He had decided that George was innocent; and, confronted by this scrupulous and exhaustive summary, he still refused to believe in George's guilt. He took Brown's account as an attack on his own integrity. He answered with such insolence, such vehement and unjust accusations that the friendship which had lasted since they were boys at school was, by this single letter, damaged beyond repair.

> My dear Dilke [answered Brown on March 31st, 1830],
> You have wounded me to the quick. I could not have believed that any one I am acquainted with, far less you, would treat me, both in matter and manner, with such injustice ... You have it in your power, you aver, to prove every thing in George's favour – do it then, and I will bow to him, honour him, make him every amends in my power. I shall be rejoiced to find, by conclusive evidence, that my Keats's brother did not behave as I believe he did, that he did not borrow money without an acknowledgment, and then declare himself a creditor – and that my Keats was not so weak and shallow as to accuse a brother of what he never committed; for this knowledge I would willingly sacrifice that part of my character, which you allow to be attacked, – I would confess myself indiscreet, defaming, – heinous, if any one insisted on the epithet; but it is enormous to expect that I should forfeit one iota of my good name in order to uphold that of the swindler of my friend ... You have, virtually, accused me of defaming George; this you have done, publicly as you could, short of printing; be rational enough to examine if the accusation you have made is not grounded on a mistake.[8]

Part of Brown's letter has been destroyed; it was apparently his answer to Dilke's 'sheer rudeness', a personal attack which he was prepared to forget. But 'I call, seriously, on you', the fragmentary letter ends, 'to make your words "most cruel severity" – good, or to explain how you had been inadvertently led into error.' Dilke never answered.

Both Dilke and Brown were dogmatic, inflexible in their regard for truth, both were intensely aware of their dignity. Each accused the other of ending the correspondence. 'I regret this,' Dilke admitted to George, 'because our intimacy and friendship *was of five & thirty years standing* ... I do not upbraid myself.' Brown, whose friendship with Dilke had been so bound with that of Keats, saw the clouding of a memory; and he was long disturbed by 'plaguing reflections; for the whiffing away a friendship of thirty years in rageful words is as grievous as it is foolish'. Some of the correspondence between Brown and Dilke has probably been burnt; but, studying what is left, examining the emotions and facts, the intentions and results, the judgment must be given to Brown.

*   *   *

'Dear Sir,' he scribbled to Robert Finch, on a hotel invoice, in April 1830, 'I wish you would come and dine with me, tomorrow or next day, at any hour you choose. Welcome to Florence.'[9] Finch arrived, the personification of prosperity. He had, since Brown first met him, inherited a fortune, and the one-time curate of Hampstead now occupied 'an enormous palace' in Rome, gave grand dinners, and drove about 'like an Ambassador'; with pleasant anticipation, Brown decided to go to Rome in October. In the meanwhile the summer passed happily, in Via Maggia, where Landor visited Brown almost daily, and in Landor's garden, 'very cool and green, and full of chestnut trees', where work continued 'at the rate of fifty things at once; oh! such planting and transplanting, such watering, such nursing of flowers', said Brown, 'and such choice grafts! In conclusion, when the conclusion shall arrive, he will make it a beautiful place.'[10]

He himself was engrossed at last in writing Keats's life. 'What I stand in need of,' he told Hunt, 'is an account of Keats when a school boy; and if I knew C. Clarke's address, I would write to him for information. I really think you are bound to induce him to send me all he can. I want to make out, as far as I can, the development of his mind. Both he and Tom have talked a little to me on this subject ... Can Clarke tell me what parish Keats was born in, for I think you have given a wrong birth day ...' And Brown was not only writing his memoir of Keats; he was satisfying an old ambition, and diligently preparing a book on Shakespeare.

By June he had written sixty pages; and he was 'astonished' at the autobiography he had found in the plays, while the sonnets offered such a key to Shakespeare's life that he felt ashamed to be the first to discover it. Landor declared it treasure trove, and 'Landor swears, out and out', the gratified critic told Hunt, 'that no man ever understood Shakespeare like myself; this is the greatest compliment, true or not, that I have ever received.'

*   *   *

As the year 1830 drew to its close, the circle of Brown's acquaintances was changing. In September, Robert Finch, driving in his ambassadorial carriage, in heavy rain, caught a fever and died. 'He was, Mayer says, only 46 years of age', noted Crabb Robinson: 'Can that be? He looked 60.'[11] On September 18th the same dogmatic, uncharitable diarist, who dismissed Landor as 'a man of unquestionable genius, but very questionable good taste', called on the Nicholsons. 'A Mr *Brown* there,' he scratched away in his journal, 'said to be a friend of Hazlitt Cobbett &c. – In the dark I co^d not see his face & only noticed his decisive tone of voice and abrupt dogmatical assertions. He talks as if he would impose on others by his manner and most likely does. He *may be* a clever man. Of course a radical as all of that stamp are.'[12] One remark on Brown's friendships needed qualification even as it was written: that very day, Hazlitt had died.

'Mr Brown knew Hazlitt', Crabb Robinson recorded, soon afterwards. 'Congeniality of opinion made them intimate. Hazlitt left his books with Brown. They are of no value ... Brown spoke highly of Hazlitt's wife as a gentlewoman. She fell in love with him on account of his writings. She parted on account of the ill-conduct of the boy. Brown related anecdotes of Hazlitt's personal cowardice, as well as of his slovenliness, and says he was the worst-tempered men he ever knew. He related an anecdote of Lamb, but not one of the best. There being very free conversation on religion, Lamb said very gravely [an erased sentence in shorthand about the Virgin Mary]. Lamb's taste,' added Robinson, 'particularly after dinner, was not very pure.'

There had been a proposal that Robinson should travel to Rome with Brown; but, not for the first time, Brown's independence earned him the displeasure of another assertive man. 'Our party will not be formed,' the diarist continued, 'and Mr B: seemed so self willed that I have no great wish to travel with him. But I shall be better able to speak of him to-morrow. He has asked me to dine with him.'

Dilke had acknowledged long ago that Brown put one in good humour; and the dinner mellowed Crabb Robinson considerably. Over his glass he grudgingly admitted: 'Brown amused me. He is a man of talents – he sho^d me a MSS abo^t Shakespear's Sonnets – which he thinks he has found a key to – and he means to publish his speculations on the subject. I promised not to *talk* about his discovery – before his book appears.' Being a natural gossip, he then explained it in shorthand.

Two days later, equipped with details about Robert Finch, whom

Brown had discussed with him, he went to Landor's and gossiped about Brown, 'of whom the Ls do not speak very well, at least without strong disapprobation of his manner of bringing up his child.' His mind was full of this 'speculator in education' as he returned from the Villa Gherardesca; the fireflies on the road were yellow, like sparks from the moon, and, the moment he reached Florence, Landor's mastiff left his side.

'SOME GREAT FRIEND OF KEATS ...'

B Y the turn of 1830, Trelawny's autobiography had given Brown
another chance to foster Keats's fame. Searching his store of unpublished work, he offered a quantity of quotations as chapter-
headings; and Trelawny was the first to use the manuscript of *Otho the
Great*, *King Stephen*, and *The Cap and Bells*. Landor, Kirkup, and Lady
Burghersh, wife of the British Minister in Florence, had given their
opinions of his book, and Mary Shelley edited it and arranged for
its anonymous publication in 1831; yet none of them offered so much
help as the 'plain downright Cockney critic, learned in the trade of authorship', and it was with Brown that the profits of both editions were
shared.

Brown himself, by the autumn of 1832, had moved to a villa near
Florence, probably Galileo's home to which he had long aspired. There,
for a few short weeks, he was joined by an English lawyer well versed in
languages and classical literature, who had travelled south to ward off
consumption. Richard Woodhouse,[1] throughout his life, kept his early
devotion to Keats; one of the first collectors of Keatsiana – he had in fact
coined the word – he had copied out Keats's poems, commissioned
Hilton to copy the Severn miniature, and Girometti to make the medallion
which caught the modest genius of Keats's being. He gave a replica to
Brown, who thought this plaster reminiscence 'quite a piece of magic';
and there, in the Florentine garden which Milton may have known,
where the scarlet verbena outshone the glories of painters' shops, and the
volkamoria made the air sultry with its hyacinth scent, they talked of
Keats. Brown's 'funny odd dislike' of Woodhouse disappeared, and he
grew to 'like him much'. When, seven weeks later, Woodhouse left for
Venice and England, Brown sent an appreciation to Severn.

Tongue in cheek, he also concocted a pleasant mystery from Trelawny's book: 'At the head of every chapter are one or two quotations
from Byron, Keats, and Shelley ... Woodhouse thinks that these quotations, in so popular a book, will be of great service to the fame of Keats;
and indeed they are chosen, in number fifty-three great and small, with

much care – some great friend of Keats's must have done all this, don't you imagine so? Woodhouse has made me promise to write the life of Keats in my quiet country nook during this winter.'[2]

* * *

It was not the winter of 1832 but the following summer that became significant in the history of Keats's fame. Richard Monckton Milnes, just down from Cambridge, was making his grand tour of the Continent and had received an introduction to the Landors. He had fallen ill of malaria, and, with his usual good fortune, he had happened to do so at Florence. Landor had taken him into the Villa Gherardesca.

And by chance this unexpected guest, a young man of twenty-four, was one of the earliest and most fervent students of Keats; though the collected poems had not then been published in England, he and his friends had, long ago, at their own expense, reprinted *Adonais*. As he sat convalescent on the mimosa-scented terrace at Fiesole, watching the fountain playing and the light upon the lemon trees, upon the four hundred rose trees in Landor's garden, he was joined by 'Mr Charles Brown, a retired Russia-merchant, with whose name he was already familiar'. Milnes had already been to Rome and learned every detail which Severn could give him; now, from Brown, he heard of Keats at Wentworth Place, and the creative years. As Brown spoke, too, of the achievement which Keats might have known, Milnes's imagination 'stood astounded'. Brown told him, finally, that he had saved a wealth of poetry which he would publish on his return to England.

* * *

For some time Brown had been sick for home. It is said that he had already paid brief visits to England: that he and the Hunts had dined together one Christmas Day and that Lamb had been a guest. (When the plum-pudding arrived, Lamb inquired in his hesitant way how many sides there were to a pudding. Everyone else agreed that a round pudding had no sides. 'Th-there are t-two sides', insisted Lamb: 'The inside and the outside.'[3]) Perhaps the society of Hunt, the grateful warmth of Lamb, a meeting with Rice or Haslam or Reynolds, a sight of the green country, had helped to persuade Brown to leave Italy. In 1834 he was faced with more urgent reasons: Carlino was fourteen, and needed an English edu-

CARLINO AT THE AGE OF NINE
From a sketch by Seymour Kirkup

JOSEPH SEVERN
From a drawing made by John Partridge in Rome
in November 1825

cation; he himself must attend to financial affairs. And, suddenly and disastrously, his health grew worse.

A few years earlier, determined not to be 'fat-suffocative', he had been the joke of his friends for his tireless walking round Florence, for the carriage drives which were merely excuses for walking further afield. One day in 1834, in Vieusseux's library in the Via Tornabuoni, he had an apoplectic fit from which he never fully recovered; and in time he also suffered from epilepsy[4] and dyspepsia, and from what he called 'a hell of nervousness'. It was characteristic of the man that he still worked to capacity: he was 'one of the most dauntless and energetic sufferers among literary workers since Defoe'.

His farewell to Italy was overcast. A few nights before his departure he dined at the Villa Gherardesca, where Julia Landor, who had given her husband 'anything but a life of bliss', accused him, in Brown's presence, of 'excessively bad behaviour'. For nearly an hour, while Landor sat in utter silence, she upbraided him. She refused to let Brown make her apology.

Some days later, Landor sought the counsel of the friend for whom he 'always felt the highest esteem'. Brown, on his way home, answered from Genoa: 'There are certain words, which, once uttered, cancel every obligation [even if they are] uttered by the wife of my friend ... I never once saw you behave towards Mrs Landor otherwise than with the most gentlemanly demeanour, while your love for your children was unbounded. I was always aware that you gave entire control into her hands over the children, the servants, and the management of the house ... All this I have more than once repeated to Mrs Landor in answer to her accusations ... which I could never well comprehend.' Supported by the unfailingly honest verdict of Brown, Landor ended his marriage of twenty-four years.

The Villa Gherardesca had no master; and in Florence, in the spring of 1835, there remained few memorials of Brown. His property had been valued and sold. The bed on which Shelley had slept, which had been jealously guarded by Mary Shelley, then Leigh Hunt, then Brown, was bought at last by Kirkup, in the hope that Shelley would appear to him in a dream.

PART FOUR

No. 2, At Laira Green

II
'THE STRAIGHT LINE OF MY DUTY'

A CLUSTER of cottages, Eagle House – Miss Trader's Boarding School for Young Ladies – and the convivial sign of the Laira Arms were all that marked Laira Green, on the banks of the Plym. It was part of the rambling village of Egg Buckland, two miles from Plymouth; the only event in Laira during the year was the June fair on the green. To this 'peculiarly attractive and respectable neighbourhood' Brown retired in the early summer of 1835. He settled happily in a cottage which boasted a quarter-acre of garden and a greenhouse.

The cottage became a centre for visitors: retired naval captains like Branch, or Howell, or Trader – presumably a relation of Miss Trader of boarding-school fame – or Bowker, who was 'neighbourly, but an obstinate old fool'. For if the reception was kind, the criticism was free: the Misses Renfry, who came for 'an evening *spread*', included 'talkative Jane, ... a horrible bore'. Some of the neighbours were 'rather dull and very sickly'. They were 'a strange unliterary set – tories into the bargain. I am on the best terms with all,' wrote Brown, 'but of what avail?'

His closer friends he made, as usual, through his taste for literature and his new interests in astronomy and geology. The members of the Plymouth Institution, which he soon joined, included the intellectual elite of the town. The president and founder, Henry Woollcombe, was an antiquarian from choice and a solicitor by profession, while the Rev. Richard Luney combined his duties as lecturer with the curacy of St Andrew's Chapel and a Young Gentlemen's Private Boarding School in Windsor Terrace. Dr Edward Moore, the secretary, was surgeon to the Royal Eye Infirmary, and George Wightwick, 'that scientific gentleman and able architect', lectured on Pope and Shakespeare, and 'sent up a very grand design for the Nelson Monument'.[1] Brown's particular friend was a retired colonel, Charles Hamilton Smith, a 'delightful gentleman of high talents and extensive acquirements'. Within a few months of his arrival at Laira Green, 'our acute and industrious townsman, Mr Brown', was himself lecturing at the Plymouth Institution on Shakespeare's *Sonnets*. His talk on 'The Intellectual History of Florence' was received with 'unusual hand applause and high compliments', and when the yearly elections took place, he found himself curator of the library.

Assured of appreciation, Brown determined to give the talk for which he was supremely qualified: he would speak on *The Life and Poems of John Keats*. The writing of the Life was to him the fulfilment of a duty. Once he had been able to remember Keats with thanksgiving and without pain. Yet many times he had abandoned his biography for grief; and now, nearly sixteen years after Keats had died, when he compelled himself to write the 'most plain unvarnished tale', his head ached as he wrote, and he cried 'like a child'.

At seven o'clock on December 29th, 1836, in the spacious hall of the Plymouth Athenaeum, Charles Brown delivered the first public lecture on Keats. For three hours he told his life and discussed his poetry; and in that west country from which, perhaps, the ancestors of Keats himself had come, the story was given 'a remarkable reception': not as any appreciation of Keats, but as the life of a poet, told by his friend. Unwillingly, for he had sought to avoid it, Brown himself was exalted in the telling. But it was the early dawn of Keats studies; in the audience of a hundred, most of them learned men, only one person had read Keats's poems; and he, who was 'enthusiastic in their praise', was the son of Coleridge. Even the lecturer believed that the *Quarterly* had helped to destroy his friend, and some resented his 'exposure of the Tory critics'.[2]

Among the later records of the Keats circle, one of the most touching is that of the militant, unswerving devotion of Brown. 'His fame is part of my life', he would write of Keats. 'He was dearly beloved, and honoured as a superior being by me. Now that twenty years have passed since I lost him, his memory is still my chief happiness.' Those who had dared at the lecture to support 'the Tory critics' received the full force of his anger. Indeed, so tenaciously did he hate the reviewers that from the moment he believed that Lockhart had criticized Keats in *Blackwood's* with the connivance of Sir Walter Scott, Brown refused to have Scott's works on his shelves. He carried his Keatsiana on all his ramblings, 'whether to Rome or to Mecca'. In the cottage at Laira Green were his drawing of Keats at Shanklin, the Girometti medallion, two replicas of the Severn miniature, and Severn's sketch of Keats on his death-bed; and one of Brown's first actions as a member of the Hanging Committee was to display the portraits at a local exhibition, the earliest in which Keats received prominence.

In his mind he still turned over the poet's epitaph, the question of a national memorial. Many Keatsians in Rome had offered to subscribe for a monument, and Severn had determined to commission one: the Girometti profile should be reproduced, and 'the most beautiful laurels and cypresses' should commemorate him. For three months Brown pondered Severn's letter:

> How could I resolve to disturb the pleasant dreams in which you then were? You were resolved on a fine monument to Keats, and I utterly disapproved of it. If his Poems should induce his countrymen to erect a monument to him, my joy would be great; but I cannot approve of such an honour, in a questionable shape, by his *personal* friends, paid to him *as a poet*. On this ground I must decline having any thing to do with the monument, – except on one point. This point is that not one word shall be there except those contained in his dying request – 'Here lies one whose name was writ in water.' ... I am convinced of the error, the sort of profanation of adding even a note of admiration to his own words.

Throughout his later years Brown continued to follow 'the straight line of his duty to Keats's memory'. He still longed to publish the poet's life; and Severn acclaimed the thought of the memoir and discussed it with the ubiquitous Crabb Robinson, and with Wordsworth, who was visiting Rome.[3] Suggestions came thick and fast from Italy: Brown must send *Otho the Great* by return of post to be performed in Rome, Severn was 'stirring up' for a new edition of Keats and Shelley, Gibson had made 'a liberal offer' to sculpt a marble group of the two poets to be erected in London. Severn grew impatient: 'Here I have heard and heard of Keats's Life which you are doing: I have written and written to you about it, and now I hear nothing more, now, when the world is looking for it, and the tragedy. Why, you would be astonished, were you to know the many who come to me as the friend of Keats, and who idolize him as another Shakespear ... *The time has come*, and I FEAR THE TIME MAY PASS ... Now tell me what you have to say by way of excuse. It cannot be, save that you do not know how high Keats's fame has risen.'

But in England there remained no general interest in Keats. Brown, seeking a publisher, offered his Life to Saunders and Otley; they sent him 'rather a cool reply'. Sometimes he thought of printing a limited edition, merely for love, sometimes he felt inclined to give the manuscript to the British Museum. 'There is no call for it at present,' he lamented to Severn, 'so that it may remain quiet till I am "quietly inurned". I have done what I conceived my duty, and I can leave it to another generation, if, after my death, he should then be more considered by the many. I cannot bear the thought of its being printed and received as of little interest except among a few.' He was too mindful of Keats's fame to force him on the public; the reception of his lecture, like the remarks of publishers, the comments on Keats in contemporary works, suggested that his fame did not yet stand high enough. 'I would almost rather it were published after my death', wrote Brown of his memoir, 'than that it should disturb my tranquillity, from attacks, whether against him by his revilers, or against me.'

It was largely the unpublished poems which delayed the appearance of Brown's biography, the flowering of Keats's fame. George Keats, still burning with animosity, had empowered Dilke to forbid their publication. On this legal point, Brown consulted Monckton Milnes, who sadly confirmed George's power of interdict. It seemed that only George's death would release his brother's poetry.

At last, however, in May 1838, Brown found himself in London; and, suppressing his pride, he called on Dilke. He was told that George wanted to buy the poems 'if they could not be otherwise obtained. My reply', he told Severn, 'was most conciliatory on this point, putting all thoughts of profit aside. I desired to publish a few here. Dilke told me he knew of no objection *now* to my publishing the whole.'

Within a few weeks *The Plymouth and Devonport Weekly Journal*[4] printed the 'Sonnet. – To the Nile. (From the unpublished Poems of John Keats.)' It was followed by twelve other poems, hitherto unknown; the impromptu stanza from Keats's Spenser made its appearance in a political leader. And on September 27th, 1838, through the devotion of Brown, in this provincial paper of which the name is scarcely known, the Bright Star Sonnet was given to the world.

THE ORIGIN OF ROBERT WYDEL

THE fame of Keats was not the only literary cause which Brown espoused at Plymouth. Light verse, political satires and leaders enlivened the local press. He remained a prolific translator, he was strongly tempted to turn all Goldoni's comedies into English, and he wrote a study of the Venetian dramatist. His love of books remained eager and critical: the news that Carlino was writing an opera brought a torrent of advice from the author of *Narensky*. His letters were punctuated by requests to return his Apocryphal New Testament, his volume of Tillotson's *Sermons*, his *Guida di Firenze*; and Dr Dionysius Lardner, the editor of the *Lives of the Most Eminent Literary and Scientific Men of Great Britain*, received a stern letter from him for blackening Shakespeare's character. At the Plymouth Institution he lectured on 'The Learning of Shakespeare', on 'Shakespeare in Reference to his Knowledge and Dramatic Art'; by the time he spoke on Milton's *Comus*, he was a vice-president of the Institution. He considered dramatic themes for Leigh Hunt, including 'a romantic tale of love and murder' in fourteenth-century France. 'The tale is full of the strongest passions, leading through woful errors to death. The scene at Giran's castle between the lovers ... the baffled bridegroom ... the supernatural agency ...'

It is strange that such adolescent taste should be found in a critic who studied Shakespeare with an original mind. Yet within a few months of this letter, in 1838, Bohn of King William Street published *Shakespeare's Autobiographical Poems*, by Charles Armitage Brown.

*　*　*

Brown had adopted his brother's Christian name, for Trelawny had informed him that Brown was just the name of a tribe. The volume had to be printed and published at his own expense; it was, like his *Life of Keats*, a work of love. It must have reflected the suggestions of Dilke and Hunt, and of Landor, to whom it was dedicated. It was the culmination of Brown's lifelong study, and it owed something, surely, to the profound understanding with which Keats himself had dwelt on Shakespeare's work.

Brown suggested that Shakespeare was a lawyer's clerk, that *Venus and Adonis* and *The Rape of Lucrece* were written before he came of age, and that Marlowe had written *Titus Andronicus*. But his chief discovery, he claimed, was that of the meaning of the sonnets. 'This key, simple as it may appear, unlocks every difficulty, and we have nothing but pure uninterrupted biography.' He believed that the printers had divided the poems wrongly in 1609, that they were not sonnets at all, but six separate poems, each ending with an *envoi*. In the first, stanzas 1-26, Shakespeare persuaded his friend, William Herbert, to marry; in the second (27-55), he forgave him for robbing him of his mistress; in the third (56-77), he deplored his coldness and warned him of life's decay. Then (78-101) he complained that his friend preferred another poet's praises, and reproved him for faults that might harm his character. In the fifth poem (102-106), the poet excused himself for his silence and disclaimed the charge of inconstancy. The sixth and last poem – Brown maintained – was addressed to Shakespeare's mistress, on her infidelity.

In a thorough chapter, based on internal evidence from the plays, Brown suggested that before *The Merchant of Venice* was produced, Shakespeare had been to Italy: indeed, he traced the poet's journey from Venice to Pisa, supporting his theory with abundant detail. He wrote wisely on Shakespeare's learning, his dramatic knowledge, his moral character, and finally offered notes on each of the dramas.

* * *

Shakespeare's Autobiographical Poems received some gratifying reviews. 'It is no small advance in the progress to the right understanding these poems,' said *The Gentleman's Magazine* of Brown's discovery. 'We cannot withhold the tribute of our sincere admiration of one of the most original and elegant of the volumes which have appeared in the department of Shakespear criticism. The writer has evidently a mind richly cultivated, and enthusiastically devoted to the study of our greatest poet.'[1] 'In closing this volume,' said *The Dublin Review*, 'and recommending it strongly to the reader's perusal, we are fain to add that we shall look to any further production of the same pen with high interest.' *The West of England Magazine* reviewed the book twice; and the following year, when a new edition of Shakespeare was published, *The Plymouth and Devonport Weekly*

Journal pointed out that 'most honourable mention is made of the very valuable work by our acute and industrious townsman, Mr Brown.'[2]

However, Brown's assertive tone was sure to rouse criticism; and nineteenth-century critics did not hesitate to turn literary judgment into personal unpleasantness. By some misfortune, too, his book appeared at the same time as *Letters on the Natural History of the Insects mentioned in Shakespeare's Plays*. A comparison was tempting, and *The Monthly Review* took the two books together: 'According to Mr Brown's mode of interpretation, would it not be reasonable to assert that Shakespeare had been a lecturer on Natural History? ... While we think that Mr Brown is more ingenious than sound or satisfactory, he sometimes acts the part of an original and sagacious critic.'

It was obvious, however, that such gibes would count little beside the verdict of *The Athenaeum*. Dilke was now editor; and by his choice of contributors, his business sense, his resolute integrity in an age of literary abuse, he had raised the magazine high among contemporary journals. For several weeks, Brown had carefully advertised in its columns;[3] he had surely, on his visit to London, told Dilke himself of the work on which he was staking not only his reputation but much of his limited money. On July 21st *The Athenaeum* condemned the book:

The title-page alone [wrote the critic] sounds a note of preparation which must startle the dull ear of the public. We have neither time nor inclination, however, to test the accuracy of Mr Brown's speculations, and must therefore content ourselves at starting with a general reference and a few passing words of comment.

Mr Brown, we will admit at starting, is a pleasant and ingenious essay writer, and seems to delight in this sort of holiday pastime. We have discussions on all the old subjects connected with Shakespeare, ... down even to 'his learning', – a question we had thought with Johnson, was for ever settled ... Among other fanciful speculations, Mr Brown comes forward in support of the hypothesis ... that Shakespeare was originally a lawyer's clerk. But he adduces not a single novel fact in support of this opinion; he simply takes his text from one of Nash's works, and illustrates it by quotations from Shakespeare's Poems, to which others, more cautious, had only and generally referred. Mr Brown runs on with fifty other quotations, some more and some less pertinent, if that be possible.

Mr Brown insists on Shakespeare's having visited Italy, and sets out by stating, 'that nothing can uproot my belief in his having been there'. So that point is not to be argued; – otherwise, as he deduces what he considers his strongest evidence from *The Taming of the Shrew*, we might remind him, that Farmer doubts whether the play was written by Shakespeare at all ... Let us, however, come to the revelation which is to unlock every difficulty. Here it is [the reviewer quotes Brown's redivision of the sonnets] – at least, we can find no other. We really do not understand this ... What Mr Brown can mean by stating that it never crossed the mind of any one that they were 'divisible poems in the sonnet stanza', we are utterly at a loss to conjecture ...

There is one point in Shakespeare's life [*The Athenaeum* concluded] respecting which Mr Brown hazards a conjecture which, we have no doubt, further enquiry would tend to confirm. He is of opinion that Shakespeare's wife was provided for during his lifetime, and that explains the bequest to her in his will ... This seems plausible, and is certainly worth a thousand conjectures respecting the sonnets.

The Athenaeum review destroyed the last vestige of Brown's loyalty; he sent Dilke 'a declaration of war'. And 'thus', he wrote to Severn, 'during the winter, I can, without remorse, draw him at full length in a novel. He is a capital character for one.'

* * *

In *Walter Hazlebourn* Dilke was therefore drawn by a man who had been his close friend for some thirty years and had found himself at last despised and betrayed. But it was not merely personal animosity which made the likeness so sharp. Brown's recollection of Keatsian days had been bruised by Dilke's insolence. It was this, as much as the insult to himself, which inspired the bitterest passages in his writing. As in all cartoons, the weaknesses are exaggerated, and occasionally there may be a flagrant untruth; but the portraits of old Mr Wydel and Robert remain unmistakable likenesses of old Mr Dilke of Chichester and his elder son:

The house I most gladly entered [wrote Brown of his youth] was Mr Wydel's ... With the old gentleman I was a favourite, and, indeed, with all the family. Even the headstrong and violent son, Robert, who seemed to take a delight in disturbing the peace, was kind to me; and I liked his wayward jollity, and the sparks of generous feeling that, now and then, appeared to emanate from a good heart, somehow repressed in its right course. Gerald did his utmost, and my small influence was added, to screen Robert's excesses from his father's knowledge, or to palliate them when discovered. Once when we were pleading in excuse for this son's misconduct, and urging everything we could think of in his favour, the father replied. – 'You know little of Robert. I hope he has, as you say, much goodness of heart; but of this I am assured, – it will never appear when his vanity stands in the way. Besides, I cannot forbear thinking him selfish ...' Though I almost felt at the time a touch of resentment on hearing so harsh a judgment by a father, the words have often recurred to me, especially when I was a sufferer from his character, as true in every respect ...

Our Sunday evening happiness at the Wydels' was, indeed, now and then, disturbed by the behaviour of Robert. As I mixed more in the world, my feeling towards him was gradually, though not entirely estranged. I began to discover that a reputation for goodness of heart and generosity was not a sufficient compensation against overbearing opinions, pompous and affronting language, and bursts of savage temper. It is not pleasant to draw an unfavourable portrait of one whom I wished to regard with friendship; but, should I omit to make his character understood, his after conduct might appear inexplicable. As a boy, either the right course was not pursued with him, or he baffled every means of instruction, for he left school with no learning whatever. His father, who had intended him for the law, seeing the purpose hopeless, used his interest to obtain for him a situation in a Government-office; which, as Robert grew older, he heartily despised. In this humour, he laudably endeavoured to teach himself Latin and French; but it was too late, or he was incapable of so persevering an effort. Consequently he railed against all languages but his own, in which he read much on every subject; till he felt inspired to become a literary man and, if possible, to set up a popular periodical work. It was of this gradation of his progress that I am now speaking. He was fond of dashing company, and in order to be admitted into that circle, he could dissemble and be tame. Otherwise, he was never of the same opinion with any one present; much addicted to boasting, and not always scrupulous in his assertions; sure to come out with some unheard-of judgment on literature, and to praise to the skies some unknown modern author; a contemner of rank, just then,

NO. 2, AT LAIRA GREEN

because he was busy with Rousseau's *Contrat Social*, which he was vainly endeavouring to understand by the help of a dictionary. Bereaved of other qualities, he would have been utterly impossible; but, when his bad temper was at rest, he was often social, jolly, and it was a pleasure to hear him speak and expatiate on some generous act that had come to his knowledge. Add to which his person, if not handsome, was imposing; being tall, though rather fat than stout, and heavily built ...[4]

The unfinished manuscript of *Walter Hazlebourn* was sent to Hunt, who made a few pencilled suggestions; kind though he was, he thought it ponderous stuff.

Brown never finished it, but a weight was off his mind.

13

'TO LIVE UNBLEST ... '

SOMETIMES, in the late 1830s, Brown recalled the past more happily:
Walter Savage Landor would descend on Laira Green. Landor's keen
eyes, high-vaulted forehead, his 'thick white fringe of backward-
flowing hair' lent him the appearance of a prophet, and his smile of
inexpressible sweetness disarmed the most timid acquaintance. 'All the
women-kind' of Plymouth fell in love with him, Colonel Smith's
daughters confessed their passion, and Brown declared that no woman
could safely go near him.

Often, as they walked beside the Laira and the Tamar, they would talk
of Shakespeare, and Brown mentioned the glad applause which had
greeted him, in one of his lectures, when he said that Shakespeare had
£7,000. He thought the anecdote revealed a good deal about humankind,
but Landor declared 'that it only showed they comprehended £7000
better than a wilderness of *Othellos*'.

And so, together, two middle-aged men of letters, they walked on
along the Laira banks; and, to Brown, these moments seemed to touch the
heights of his past. He declared he had not been happier when, twenty
years earlier, he had walked with Keats.

*   *   *

Landor's visits only deepened Brown's usual loneliness and frustration.
'This Elizabeth will drive me mad', he grumbled about his housekeeper.
'She has been even rummaging my cupboards for articles to set off a
mantelpiece.'[1] Elizabeth had her merits and was 'extremely attentive'
when he walked home one night from the Plymouth Athenaeum, weak
from *cholera morbus*. But her ministrations were no substitute for those of a
wife; and in *The Plymouth and Devonport Weekly Journal*, over his initials,
there appeared a pathetic sonnet on the loneliness of bachelors:

> To have a house, and yet to boast no home;
> To boast of freedom, and to wish it less;

To lose all heart for roaming, yet to roam;
To live unblest in single blessedness;
To wince beneath a thousand petty ills;
To give directions for my board and bed;
To check my tradesmen's and my washing bills;
To order how I will be comforted;
To fall in sickness, and with no one nigh,
Unless a venal nurse, no one to care
Whether I'm well or ill, or live or die,
Except my anxious nephew, my next heir:
Such are the comforts of a single life, –
My comforts! – no, I've none without a wife.[2]

Brown had little pleasure in solitude; and there was a poignant difference between his claret days at Wentworth Place and the time when he lived, 'most modestly', 'without factitious luxuries', and advertised for someone to share his life:

THE ADVERTISER, living alone, is desirous to receive into his house, as BOARDER and LODGER a Gentleman, who will not be required to expend more than is requisite to defray the extra expence of his presence. The residence is about two miles from Plymouth. A gentleman of literary or scientific pursuits, and of liberal principles, would be acceptable; as the advertiser seeks for a companion, by no means a boarder and lodger for profit.

But there was no answer to his advertisement.[3]

*   *   *

Much of Brown's loneliness was explained by the absence of his son, for in 1838, a boy of eighteen with a talent for engineering, Carlino was searching London for a job. Brown naturally enough suggested work with an engineer, but Carlino wanted a government post, and, looking round for a patron, he remembered an acquaintance of his father's: Richard Monckton Milnes. The idea brought a brisk reply from the radical Brown: 'You could have hardly pitched on any M.P. less likely to forward your interest than Mr Milnes; I have no claim on him whatever; and if I had the greatest, he could do nothing; he is an absolute Tory, votes constantly against Ministers, and is industrious in acting and speaking in the House against them ... Pray do not lose your hopes, your time, your energies in a vain pursuit. Rather inquire if there are not good prospects in France as an engineer.'[4]

Within three weeks, however, Brown's hopes had shifted to Italy, and a paragraph from the papers was on its way to Carlino: ' "Mr Stephenson, the celebrated rail-road engineer, has been engaged by the Florence and Leghorn Railroad Company to make the requisite surveys and plans for that line. Two English engineers have already arrived at Florence to commence the preliminary works." Now an enquiry into this may lead to great good.'[5] But the prospects proved unattractive. Early in 1839 Carlino was thinking of Germany, and the patient Brown was giving him counsel, while Mancur materialized once more and, not knowing the wound he touched, suggested that Carlino might ask for help from Dilke. Brown exploded:

My dear Son,
    Remember me to Mancur, with my love to his wife, if they should be yet in town. Tell him that I have a letter of his, written fifteen years ago, full of detestation against the selfishness and pomposity of Dilke, and that I wonder he can recommend any one to call on him. Were you to do such a thing, or to return his greeting otherwise than with contempt, I must – I could not help it – consider you as ranked among my enemies. No explanation – nothing could ever after reconcile me to such conduct. If he should accidentally meet with you, and civilly accost you – spit in his face ... His infamous treachery towards me last year ought to make any friend of mine despise him. Nor, if he could, would he be of any service to you in any of your views; his own selfishness, and his jealousy (long entertained) of me would prevent it. Nor with his piggish son ought you to exchange a salutation. He, pig as he is, sways his father on certain points; and I have traced some of the father's acts against me, in my thoughts, to the son's instigation.[6]

                    *   *   *

At last, by July 1839, through the influence of his uncle, William Brown, in Midhurst, Carlino was on probation to Chorley, a local engineer; and Brown had settled down to retirement. Though he had sprained his hand 'over-gardening', the old enthusiasm remained from Wentworth Place:

the amateur who had walked round his Hampstead garden, 'hands in Pockets making observations', delighted in his greenhouse; and 'my strawberries are now full of fruit', he boasted, 'because I had grubbed up so many useless apple-trees'. One of his plants displayed such profusion of blossom that he sent it to a local flower show.[7] Life at Laira Green was contracting: some of his neighbours had gone, their possessions had been auctioned, their cottages remained uninhabited, and a favourite cat was Brown's most frequent company. In the summer of 1839 his vice-presidency of the Plymouth Institution came to an end: 'Down with your pride, for you are no longer the son of a Senior Vice!' All his ambitions, now, were centred in Carlino: 'Heaven prosper you, my dear boy – and Heaven will, if you exert yourself, giving no cause of offence.'[8]

Soon after he wrote, Brown heard that Chorley had engaged Carlino on false pretences; he was in fact no engineer, only a simple millwright, unable to give him training, and after three years' apprenticeship the boy would remain unqualified. 'I cannot consent,' wrote Brown to William, 'that he should make so great a sacrifice.' Constructive as usual, he observed that Henry de la Beche, director of the Geological Survey of Great Britain, had been asking for assistants; the pay was 'good', from four to eight shillings a day. There was no certain future in the work, but 'Mr Delabeche is a kindhearted liberal man, and with much influence, not likely to abandon a youth, were he partial to him for assiduity and talent'.[9]

Carlino saw no advantages in the work with De la Beche; he had begun to think more favourably of Chorley. 'You must do as you please,' his father answered resignedly, 'making use of all the foresight and wisdom you possess.'

* * *

Brown himself, 'a simple plodding fellow', continued to work steadily. The Cockney critic, learned in the trade of authorship, was cultivated by publishers, who sent him books to review. The latest additions to his library brought him memories: the volumes on British America recalling his farewell to George Keats nearly twenty years ago; and *The Edinburgh Review*, with its criticism of Shelley, resurrecting Ariel in the Vale of Health, and conversations with Hunt in Italian days. 'We believe,' wrote Brown, 'somewhat against the reviewer, that Shelley's talent was chiefly dramatic, and that he himself was aware of it. Nay, we have heard, on tolerable authority, that he was preparing his mind for the production of English Historical Dramas, on those regions which Shakespeare has left untouched.'

But despite the journalism, despite the fact that he lived '*most moderately*', Brown was not financially comfortable. The cottage needed a coat of paint, Abby must have her allowance, Carlino wanted pocket-money and £20 a year for apprenticeship fees in unprofitable work. Even if Carlino were to be Chorley's partner, Brown would have to finance him. 'To confess the truth, it was a hard case for me to support a son till he was five and twenty … To avoid this anxiety, I chose to write for a newspaper; which I may continue to do, for both our sakes. Add to which, I laid down a stricter rule of economy, while living by myself. All this I did, and would continue to do cheerfully for your sake, provided it were really for your sake.'[10] Brown counted the extra pence on postage, the cost of an outside place on a coach, but he denied nothing to Carlino. 'I must always have a sufficient income … As to the rest, all is yours; I do not refuse to help my son during my lifetime.'[11]

There was a certain melancholy about the letter. Had he suffered another bout of illness? He insisted that he might enjoy another fifty years, but a new thought had entered his mind: he was making plans for his funeral.

For, whatever his assertions, he remained uncertain of health. Apoplexy and epilepsy had left their effect and might at any time return; often he felt 'in a hell of nervousness'. But in the instructions he sent Carlino, he made his decisions calmly, with his old defiant good sense:

It is my earnest wish to be buried like a parish pauper, the expence being a trifle, something like 9/–. Let the bearers of the body have a guinea each. Allot £20 for the burial and the poor, saving as much as possible out of that sum for the mere putting me underground, and divide the remainder among the poorest and most deserving of my neighbours. Do not let any foolish pride on your part prevent this. Should my body be thought of any use to science, you had better give it to any surgeon, or any anatomical school, and save all expence of burial, leaving the whole £20 available for the poor … It is good to endeavour to be useful to science, that is, to our fellow-creatures, even after death.[12]

Soon after the letter was sent, some stirring news arrived: Mancur, still eager to help, had discovered a Mr Dobbs, an engineer at Aix-la-Chapelle, who offered Carlino a situation. It was 'most advantageous in every respect'.[13] Indeed, Mancur's nephew, who once worked with Dobbs, was now 'setting up no less than eight steam engines in different parts of Germany'. The nephew had left a vacancy; and Mancur had described Carlino in such terms that there seemed little to do but 'send Charles off at once by the Ostend steamer ... Now as to the expence of his living', said Mancur, 'I should say £40 a year is enough; clothes I can say nothing about; but Charles must make up his mind to wear a Jacket &c &c in the factory.' Satisfied that Carlino was not morally bound to Chorley, Brown wrote to Dobbs and awaited the result. 'There is no cold water thrown over my hopes except this. Poor Mancur's swans have hitherto invariably proved to be geese.'[14]

The work with Dobbs was, alas, yet another goose 'tricked out swan-fashion'. Dobbs sent an ambiguous answer: 'I have advised to refer to a better opportunity for coming over.' '*Whose* coming over?' Brown asked Carlino, '*his* or *yours* – take it either way, *you* are not to go over *now*.'[15]

*　*　*

The new year, 1840, opened with a pleasant task: the captain of H.M.S. *San Josef*, lying off Hamoaze, wanted help with a pamphlet on naval progress, and Colonel Smith dispatched him to Laira Green. Soon afterwards, Charles Brown, an obliging journalist, who prepared the pamphlet gratis, was invited to dine in the wardroom. Some twenty years earlier, in the Solent, he and Keats had admired the discipline of the Georgian navy; and Brown was much gratified now by a sight of the latest Victorian devices, and the 'first-class boys' who 'went through their lessons in gunnery, with geometrical elucidations'.

The year brought less welcome events: a disturbing influence, in the person of Miss Renfry – 'my horror' – made itself felt in the cottage. 'She will,' wrote Brown, 'exterminate me.' Her visits were frequent, her conversation endless, and her purpose was suddenly revealed by the housekeeper: 'Crazy Jane' was in love with him. 'She has been weeping in sorrow at my indifference,' Brown explained to Carlino. 'Even though you should intreat me to make her your mother-in-law, I should be obstinate. Do not waste your labour in trying to make me as crazy as herself.'[16] He was fifty-three, and still lonely. 'My comforts! – No, I've none without a wife.' Secretly, perhaps, he enjoyed the compliment. But he remained Abby's husband, at least in name; and Jane Renfry went the way of Euphemia and Lady King.

* * *

Other problems were less easily settled. Brown found himself in increasing financial difficulties. A tenant had fled, owing him considerable rent.[17] He had paid for the printing of his book, but his publisher was slow in making payment; and Carlino had rashly discussed his father's troubles with May, the proprietor of *The Plymouth and Devonport Weekly Journal*:[18] confessions which, as Brown was afraid, scarcely enhanced his prestige. May had once offered to use his influence in Carlino's favour;[19] now his conduct changed abruptly. He delayed payment for contributions.[20] He rejected a criticism of the National School Society, for 'he [May] would not, he said, any more offend the Churchmen'. Brown refused to write again for the *Journal* that month, and sent the article to *The Devonport Independent*. He followed it with 'a song of 12 stanzas, ridiculing episcopal inspection of Public Schools ... It really is a song that pleases me'.

And the editor of *The Devonport Independent* was obliging; he printed not only Brown's lines on *The Church in Danger*, but

THE TORIES' CONFESSION

An Excellent New Ballad, unaccompanied by Cant.
Tune. – 'The Vicar of Bray, Sir'.–

In George the Third's prodigious days,
    When folks from reason wander'd,
How easy was it then to raise
    Grand loans by Tories squander'd!
These fell like golden rain on us
    Who well approved the system,
And thus were Tories prosperous
    With no one to resist 'em.

For this is law of ancient date,
    To last while Tories live, Sirs –
Corruption ever rules the State
    By power Conservative, Sirs! &c. &c.[21]

The balladmonger's radical verses also appeared in the *Western Times of Exeter*.[22] May apologized for his hasty words, and Brown continued, graciously, to send him contributions.

But middle age and failing health had not lessened his pugnacity, for while the battle of journalism ended in triple victory, he was hotly engaged in 'a Star Chamber matter' with the Plymouth Institution. He felt there was 'strong Tory feeling' against him; he felt compelled to write a 'quiet and resolute' letter to the president. 'Educated from my childhood as I have been,' it began, 'and accustomed to a gentlemanly demeanour from all ...'[23] Only the secretary's written apology or his resignation could content Charles Brown.

*　*　*

In August he went to Midhurst, where Carlino complained that Chorley was giving him inferior work. Brown made Chorley promise to give him scope for his talents. The promise was not kept. A few weeks later, Carlino had finally left him, and was making a tobacco-cutting machine for Trelawny.

14

A TRUE LOVER OF KEATS

THE news was sent in a letter from Brown to Richard Monckton Milnes. Whatever his earlier conviction that he had no claim on him, they had, by admirable fortune, been drawn together. Brown had rewritten the diary of his Scottish tour, his recollections of a Keatsian summer; the first four chapters had been accepted by the *Journal* and posted to Monckton Milnes. The generous devotion which had led Brown to publish without payment, led him also to send some lines from *Lamia*, in the writing of Keats.

Milnes, for all his multitudinous interests, is remembered best as a Keatsian. Before the collected poems of Keats had been published in England, he and his Cambridge friends had studied him and printed, at their own expense, an edition of *Adonais*. Now, in 1840, when the author of *Hyperion* had still to be acknowledged 'among the English Poets', and the London publishers told Brown that Keats would prove a losing speculation, Milnes answered him with a prompt, far-sighted request. 'You ask of me,' replied Brown, 'what I am so desirous to give! – a life of my dear Keats, with all his unpublished poems.' The apt enthusiasm of Milnes was to solve a problem which had lasted two decades.

*　　*　　*

For many months, the thought of emigration had hovered in Brown's mind;[1] *The Plymouth and Devonport Weekly Journal* had sung the praises of South Australia, advertised the sailing of the fine barque *City of Adelaide*, and printed joyful letters from early settlers. Early in 1840 it announced a pamphlet, 'The Colonization of New Zealand from the Counties of Devon and Cornwall', published by the directors of the Plymouth Company of New Zealand. Many of Brown's neighbours seem to have emigrated: Captain Howell, the Traders, the Berrys, Captain Branch; the Addis family had sailed two years ago. In 1838 Carlino himself had thought of leaving for New South Wales. Late in 1840, when he had heard a lecture on colonization, when Carlino's hopes in Germany and Italy, France and America had been abandoned, and his work in England showed no future, Brown himself took the initiative. Uncertain though he was in health, he determined for Carlino's sake to emigrate to New Zealand: 'That way fortune lies.'

He bought land near Taranaki, and machinery 'from pins and needles up to a Saw-mill and a steam-engine'. He and his son would go into partnership, Brown to keep accounts and Carlino to work: 'Shares equal,' Brown announced to Richard Monckton Milnes.

One other item, he considered, should be shipped to Taranaki: a wife for his son. It is said that Carlino proposed to Hunt's daughter, Julia, but she was too devoted to Hunt to consider emigration. Brown, disappointed, still urged him to marry: and as Carlino would be busy, and he himself would be lonely, it seemed obvious who should choose the daughter-in-law. 'Hadn't you better marry her yourself?' Carlino asked. The answer was decisive. 'You forget, my boy, I have a wife.'[2]

* * *

ELIGIBLE INVESTMENT
In the Neighbourhood of Plymouth

TO BE SOLD BY PRIVATE CONTRACT, on Terms very Advantageous to the Purchaser,

ALL THAT

FREEHOLD COTTAGE

being No. 2, at Laira Green, near Plymouth, now in the occupation of Charles Brown, Esq., containing two Parlours, two Kitchens, five Bed Rooms, a Pantry, China Closet, and other offices.

A PLEASURE GARDEN, with a GREEN HOUSE, and a KITCHEN GARDEN, form part of the Premises, which altogether include nearly a quarter of an acre, and being Extra-Parochial, are altogether exempt from Rates and other charges (with the exception of the Assessed Taxes).

The Premises appear to be in every way suited for convenient family residence, and from the respectability and peculiar attractions of the neighbourhood are particularly recommended to any one desirous of settling in the vicinity, or of retiring from the town.

For further particulars, apply at the Cottage; or at the offices of

MR ALFRED ROOKER, Solicitor,

Green-Street, Plymouth.

Dated, Jan. 13*th*, 1841.[3]

* * *

Brown and Carlino paid a final visit to London; perhaps, at Hunt's suggestion, they drove to Hampstead, saw the altered Wentworth Place, the familiar Heath. Soon afterwards, Brown took his supreme decision, and offered Monckton Milnes the task of establishing Keats's fame. He could have made no wiser choice: for Hunt, despite his devotion, was inclined to remember Keats as a stricken consumptive, and Severn – Brown told him frankly – was an inadequate writer; Taylor was disqualified by selfishness, for he had refused to publish a second edition of Keats or to relinquish his copyright; Dilke and George Keats were out of the question. 'As I am on the eve of quitting England for ever, I considered it would be my wiser plan to confide in a true lover of Keats, and place the Life and Poems in his hands, to act in my stead. Such confidence,' Brown wrote to Milnes, 'I am ready to repose in you, if you will undertake the task.' Milnes accepted by return.

'Fevered and nervous', Brown set himself to revise his Life of Keats for the last time. The sight of Keats's writing, even his own account of his Keatsian years, moved him, now, unbearably. It was almost twenty years to the day since he had heard of the poet's death; yet he felt 'quite unable' to concentrate on his memories. There were only two points he asked Milnes not to change: his exposure of *Blackwood's* and the *Quarterly*, and the history of Keats's illness, as Severn had recorded it. He rejected the final chance of incriminating George; in the last reckoning, the brother of Keats was 'entirely spared'.

* * *

On March 19th, 1841, the day on which Brown relinquished his task as Keats's biographer, he and his son attended a farewell dinner to the cabin passengers of the *Amelia Thompson*, the ship in which Carlino was to sail.[4] Among their fellow-guests at Whiddow's Royal Hotel was an emigrant who seemed a link with Brown's Italian days: John George Cooke, late of the 11th Regiment, a friend of Trelawny's.

> The Chair was taken at six o'clock by Thomas Gill, Esq., Sub-Governor of the Plymouth Colony of New Zealand. About forty gentlemen sat down to dinner, which was served up in Mrs Whiddow's usual style, and consisted of every luxury that could be desired. The healths of the 'Queen', the 'Queen Dowager', 'Prince Albert', and the 'Royal Family', were drunk with the usual honours.

Thomas Woollcombe, whose presidential voice had resounded so often in the Plymouth Athenaeum, paid tribute now to the emigrants, 'those bold and energetic men'. They were 'departing from their native country on a mission which he firmly believed would end in bringing great glories to this country'.

Then Mr Charles Brown, sen., of Laira Green, begged to make a few remarks before the company separated. He was not going himself in the Amelia Thompson, but he was nevertheless equally interested on account of one ... whom he intended speedily to follow. He could see clearly that in matters of this kind no good could be accomplished unless every man acted *truly* for himself. If every man acted well for himself, he would also act well for the community. Indeed, the speaker begged to say that there was one case in which, when a man spent twenty shillings for the public benefit, he gained twenty pounds for himself: he alluded to the promulgation of education, not only amongst the whites, but also amongst the *Browns*.

The speaker's post-prandial mood had not changed with the years.

Then 'Mr Charles Brown, jun., proposed the health of the officers of the company, which was drunk with enthusiasm', and the party 'separated at an early hour of the evening'. Next day Carlino boarded the *Amelia Thompson*; and on March 25th, when it had stayed five days wind-bound in Plymouth harbour, the ship got under weigh. As it passed the *Impregnable*, lying in the Sound, it 'was greeted by every soul on board, the ship's band playing the National Anthem'.

*   *   *

Laira Green,
21st March, 1841.

My dear Severn,

Welcome to England! An impudent congratulation, you will say, from one about to go to the other hemisphere at the beginning of May. You press me, with your wonted kindness, to go and live with you, instead of pursuing my plans. You tempt me, but I cannot, must not ... The die is cast ... You *blame* me; but are you acquainted with the probable great advantages, not so much, perhaps, in money getting at my time of life, but in happiness?

*   *   *

Eight days later, Brown sent, by coach, a final parcel to Milnes; it contained all the poems of Keats in his possession. Some of them he had published, others he thought unworthy of Keats's genius. Yet however shrewd his other judgments on literature, there was one poet whom Brown could not assess. Two decades ago, as he had awaited the news from Italy, he had felt the presence of Keats at Wentworth Place; now, again, in his middle fifties, he felt that Keats was with him.

Any other Poet's works I can coolly criticize, from Shakespeare downwards, but I feel there is no cool judgment in me while I am reading anything by Keats. As soon as I begin to be occupied with his MS poems, or with the Life I have written, it forcibly seems to me, against all reason, that he is sitting by my side, his eyes seriously wandering from me to the papers by turns, and watching my doings. Call it nervousness, if you will; but I am unable to do justice to his fame.

Implicitly do I rely on your judgment [Brown wrote to Monckton Milnes] as a friend to his fame, and as a brother poet; and gratefully do I acknowledge, in the name of Keats, your good will and kindness.

The momentous parcel left his care. Apart from a few relics which he would take to New Zealand, the material link had been cut. But, as Forster would acknowledge in his book on Landor, Charles Brown would be remembered 'as long as a reader remains for the most sorrowful story in our language, the brief life and pitiable death of the author of *Endymion*'.

* * *

Brown spent his last few months in England arranging financial affairs; the cottage at Laira Green was sold for £225.[5] In his golden dream he saw his strip of New Zealand soil with a water-course for the saw-mill, and a boulevard stretching before his house. 'Tomorrow,' he wrote to Carlino on April 13th, 'I shall wish myself many happy returns of the day in New Zealand.' He would be fifty-four. With satisfaction and courage he addressed the letter to 'Messrs Chas. Brown & Son, New Plymouth, New Zealand'.

On June 22nd, 1841, while Plymouth buzzed with election preparations, the *Oriental*, 506 tons (Captain William Wilson), sailed for New Zealand. In his small green notebook, Charles Brown began his record of emigration: 'At noon, quitted by pilot in Plym[th] Sound.'[6]

PART FIVE

Charles Brown the Emigrant

15

THE WAY TO MARSLAND HILL

THUS it was that the generous man who had befriended so many, who had given his stalwart affection to Hunt, to Severn and Landor, who loved the life and fame of Keats with devotion, was drawn across the world for the sake of his son. In days when New Zealand remained an unknown land, a hazardous prospect at the end of a perilous voyage, it needed no common fortitude to emigrate; and to do so in middle age, to forsake the well-earned peace of book and garden, of tranquil recollection and the Devon hills, demanded all Brown's native resolution. 'Citizen of the World' he had called himself; but that did not make it easier to bid farewell to his family, to Hunt and Severn, the last of the Keats circle, knowing that, at the far end of the earth, he would not see them again. The *Oriental*, making its slow way down the Channel, follows, touchingly, in the course of the *Maria Crowther*.

All Brown's remaining hopefulness, vitality and assurance, the qualities which had refreshed and encouraged his friends, he brought to this last adventure; wholehearted and practical as ever, he had invested in it to his capacity. And, cabined and confined upon a ship that was to touch no port until it reached New Zealand, he buoyed himself, in failing health, in his sleepless nights, with the golden promises of the Plymouth Company, the joyful testimonials he had seen in the English papers, the enchanting lectures, the endless prospects of happiness for Carlino and himself in the new, inviting world.

In November, after five months' imprisonment on the primitive ship, he reached the rugged barren coast of New Zealand, and 'the penal settlement of the Plymouth Company'.

* * *

An earlier ship, the *Regina*, had been smashed on the rocks; New Plymouth had no harbour of its own. The country was wild; no houses had been built, let alone the boulevards and mills of which he had dreamed. Of the seventeen cabin passengers, only three – and he was among them – would go on to Taranaki. Captain Wilson landed them with 'great despatch'. Brown's only consolation was to rejoin his son. The full weight of disillusionment fell on him. The survey of the settlement was made, and the sections distributed; the immigrants, including Brown and Carlino, camped near the beach. Within a few weeks, he thought of returning home.

The settlers had been promised a port for their money; the nearest port was Port Hardy, a hundred miles away, on an island so difficult to approach that ships no longer attempted it. The New Plymouth coast was too dangerous for the company to land supplies; stocks were diminishing, and soon, unless they could live on fern-root, it seemed that the immigrants would be threatened with famine.

By December, Brown was 'irretrievably sinking'. Unrest was general; the labourers called public meetings to decide on some course of action, and he was asked to preside. In January, the land purchasers and company's agents assembled, and the crisis came: Brown asked the chief surveyor where the port of New Plymouth was. Carrington replied that the harbour was Port Hardy. Brown recorded the answer and the signatures of three witnesses. 'Then I and my son declare ourselves ready to proceed, and thus fulfil our part of the agreement.' Everyone stood silent. 'I am aware', Brown continued, 'that Port Hardy is in D'Orville's Island, which is little more than a craggy steep, yet, to fulfil our part of the contract, we declare ourselves willing to go.' 'But, Sir, it is an impossibility; there is not land enough there for half a dozen houses.' 'The possibility rests with the company,' Brown answered. 'We will try if it is more possible for them to return our purchase money, our amount of freight, our loss on the goods and machinery we have bought, and our other losses, which we will specify before going into a court of law.' The meeting broke up. Brown sent his account of the battle to Trelawny, asking him to publish it as a warning. On August 31st, 1842, this document of rebellion was printed in *The Times*.

* * *

There remains but a record of frustration, of pathetic quarrels in which

Brown was condemned as 'ungentlemanly and insulting', and registered his protest.[1]

The Plymouth Company did not fulfil their responsibilities; even letters were withheld and censored and delayed. Brown had instructed Skynner, his lawyer, to sell his English property, but Skynner sent no account of a sale; and though Brown had invested much of his small capital in the New Zealand mirage, and in the settlement, where money was scarce, he could only sell his investments at great loss, by February he felt he must sell enough to pay for the voyage home. In a poignantly uncertain hand he ended that he might not survive the journey. Perhaps, if he returned to England, he would have to go to the parish for an existence. If Skynner failed to send the money, he might, in that primitive settlement, die of want.[2]

There remained one other possibility: that his life might come full circle: that he might return to the joyous company of Severn; that there, in England, with the friend who loved Keats, still, with vigilant devotion, he might spend the brief time that was left. Gratefully, now, Brown remembered the invitation which Severn had given him, and, from the coast of Taranaki, a hemisphere away, his thoughts returned to the eager circle of friends. Often he spoke of writing his reminiscences, a record of all the men of letters, the actors, wits and artists, the singers and the engaging dilettanti who, in the last half century, had walked beside him.

'The shepherd of all the vagrant amusing stories of his day' never gathered his flock together. He had another stroke; and on June 5th, 1842, Charles Brown lay dying. It is said that some Baptist emigrant attempted to comfort him with thoughts of the Saviour. 'For the love of God, sir,' answered Brown, 'speak to me no more about that *man*.'

He died a Deist, and they would not bury him in consecrated ground. Carlino and Cooke, Trelawny's friend, followed his coffin up Marsland Hill, overlooking the sea. Charles Brown, the dearest friend of Keats, lies solitary on the cold hillside; 'and there, under the beautiful shadow of our glorious mountain Taranaki, after life's fitful fever, let us hope he sleeps well.'

BOOK TWO

CHARLES WENTWORTH DILKE

16

GUIDE, COUNSELLOR AND FRIEND

HE was the most scrupulously honest man I ever knew – but wanted nobleness to lift this honesty out of the commercial kennel ... He could do generous things too – but not after the fashion of the world and therefore they were not appreciated by the world. His sense of justice led him at times to do acts of generosity – at others of meanness – the latter were always noticed, the former overlooked – therefore amongst his early companions he had a character for anything rather than liberality – but he was a liberal.

THIS was the tribute to Charles Brown that Dilke would write, six years after Brown had died. It was only a private annotation in Milnes's work on Keats, but the grateful thought remains that Keats brought Dilke, at last, to do this justice.

Since March 1821, when he had learnt the end of the 'most affectionate friendship' of his life, Dilke had shown his practical devotion to Keats's memory. The man who – even Brown admitted – could make himself forbidding, had pitted himself against the forbidding Abbey; and when Fanny Keats came of age, it was Dilke who dealt with her former guardian and ensured, at last, that she had her fortune. 'On a further examination of Mr Abbey's behaviour,' wrote George Keats to Dilke in 1826, 'I am confirmed in your opinion of him and can see in prospect his complete downfall.'[1] George's prediction was fulfilled: by 1827, Abbey was largely indebted to Dilke and Rice, two years later he mortgaged his London property, by 1833 he had vanished from Walthamstow. His life ended in downfall and mystery, and there was no record of regret when, on March 23rd, 1837, at a meeting of the Worshipful Company of Pattenmakers, the Clerk reported his death.

Dilke did not only have to solve the protracted problem of Abbey, there was also the problem of Valentine Llanos. Fanny Keats's husband disputed a bill with Rice and Reynolds, her solicitors, and borrowed some £2,000 from her to promote an abortive bridle-bit patent. Dilke was so vexed by Valentine Llanos's lack of tact and sense that he put Fanny's

H   113

marriage settlement funds in the Court of Chancery, and slightly with-
drew from his position as confidential adviser.

Yet from her departure for Spain in 1833 until her meeting with
Severn in 1861, his correspondence with her was almost her only link
with Keats's history; as for his correspondence with George, in America,
it continued sporadically until George's death. Dilke looked after his
English interests; and eight years after his controversial visit to England,
George gratefully declared: 'You are the man of all others to whom I am
most closely allied in feeling, you have had confidence in my integrity
when others have condemned me unheard.' Far away in Louisville, the
emigrant mill-owner regaled himself with memories of the country-
dance he had named after Maria:

> My dear Mrs Dilke,
> ... You are still the same lively chatty being, you were in 1818, pray
> remain so untill I can come and talk with you, and laugh with you,
> and dance with you. I beg likewise you will not endeavour to im-
> prove your husband, I am satisfied with him as he was, even to the
> taking of snuff ...
> ... I look to Mr Dilke as my anchor in my native sod, and so long
> as my cable of love of Country, and kindly feeling lasts, I shall cherish
> a hope that I shall one day haul my vessel to his hearth.[2]

Often he dreamed of sitting, once again, at Dilke's fireside, often he
urged him to bring 'merry Mrs D.' and Charley to Louisville, often he
emphasized the benefit of the long sea voyage to Maria. But Dilke could
not tear himself from London, George could not leave his saw mill in
Kentucky, neither of them crossed the Atlantic, and their correspondence
continued, all the more revealing as the erratic letters had to contain such
concentrated news. It was to Dilke that George poured out his own ideas
of his brother, when Hunt created the illusion of a weak, dependent Keats.
It was to Dilke that he explained his brother's finances when, in 1830, he
heard of 'the threatened life of poor John by Brown, involving the
sacrifice of my good name'. Perhaps, if Dilke had urged him further, he
would have written the memoir he had planned; for 'what fools we mor-
tals are, and how we are straining for ever so small a niche in the temple of
Fame, I claim being the affectionat[e] Friend and Brother of John Keats'.
When he spoke of John, a decade and more after he had seen him, his
thoughts still caught fire.

And, through his correspondence with Dilke, posterity keeps in touch with the Keats circle: 'My dear Sir,' he complained to Dilke in March 1826, 'Altho' there was not a jot too much in your well filled letter on the subject that composed it I was most anxious as I travelled thro' it to come to something about yourself and John and Books, and Authors, and Rice and Reynolds and gossip ...' In March 1828, in Chichester, where he and Maria were staying with his mother, Dilke finally found leisure to answer: 'Severn was very well when I last heard of him ... and he *talked* of paying England a visit this summer – Hunt has just published a sad tweedling book about Lord Byron and his contemporaries – Rice and Reynolds are both well ...'

Poor Rice, with his clinging illness, his Swiftean wit, his inevitable friendliness; his vivacity would soon grow less, his pallor more alarming. He would be only forty when he died in 1832, and was lost in tantalizing oblivion. As for Reynolds, his life would be a wretched falling-off from his Hampstead days:

> I once had thought to have embalmed my name
> With poesy – to have served the gentle Muses
> With high sincerity; – but life refuses ...

So he wrote in his thirties, in his *Sonnet to Retirement*.[3] In 1847 he went to Newport, Isle of Wight, as Assistant Clerk to the County Court. 'The law spoiled his literature, and his love of literature and society interfered with the drudging duties of the lawyer. The contest ended only with his life.' He died on November 15th, 1852, knowing well where his devotion lay. On his tombstone he is called 'The Friend of Keats'.[4]

There was another friend of Keats, of infinite importance, whom Dilke remembered constantly: he was the trustee of Fanny Brawne. Since the poet's death, her consolation had been her growing friendship with his sister; and, certain of being understood, eager to confirm her strongest bond with Keats, she had written to her with touching spontaneity. She had fought – with help from Maria Dilke – to break down the walls that Abbey built round his ward, she had encouraged, gossiped, entertained; she had fostered the girl's romance with Valentine Llanos,[5] she had disclosed her own deepest feelings, she had shown all her young vivacity, all her adult, steady understanding; and when Fanny Keats came of age at last, and the correspondence ceased, the Brawnes took her under their wing until she married.

For Fanny Brawne her youth became a time of repeated mourning: in 1828 her brother died of consumption, in 1829 her mother lit a guest across the garden; the candle set her dress ablaze, and soon afterwards she died. The Dilkes felt for her in her tragic series of misfortunes. The motherly Maria was fond of the courageous girl, and Dilke respected her integrity, and 'admired her very much in society'. 'My dear Brown, for my sake, be her advocate for ever.' So Keats had urged, on his journey to Rome. Had he not said likewise, to Dilke, in his last letter to him?

'The Brawnes are still single,' Dilke told George in February 1833, '& residing with an uncle & cousins in France.' In France Fanny Brawne had met her future husband. Four months later, on June 15th, 1833, she married a boy of twenty-one, Louis Lindon. Fanny Llanos 'neither understood nor excused' the marriage: an attitude both ungenerous and blind. The Dilkes remained friends of Fanny and her husband. They knew that Fanny Brawne was too vigorous to remain content with memory. They knew that she, who had loved Keats with devotion in her youth, would love the remembrance of him all her life.

17

THE GRAVE EDITOR

YOU have heard it appears that I am Editor of a Periodical [wrote Dilke to George, in 1833]. This is true enough. – It originated in an after dinner talk – I embarked on the work without forethought, or preparation – I was told that the Athenaeum was for sale on Monday, bought it on Sunday, and thought it out on Saturday – the Labors of the first twelvemonth almost put me into the grave – my wife says they have added ten years to the heavy score standing against me – Be that as it may, I believe I may now say I have succeeded – and succeeded where so many have failed.[1]

THE editorship of *The Athenaeum* was by no means the first of Dilke's literary ventures. His writings, if anonymous, were many. 'Some thirty or thirty-five years since,' recorded *The Men of the Time* in 1852, 'Mr Dilke was a contributor to the *Westminster Review*, and the *Retrospective Review* under the editorship of Mr Southern, our present minister at the Brazils.' In the 1820s he wrote for Colburn's *New Monthly Magazine*, and he contributed, as Thurusa, to *The London Magazine*, in the days of Lamb, Hood and Reynolds. But if *The London Magazine* encouraged his literary tastes, if Bentham's *Westminster Review*, that organ of the philosophical radicals, gave him a chance to air his politics, if, in 1821, in 'The Source and Remedy of the National Difficulties', an open letter to Lord John Russell, he proposed the repeal of the Corn Laws, the abolition of all laws affecting agricultural produce, it was still as editor, rather than author, that he made his mark. It was the editorial chair that felt most comfortable to the dogmatic man. As an editor, Dilke could assert all his principles, he could command his contributors and his public.

The Athenaeum had been founded in 1828 by James Silk Buckingham, the traveller and miscellaneous writer; and after a period under the aegis of Carlyle's friend John Sterling, it became the property of a small company, consisting of Dilke, Hood, Reynolds, Allan Cunningham, the stalwart Scottish poet, and Holmes, the printer. In 1830, Dilke became editor, and undertook 'the heavy and too often thankless task of conducting a critical journal, in which the truth, as far as he could find it, should be honestly told'.

As an editor, he showed the firmness and business acumen that Mr Abbey had long ago discovered. Early in 1831, Reynolds was horrified by his decision to halve the price of the journal:

> My dear Dilke,
> You astound me with your fall. It is more decided than Milton's 'Noon to Dewy Eve' one! From 8d. to 4d. is but a step, but then it is also from the sublime to the ridiculous ...
> Dear Dilke, Hood and I have been calculating this afternoon, and the result is appalling ... We are quite against the total change in our paper-constitution which you threaten.

Reynolds, Hood and Cunningham gave up their shares in the magazine, and the financial responsibility fell on its printer and editor. But the price of *The Athenaeum* was halved. Dilke, as usual, remained inflexible, and 'I think this first day, and these first hours,' he reported to Maria, 'the experience has succeeded well. You remember that at the outset we professed we should be well pleased if at starting we *doubled* our sale. We have already *trebled* it.' Early in 1832 he published the formal statement: 'Our success has exceeded even our own sanguine hopes. It has been more rapid and triumphant than was perhaps ever known. From a comparatively low state of existence the *Athenaeum* has risen to a sale exceeding that of *any* literary paper.'

*   *   *

Dilke attracted a constellation of contributors. Lamb, 'your Laureat', gave *The Athenaeum* some of his last pieces, and quibbled at proof-correction: 'I have read the enclosed five and forty times over. I have submitted it to my Edmonton friends; at last (O Argus' penetration) I have discovered a dash that might be dispensed with.' (Alas, he was too stricken to write, as Dilke had asked, on the death of Coleridge: 'I am totally incapable ... I do assure you I am incapable ...') Barry Cornwall wrote for Dilke, and Reynolds contributed poems and letters. In 1830, Dilke asked H. F. Chorley,[2] as a young Liverpool writer, to report the opening of the Liverpool–Manchester Railway; and in 1833 Chorley asked for a staff appointment. Dilke's reply was characteristic: 'I would consent to take my chance of your being more or less useful to me, and would give you £50 *for six months' services* ... I should require you to live in my immediate neighbourhood and to give me your assistance in any and every way I might suggest.' Chorley accepted the deterrent proposal – he even lived with the Dilkes for some time – and he became a distinguished music critic; and though, he wrote later, 'no two persons could be more unlike in many matters of taste, opinion and feeling than the late honoured Charles Dilke, and myself, it was impossible to know and not respect him, however so many were his prejudices (and they were many), however so limited were his sympathies (and they were limited).' As usual, 'merry Mrs D.' gained more than respect: in 1844 Chorley gave her 'a little trinket ... for an amount of cheerful and unwearied kindness which has thrown the charm of home over my London life'. Among his fellow-contributors was that wild Irishwoman, Lady Morgan, who had 'a genial love for Art, limited by the most inconceivable prejudices of ignorance'; as for her attempts at autobiography, they were, said Chorley, 'like their writer, so made up and rouged for effect as not to have taken a permanent place in the library of Female Biographies'. But where Chorley ridiculed, Dilke admired; and when Sydney Morgan duly quarrelled with Colburn, he invited her to write for him.

More than two hundred men and women wrote for *The Athenaeum* under Dilke. Elizabeth Barrett contributed poems and occasional reviews. The Howitts sent frequent articles, and in 1833 Dilke mentioned Douglas Jerrold and Thomas Lovell Beddoes among his contributors. He also enlisted – a bold innovation in English journalism – the assistance of distinguished foreign writers.

* * *

Dilke, Keats had written, years ago, 'is a Man who cannot feel he has a personal identity unless he has made up his Mind about every thing. The only means of strengthening one's intellect is to make up ones mind about nothing – to let the mind be a thoroughfare for all thoughts ... Dilke will never come at a truth as long as he lives; because he is always trying at it. He is a Godwin-methodist.'

Keats, in his native generosity, had seen beyond the set of prejudices. But Dilke's intransigence and self-righteousness increased with worldly success, and they certainly made him enemies. When Brown last called on him, in 1838, he lamented to Severn that 'Dilke is altogether unpleasant towards myself. He is dogmatical, conceited, and rude. Success has turned his brains ... I would rather not henceforth be in his company.' A few weeks later, when *The Athenaeum* damned his book, he added – 'It was all *malice prepense*. My fault has been in not lauding his literary talents, which was out of my power. I could praise his talents in obtaining success, but no more. My conscience has undone me with him.' In a final letter to Dilke, Brown 'told him plainly he was generally regarded as a blockhead, quoting Charles Lamb's adjective — a Dilkish blockhead'. The comment must have cut Dilke to the quick. But Severn's biographer repeats Lamb's opinion: Dilke lacked 'real discrimination and taste'. There was a sad amount of truth in Brown's words, and in the portrait he drew of Robert Wydel; and 'old Dilke of the Athenaeum', as Thackeray called him, was heartily disliked by others besides Brown. 'You may say,' wrote Dilke to Severn, 'do I pretend to know more of Keats's affairs than Keats himself? Yes, I assuredly know more than all the Keats put together.' Severn must have been vexed by the smug omniscience. But Dilke was always convinced he was right, that he alone was informed, that he alone had a conscience. In the early days of *The Athenaeum* he had a long correspondence with the dramatic critic, Charles Dance; all the principles of dramatic criticism were discussed, and Dance – who presumably showed independence – resigned.

Dilke left no doubt of his authority, and there was a certain coldness between him and Reynolds when Reynolds asked to review a book and Dilke inquired if he knew the author or publisher; Reynolds returned the book 'that you may consign it to some independent hand, according to your religious custom. I, alas, know author *and* bookseller!' Dilke's principles remained religious: Chorley was reprimanded for naming a contributor to Miss Mitford, and humbly acknowledged his transgression. As for the Paris correspondent, who accepted advance sheets of books from publishers, he received a devastating note: 'It is no use for you to send me reviews at present.' Robert Montgomery, the poet, who dispatched his works to Dilke's private address, had them swiftly returned; and if Mrs Gore, the novelist, thought she had found a devious means of ensuring a good notice, she was mistaken:

> You will receive in a day or two [she wrote] a novel of mine, called *The Sketch Book of Fashion*. I should feel greatly obliged if you would not notice it at all ... As you may imagine there is something mysterious in this Medea-like proceeding towards my own offspring,

I ought to add that general condemnation has rendered me somewhat ashamed of my sickly progeniture of fashionable novels, and
that I now have in the press a series of stories founded on the
history of Poland, which I hope will prove more worthy of
attention.

The Polish tales were duly condemned.

*   *   *

Dilke's main principle, as an editor, was to show independence: to criticize
books regardless of writer and publisher. He determined to break down
the system of publishing 'puffs', whether or not the publishers sent their
books or advertisements. The principle was a sound one – and, at the
time, a novelty; but it was characteristic of him to carry it to an extreme.
While he edited *The Athenaeum* he hardly ever dined out, in case he made
acquaintances who might seem to compromise him. He expected his staff
to observe the same code of honour; and if he let Chorley go to Lady
Blessington's, 'because she is Lady Blessington', he refused to let him go
anywhere else.

However, the literary world converged, more or less successfully, on
the Dilkes at 9, Lower Grosvenor Place. 'Esteemed friend', wrote William
Howitt, the Quaker topographer, from Nottingham,

> I was much obliged by thy polite invitation to thy party the night
> I arrived in town. The fact was that I ... made several attempts to reach
> thy house, but owing to the immense distances of London, and the
> want of punctuality in London people, I found it impossible to com-
> plete my business and see my friends ...

Miss Mitford, from Three Mile Cross, was more fortunate. In July 1837
she spent the evening with Thomas Barnes, the editor of *The Times*, and
found Dilke on a rare excursion into the outside world. 'The persons
whom I was most delighted with', she told her father, 'were Mr Dilke
and his wife. He is ... one of the most perfect and accomplished gentlemen
that I ever knew.'[3] Two years later she bustled to London for 'ten days
crowded with gratification', and commissioned a friend 'to get me a fly,
that I may go and see ... the Dilkes'. It was, no doubt, in a fly, that she
bowled along, respectably, to dine with them on June 1st. The Dilkes

were fashionable indeed: 'Yesterday a charming dinner made for me at Mr Dilke's', noted Lady Morgan on July 2nd, 1832. 'Amongst many celebrities, Hood (of the *Comic Annual*), a very grave person, looking the picture of ill-health, was presented to me. Morgan quite happy – good music in the evening. The cordial hostess full of kindness – pretty house – full of good pictures and curiosities.'

Hood was among Dilke's closest friends. 'Consult Dilke' was a recurrent phrase in his letters. It was to Dilke he unburdened himself when domestic troubles oppressed him, it was to Dilke he described his wife's oppressive family: the Reynolds's in Little Britain, whom Keats had often visited. Old Mrs Reynolds, 'if sometimes wrong-headed ... is always', said Hood, 'right-hearted'. But 'My dear Dilke, I do not mean to submit to Little Britain Leading strings ... the male sex stand not on a high pedestal in L.B. Fathers – Brothers – and so forth are but hewers of wood and drawers of water.'[4]

When Hood was in England he stayed with the Dilkes; and in Coblenz he dreamed of them. 'Shall I ever', he asked, when he was writing *Up the Rhine*, 'go *down* the Rhine, and drop in at Lower Grosvenor Place? ... I drank your health yesterday, in a glass of Jane's ginger wine.' At Lower Grosvenor Place, Dilke advised him, and Maria mothered him. ('Mrs Dilke told me to have my linen well aired.') Though she was still, as Keats had known, 'liable to Illness', though she still suffered from spasms and indigestion, Maria remained 'as plump as a partridge' and believed in filling 'the cavities'. Maria remained a perpetual tonic. 'If I recollect rightly your style of singing', wrote the devoted Hood, 'you were in favour of "tollol"eration.' 'My dear Mrs Dilke, I write to you (I hope Dilke won't be jealous) *con amore*, seeing that we have always been very good friends ...' Charming Maria! As Keats and Brown had discovered, long ago, she deserved a nonsense letter to herself. He sent her one:

> Madam, ... my mane object being to get sum of the children of my hands am intending to send one up to you by the Saturdays carryer hoping you ... may be the Means of getting him into sum sittiation in London ... and the Allmity Bless and prosper you for such and as the well noon gudness of Hart of you and Mr Dilke will I trust exert in Behalf of our deplorible states ...

If only Dilke had sent him more than a 'little letteret' in answer! But Dilke remained an inadequate correspondent. 'I suppose,' Hood lamented, 'some day I shall come to "T.H. is received," at the fag end of the *Athenaeum*.'

* * *

Dilke was, as usual, occupied, and not only with his paper. He remained a clubman, even in his editorial days. In the early 1820s John Martin, the artist, and Thomas Campbell had founded the Literary Union; and the committee, wrote Martin's son, 'also included Mr C. W. Dilke, founder of the *Athenaeum*, a journal renowned for the lofty tone of its articles and the asperity of its criticism. The name of Mr Dilke sounded a note of terror in the imaginations of all humble authorlings, for it had become a synonym of merciless, critical excoriation. A house was taken in Waterloo Place. To be elected was a marked honour ...' The opening of a neighbouring club, the Athenaeum, in 1824, had gradually drawn away its members; and the Literary Union had been reformed as the Clarence Club, 'when it became more noted for its free luncheons of biscuits and bitter than for its members, who consisted of all sorts and conditions of men'. But Dilke was fond of his food. 'He is not', wrote Hood, 'a man to go about picking shrimps and teazing periwinkles out of their shells. He never met with anything he couldn't eat ... As for Dilke,' Hood added, 'you know his infatuation for everything outlandish. Doesn't he send to the further end of the Edgware Road (or where is it?) for German mustard?' Dilke duly delighted in the cuisine at 12, Waterloo Place; and when he asked what he could bring on a visit to Coblenz, even the author of *Up the Rhine* demanded 'a dish of pork chops with tomato sauce, à la Clarence!'[5]

Were they served at 9, Lower Grosvenor Place to a gratified Lady Morgan? 'Yesterday dined with some of my literary friends at Mr Dilke's', she wrote, on May 22nd, 1836. 'Kind, gay, and pleasant. After dinner, I got up and danced a *reel* with the *grave editor*.'

* * *

The dance recalls the 'pianoforte hop' that Keats himself had graced, nearly two decades earlier; and Dilke still showed his devotion to the poet. He remained the trustee of Fanny Llanos (it had cost him 'years of anxiety'), and of Margaret Brawne, now wife of the Brazilian Minister to Vienna. He remained the trustee of Fanny Brawne, Mrs Lindon; and as she followed her husband, an officer in the English Legion, to Spain –

which was then in the grip of the Carlist Wars – as she travelled with him to Bayonne and Heidelberg and Freiberg, she often corresponded with Dilke and Maria.

'I am a great friend of Mrs Dilke's', Fanny had declared in 1820. Maria had always, loyally, befriended her. She had copied out the Snooks's comments on Keats at Bedhampton; and, when Keats had died, she had come to comfort Fanny at Wentworth Place, she had swept her off to theatres and exhibitions, she had asked her to dine and stay at Great Smith Street. When Jane Reynolds sneered at the poet's 'most unhappy connection', Maria had quarrelled with the Reynolds family; and she helped to keep the secret of Keats from Louis Lindon, until, at last, some seven years after his marriage, he noticed a portrait at Lower Grosvenor Place, and asked who it was. For once the talkative Maria could find no words; and Fanny 'when we got home explained as much as was necessary'. Maria was almost the only person with whom she broke her silence, and in 1848 she was still sending her long, spontaneous letters, she was still writing freely of Keats himself. 'I can tell you', she had told his sister, soon after he had died, 'who next to me (I must say *next* to me) loved him best, that I have not got over it and never shall.'

Dilke, like Maria, knew Fanny's constancy; he warned Severn sternly that Brown's memoir made 'certain references to Mrs L. which could not but be deeply painful to her'. When, towards the end of her life, beset by financial troubles, she was compelled to sell Severn's miniature of her poet, she offered it to Dilke instinctively: 'It would not be a light motive that would make me part with it, but I have this satisfaction, that next to my own family, there is no one in whose possession I should …' Part of the letter is torn away, but the affectionate trust remains quite clear.

*   *   *

And Dilke, the advocate of Mrs Lindon, watched over the poet's fame, though he did so with less nobility than Brown. When Brown had first suggested a memoir, Dilke urged him, as the only proof that he was not book-making, to declare that he would not accept a penny of the profits. 'I never', Brown told Severn, 'thought of profit, rather of loss.' Dilke's principles were less rigid when they applied to himself: in 1841 he confessed that George Keats had given him 'full power to treat for the copyright of his brother's works, and he was most anxious to bring out a handsome edition … I fear indeed that I alone am responsible that no such edition was published. I however had but little leisure at the time ...'

Yet, for all the selfishness, the arrogance, the rivalry with Brown, Dilke's devotion to Keats still existed; and in 1846, when Milnes was preparing his work, he helped him eagerly. 'I now send all [the letters and papers] that I have preserved of any value ... I wish, with all my heart, that I could have sent any thing ... proportioned to my love for the man and care for his fame.'[6] He added details of Keats's finances and a note on Valentine Llanos; the following summer, from Bedhampton, 'where poor Keats passed his last day & slept his last night in England',[7] he suggested a date for one of the poet's letters that Milnes had sent him. When, at last, in August 1848, he ran through the two volumes 'with eagerness & pleasure', he reminded Milnes that 'whenever you are inclined for a talk on the subject [of Keats's finances], I am at your command.' He had lent him Severn's copy of the miniature to engrave as a frontispiece, and when he had bought the original, he kept it, permanently, in his room.

'If the public cry him up as a great poet,' Maria had decided in 1820, 'I will henceforth be their humble servant; if not, the devil take the public.' In The Athenaeum, Dilke and Reynolds showed their lasting awareness of Keats. In January 1831, reviewing Moore's Letters and Journals of Lord Byron, Reynolds observed with anger:

> The biographer has allowed all the ill-nature and sarcasm against Keats to be perpetuated, – without regard to the feelings of surviving relations and friends. The idle stuff of Keats's dying of the Quarterly Review is preserved carefully – although it is well known that consumption, and not criticism, destroyed him.[8]

On February 5th, in an article on criticism, The Athenaeum returned to the attack:

> Whether that craft is answerable for the death of Keats, or has otherwise materially increased the demand for coroners, it is not necessary to enquire. The general tendency to repress the aspirings of untried genius, and the occasional strangulation of works of acknowledged merit, are counts of indictment sufficiently grave.

On March 10th, 1832, there appeared an elegy on Keats's death; and on August 4th Dilke himself, roused by Medwin's Memoir of Shelley, repeated:

Lord Byron's opinion, that [Keats] was killed by the reviewers, is wholly ridiculous; though his epitaph, and the angry feelings of his friends, might seem to countenance it. Keats died of hereditary consumption ... We go as far as Captain Medwin in admiration of Shelley; but as far as Shelley in admiration of Keats.

Here and there, in his *Athenaeum*, Dilke continued to publish his loyalty to the poet's circle: a kindly notice of Leigh Hunt's play, *A Legend of Florence*,[9] a handsome article on William Hilton, and, on January 4th, 1840, a generous obituary of the same friend.'[10]

* * *

In the first years of Dilke's editorship, the circulation of *The Athenaeum* had risen; but there had been no profit from which to pay him a salary. In 1836, however, when the Navy Pay Office was abolished, he retired from government service on a pension, and devoted himself to the journal. By the 1840s it had become an established success, and no longer needed his constant exertions. He was prepared for change.

On January 21st, 1846, there appeared the first issue of *The Daily News*. It was launched by Joseph Paxton, the future designer of the Crystal Palace, as a deliberate challenge to Delane's *Times*. It was to be run on advanced Liberal lines, and support the Manchester School and the agitation for the repeal of the Corn Laws. The country was in the throes of the Free Trade struggle. The first leader – a plea for untaxed bread – was written by William Fox, one of the great orators of the Anti-Corn Law League. Such politics were after Dilke's own heart.

The paper had been bravely launched, and Dickens had been engaged as editor at £2,000 a year. Dickens's editorial powers hardly matched his powers as a novelist. 'He was the best reporter in London,' wrote Sir William Howard Russell, the journalist, 'and as a journalist he was nothing more ... He told me himself that he never thought about politics till the Revolution of 1848. He had appointed as manager his father, and if his father was not really a Micawber, he was at all events destitute of the energy and experience of Delane senior.' Dickens's sense of dignity was so exaggerated that proofs were served to him on a silver salver.

He remained editor for three weeks, after which he was succeeded by John Forster. His future biographer was no more fortunate, and by the end of March the position of *The Daily News* was critical. Dilke, the

drastic, the awe-inspiring, was summoned to the sickbed, gave the editorship of *The Athenaeum* to an old contributor, Thomas Kibble Hervey, and
'Oh!' cried Browning to Miss Barrett, on May 7th, '*The Daily News*
passes into the redoubtable hands of Mr Dilke – and the price is to be
reduced to 2½d. ...'[11] The new manager had been given a three-year
contract and absolute power to deal with *The Daily News* as he pleased.
He repeated the *Athenaeum* formula, and the circulation rose from 4,000
to 22,000.

The leading proprietors of the paper were his friends William Bradbury
and Frederick Evans – Bradbury was one of the owners of the newly-
established *Punch*. They were supported by Sir Joshua Walmsley, who
had worked with Bright and Cobden in the Anti-Corn Law League, and
would found the National Reform League. There were sometimes con-
flicts between Dilke, and Bright and Cobden. But though they might
differ, both men respected him; and Bright, some thirty years later, still
kept 'a lively sense of the intelligence and the dignity by which he was
distinguished'.[12] Dickens, writing to Dilke's grandson in 1870, still recalled
'the relations of friendship which I held both with your excellent father
and grandfather, and can never remember without emotion'.[13]

In April 1849, when his three-year contract expired, Dilke retired from
the paper. A colleague assured him that 'there is not an individual connected with the *Daily News* – who knows its true interests – who will not
look upon this day as the blackest in its calendar ... From the sub-editors
down to the smallest boy, there is not one in the office ... who does not
look upon your loss as a personal misfortune'.

* * *

Dilke's retirement from the Press had not ended his literary activities.
In 1858, with Dickens and Forster, after years of investigation, he published *The Case of the Reformers of the Literary Fund*, pointing out the
excessive cost of administration, and the faulty constitution of the manag-
ing committee. 'Honest men on an irresponsible committee are not',
thundered Dilke, 'a sufficient security against misconduct.'

His researches were not only administrative. 'Since his retirement from
the *Daily News*,' observed *The Men of the Time* in 1852,

Mr Dilke appears to have indulged himself with more quiet than
his indomitable tendency to hard work ever before permitted him to

enjoy. Now and then he may be seen in the Reading Room of the British Museum (of which, by the way, he was one of the very earliest frequenters in the days of Benjamin D'Israeli the elder) pouring over some seldom-searched page printed perhaps by a flying press during the turmoil of the Civil Wars, or, it may be, in the less sanguinary but scarcely less exciting days of 'Wilkes and '45,' when the press was struggling to be free ...

'His habits were simple and homely', recalled John Francis (son of the publisher of *The Athenaeum*), 'and he passed his time in his library or in searching for books on his special subjects among the old book-shops, with occasional visits accompanied by his son to the *Athenaeum* office ... In the autumn he would take his holiday with his son and two grandsons ...'

Dilke himself surveyed his researches with a scholar's eye: 'Gropings among old fusty MSS cannot, I suppose, be considered very *successful*, because there has been but little *result*; but to me there is pleasure in the search itself, just as a sportsman loves the hunt for the hunt's sake.' Keats had long ago found him 'up to his Ears in Walpole's letters'; now his retirement gave him years of academic pleasure.

He remained an inveterate writer on miscellaneous subjects: in 1845 he had written largely in *The Athenaeum* on mesmerism – which he disliked profoundly – and in 1846 he had turned to one of his favourite subjects, stained glass. As editor of *The Athenaeum* he had rarely written for the paper; when he gave up the post, he became a serious contributor. The former editor of *Dodsley's Old Plays* kept his affection for Elizabethan drama, but he now turned to the literary history of the seventeenth and eighteenth centuries. He was fascinated by the mystery of the authorship of the Junius letters. 'The truth, the whole truth, and nothing but the truth, was the end and object of all his enquiries and in the search for this,' wrote an admirer, 'he was indefatigable.' With his usual thoroughness he acquired a knowledge of the subject that none could rival. Unlike his contemporaries, he was not so anxious to find out who Junius was, as to show who he was not; and though he had an idea of the writer's identity, his published criticisms were entirely destructive. His first Junius article appeared in *The Athenaeum* in 1848, and in the next five years he wrote a series of reviews which were probably the most weighty contribution to the controversy. His study of Junius led him to the study of Burke and Wilkes, and he rescued Wilkes from obloquy. Dilke was 'severe when the

CHARLES WENTWORTH DILKE
From a miniature

'THE GRAVE EDITOR'
A cartoon of Dilke by Thomas Hood
published in Hood's *Up the Rhine*, 1840

'THE GRAND'. CHARLES WENTWORTH DILKE IN LATER LIFE
From the painting by Arthur Hughes

occasion called for severity; but his kind nature', wrote John Francis, 'made him far more happy when helping to add a name to the roll of fame than when removing an unworthy one from it'. In 1854 he was working on Pope, and deep in the Caryll Papers recently acquired by the British Museum; in a series of articles he solved the mystery of Caryll's publication of the letters, explained Pope's parentage, settled several matters in his early life, and identified the 'Unfortunate Lady'. This engaged him in argument with other students of Pope, and for three years he corresponded busily with John Murray, showing what the publisher called his 'inflexible truth'. Dilke's conclusions remained unshaken, and they were adopted by Pope's editors, Elwin and Courthope. He was asked to help them edit, but he felt too old for the task. However, with the love of truth that Murray had recognized, he had helped to found a periodical in which scholars might air their doubts and discoveries. In 1849, with W. J. Thoms, the future deputy librarian of the House of Lords, he had established *Notes and Queries*, to which he often contributed.

'There is one thing known only to myself', Thoms would write: 'the deep respect and affection with which I regarded that good and wise man – a respect and affection which it is my boast that he cordially returned.' At their first interview Thoms had been struck by Dilke's 'strong common sense', and 'yet more impressed by his frankness and warm-hearted sympathy'. Thoms would live to 'honour his memory on this side idolatry';[14] and when Dilke died, he paid tribute in *Notes and Queries* to his lasting integrity:

> Mr Dilke was one of the truest-hearted men and kindest friends it has ever been our good fortune to know. The distinguishing feature of his character was his singular love of truth, and his sense of its value and importance, even in the minutest points and questions of literary history. What the independence of English literary journalism owes to his spirited exertions, clear judgment, and unflinching honesty of purpose, will, we trust, be told hereafter by an abler pen.

Dilke's scholarship was lauded, with characteristic hyperbole, when, in 1881, his grandson dined with Lord Beaconsfield, and

> Lord Beaconsfield praised my grandfather, a sure way to my heart, and said that my grandfather and his own father were 'the last two men in England who had a thorough knowledge of English letters' ...

I thought Dizzy very polite and pretty in all his ways and in all he said.[15]

One episode in English letters Dilke could discuss with almost unrivalled thoroughness; and Rowland Hill, the inventor of the penny postage, living now in Hampstead, would often wander over the Heath with the

famous journalist and influential man of letters, at whose house one met every writer, to say nothing of other men and women, worth knowing. He was a charming old man, to listen to whose talk was a liberal education. Did we walk with him on Hampstead Heath, where once he had a country house, he became an animated guide-book, guiltless of a dull page, telling us of older times than our own, and of dead and gone worthies who had been guests at 'Wentworth House'. On this much-worn, initial-carven, wooden seat used often to sit Keats listening to the nightingales, and, maybe, thinking of Fanny Brawne.[16]

18

DILKE AND HIS BOY

'I CANNOT help thinking,' Keats had written, when the Dilkes moved to Westminster, 'what a shame it is that poor Dilke should give up his comfortable house & garden for his Son, whom he will certainly ruin with too much care ... Dilke has continually in his mouth 'My Boy'. This is what spoils princes: it may have the same effect with Commoners ... One would think Dilke ought to be quiet and happy – but no – this one Boy makes his face pale, his society silent and his vigilance jealous ... With all this he has no notion how to manage him.'

The whole of Dilke's existence, the whole of Charley's life – or, rather, Wentworth's life, for he now used the family name – were to confirm the wisdom of Keats's judgment. Wentworth would earn his worldly success; his relationship with his father would be a classic case of parental misunderstanding.

*   *   *

'Give my kindest love to my dear boy', Dilke had exhorted Maria. 'I cannot love him better ... I hope that he will sometime or other be the first boy in the school, and that he will soon be the first of his age.'[1] In 1826, when he left Westminster, Wentworth had duly reached the top of the school; and when Dilke had left him in Florence with Brown, and begun his homeward journey, he had sent him an eloquent letter:

> I ought to be in bed [this from Genoa], but somehow you are always first in my thoughts and last ... It is natural perhaps that I should take a greater interest than other fathers, for I have a greater interest at stake. I have *but one* son. That son, too, I have brought up differently from others, and if he be not better than others, it will be urged against me, not as a misfortune, but as a shame ... And you will not fail me. I am sure you will return home to do me honour, and to make me respect you as I do, and ever shall love you.[2]

The ambition was already mistaken, egotistic, intense. Dilke, who always made up his mind about everything, had determined to make his only son a great man, and, which was more foreboding, to stake his own reputation, his own honour and self-respect, on the result. He watched the boy's progress intently:

> You seem to have something of your father and of your grandfather in you, and to love books [he wrote, in a birthday letter]; but do not mistake buying them for reading them, a very common error with half the world ... A library is nothing unless the owner be a living catalogue to it ...
> I do not desire to have you a great Latin *scholar* ... But I do wish you to know and understand Latin as well as you do English ... Keep your mind always awake to what is going on about you ... There are advantages in travel often overlooked. But if a man hopes to distinguish himself – to be a writer, or a statesman, or to desire to be *qualified to be* these, which all men ought – then he must contrast laws with laws, agriculture with agriculture, peasantry with peasantry, and then his country may benefit by his observation and travel.
> Here's a pretty birthday letter of congratulation! Never mind, my dear fellow ... The fact is, I never think of you, but it is how to make you happy, respected, self-respected.[3]

Dilke was a living catalogue to his own 12,000 books. Dilke was a self-made scholar, a self-made man of affairs, an industrious civil servant who knew the need for self-improvement and unremitting hard work. Dilke was a Radical and a republican. Dilke had also blindly determined to see his son in his own image: to see his son achieve all his own ambitions. He refused to consider that the product of parental self-sacrifice and conventional education might be very different from himself.

Left in Florence, Wentworth grew well-versed in Italian and opera, and learned the easier delights of *dolce far niente*. At Cambridge – his own son would record – he was Dilke's despair. Dilke had seen him as a barrister (had not Mr Wydel intended his son, Robert, for the law?); Wentworth never used his LL.B., and in London he was known for not missing a night at the opera. Dilke's pride was wounded to the quick. Wentworth's behaviour belied all the principles of his education. Wentworth had not done him honour as he had designed, and this was 'not a misfortune, but a shame'.

Dilke's disappointment was the result of stubborn egotism, of the conviction that he alone must decide his son's career. He had devoted himself to Wentworth's education; he had chosen what his boy should be. That 'Dilke's boy' should become a man, with a character of his own, was unthinkable. Wentworth was, in fact, to justify all his father's attention; he was, in his own way, to become a man of distinction. But Dilke never forgave him for his failure to conform to the predetermined parental pattern. Nothing that Wentworth could achieve would now, in Dilke's eyes, redeem him.

On March 30th, 1840, at St Luke's, Chelsea, Wentworth married Mary, the only daughter of the late Captain William Chatfield (once in command of the first Madras cavalry). 'The young Dilkes are expected back soon', Hood told his wife on April 15th. 'They are at Henley-on-Thames. They are to live in Sloane Street. We have had a deal of fun, Mrs Dilke and I, about the haste of the wedding, that the cake was put in a very quick oven, &c. I told Mrs Dilke they ought to have put it in the papers thus: "*Suddenly*, on such a day, at St Luke's, Pimlico." '

Wentworth's marriage made him a lonely man in an oppressive circle of female relations. His widowed mother-in-law, Mrs Chatfield – known as Dragon – moved at once into Sloane Street, bringing not only her own mother, Mrs Duncombe, but her unmarried niece, Miss Folkard. Mrs Chatfield and Miss Folkard continued to live in the house long after its nominal master had died. Wentworth's prestige grew even less, his authority diminished even further.

The result of Dilke's disillusionment was inevitable. On September 4th, 1843, Mary Dilke gave birth to the child whom he would address as 'Dearest Numero 3': the third Charles Wentworth Dilke in existence. Mary would have another son, Ashton; but to Dilke there would always be, virtually, one child, and on this child he focused all the affection he had once shown his own offspring. He lavished upon him a solicitude all the more intense because he had irrevocably determined that Numero 3 should fulfil the ambitions that Numero 2 had disappointed.

My father loved my grandfather deeply [Numero 3 would write], but my grandfather was greatly disappointed in him, and always a little hard towards him: my father suffered through life under a constant sense of his inferiority. He suffered also later from the fact that while his elder son was the grandfather's and not the father's boy, his younger son was as completely under my influence in most matters, as I was under the influence of my grandfather.

With the ruthlessness for which he was known, Dilke ignored his son's paternal responsibilities. Mary sanctioned this domination. From the moment of Charles's birth, she became Dilke's chief correspondent, and Wentworth was completely overshadowed.

In *The Papers of a Critic*, years later, Charles would emphasize the 'remarkably warm affection' between Dilke and his son; he would record Dilke's thanks to 'dear Wentworth' for his 'kindness and attention. I am at all times very sensible of it', Dilke told his son, 'though it is only on rare occasions that I speak ...' The occasions must have been rare indeed; and in everything else he published, in the manuscript of his autobiography, in the papers he chose to keep, Numero 3 made it plain how little affection Wentworth received from his father. The parental mania which Keats had lamented long ago, had gone for ever. It was replaced by a passion even stronger. From the moment of his retirement in 1849, until his death, Dilke's engrossing occupation was the training of his elder grandson. It was a training which lent itself to the making of a statesman.

19

DEAREST NUMERO 3

IT was largely through Dilke that Charles could write: 'I have known everyone worth knowing from 1850 to my death.' At the age of seven he met them in Sloane Street and Lower Grosvenor Place. He remembered visits with Dilke to Gore House, where the gay, the superb, the luxurious Lady Blessington held sway; he had memories, too,

> of the bright eyes of little Louis Blanc ... of Thackeray's tall stooping figure, of Dickens's goatee, of Paxton's white hat, of Barry Cornwall and his wife, of Robert Stephenson the engineer, to whom I wanted to be bound apprentice, of Browning (then known as 'Mrs Browning's husband') ...

And then the gay, revolving world stopped suddenly. On November 12th, 1850, at the age of sixty, his grandmother died.[1] Maria Dilke 'was indeed a great loss to all that knew her', Matthew Snook told Carlino Brown, three years later. 'I have never liked London since.'[2]

For Dilke it was the end of a forty-years' marriage, of 'the most complete happiness'; his health was so affected that for sixteen months he abandoned literary work. For sixteen months he wandered through the remoter parts of Scotland, and along the north and west coasts of Ireland.

His one remaining pleasure was Sloane Street, and to his daughter-in-law he wrote constantly. They disagreed on fundamental principles: 'My mother', wrote Numero 3, 'had been a strong Low Church woman ... My grandfather and my father, although both of them in their way religious men (and my grandfather, a man of the highest feeling of duty), were neither of them churchgoers, nor of her school of thought.' But on one point Dilke and Mary seemed to agree: that Wentworth was 'in every way a man of less real distinction than his father, although much better known by the public'.

On May 1st, 1851, the Great Exhibition opened. Wentworth had been among the first to propose it, he had been a member of the executive committee. He had been in charge of the building and general superin-

135

tendence, and 'worked with more zeal and persistence than anyone else'. He had consulted Dilke a good deal (perhaps it was Dilke who suggested that he gave some work to Louis Lindon). Now the triumphant outcome of his labours prompted him to write to the person he longed to impress:

> *The Building.* 1*st May*
>
> My dear Father
> I cannot resist a line as I know you will be nervous. It has been a complete success.
>
> Yours affectionately
> C. WENTWORTH DILKE[3]

That August he and Mary were entertained by the French government; when the Exhibition closed he declined £3,000 and a knighthood. He received two services of blue Sèvres, voted by the Assemblée Nationale, and a diamond-and-ruby bracelet for his wife from Queen Victoria. The Prince Consort sent him his friendship medal in gold, the King of Sweden did likewise, and the King of Saxony dispatched the collar of the Order of Albertus-Animosus. In the official picture of the opening of the Great Exhibition, 'Dilke's Boy' was a prominent figure. In December he was elected Vice-President of the Society of Arts.

There is no record of delight from Dilke.

∗   ∗   ∗

But as he wandered through Ireland, Dilke remained aware of the little boy in Sloane Street; and his letters to Charles were suffused with gentleness:

> *Dublin* 1*st of October* [1851]
>
> Dearest Numero 3,
> ... Mamma tells us about benevolent fairies watching over good children. Fairies you know never existed, they are merely names by which we describe affections ... But there are loving mothers and fathers and grandmothers and dear friends who are always watching over good children ...[4]

The answer was laboriously inscribed on ruled paper:

> My dear Grandpapa
> I have been waiting to write to you till Mamma could sit by my

136

side and keep me quiet and now Grandpa she is here but my hands are so cramped with playing the Bird valse that I must say goodbye dear Grandpa.

Your affect^{ate}

CHARLES W. DILKE 3[5]

* * *

The following year Dilke took Numero 3 all over England, 'reading Shakespeare', recorded Charles, 'and studying church architecture, especially Norman ... We followed Charles II in his flight, and visited every spot that has ever been mentioned in connection with his escape – a pilgrimage which took me among other places to my future constituency of the Forest of Dean. We went to every English cathedral, and when my grandfather was at work upon his Pope investigations, saw every place which was connected with the history of the Carylls': the family of John Caryll, who had suggested to Pope the idea of *The Rape of the Lock*. Some of the boy's first vivid recollections were of staying in country places and cathedral cities with the grandfather 'under whose influence I was in childhood and to some extent have remained throughout my life'.[6] Dilke 'had a terror' of his becoming a soldier, and 'used to do his best to point out the foolish side of war', to encourage his moral rectitude, his literary tastes. In 1853 he reported to Wentworth, from Bedhampton:

Charley-boy ... is now learning his Latin verbs, and I shall soon send him into the garden. He is very good, as indeed he always is – and very desirous to be good and to be loved as a good boy. This is a great blessing and if we can only *keep up this gentle and kind nature*, it will influence him hereafter, when age is so easily misled, to his own happiness and that of all who love him.[7]

Long afterwards Dilke would thank his grandson 'for the many years of happiness which your upright and honourable conduct has given me'.[8] The happiness had always been shared, the affection always returned. When Charley was nine, his grandmother, Mrs Chatfield, reported that 'he told me that spot in the corner of the garden near the sitting room had the advantage over all the rest "because Grandpapa can look out upon it *all day*".'[9]

* * *

Dilke would soon gain a still more decisive influence over his grandson. Mary Dilke had fallen into a decline. Wentworth, now Royal Commissioner to the New York Exhibition, was called home from America. On September 26th, 1853, Mary died. 'She is a great loss to her husband,' Matthew Snook told Carlino Brown, in New Zealand, 'being a talented and literary character.'[10]

On the morning after her death, Dilke gave Charles the last note she had written him: 'Moral discipline your grandfather will teach you.' That day, Dilke and Wentworth exchanged all too eloquent letters. 'My grandfather's I shall not quote', Charles wrote, years later. 'It is about myself.' Wentworth's answer remains:

Your letter ... is like all the acts of your life towards me, dictated by your love, but I cannot allow you to come to town, it is enough that I am here ... God in Heaven will bless you for all your kindnesses to us – to me of course more especially has your goodness ever been shown by the sacrifices made in early life to give me my chance and though I am occasionally bad tempered, from over excitement, I am never, I never have been, insensible to all that you and my ever beloved, and affectionately remembered Mother went through, to make me good and prosperous. I am I know excitable, I try to controul it, I do not always succeed, by tolerating it you only make me each time more sensible, if possible, of your love. Again and again, thanks, thanks, I hope to show yet for years to come the love of

Your affectionate son

C. WENTWORTH DILKE[11]

So a man of forty-three expressed his craving for affection, his dependence on his father, his fear of him: the emotions of a maladjusted child.

*   *   *

Soon after his mother's death, Charles was sent to stay with his cousins, the Snooks, at Bedhampton.

Dear old Admiral [Dilke wrote, on October 15th],
    Hope you found all right and tight: a gallant vessel – tackle-trim – noble crew of true blue waters – guns shining and serving for looking-

glasses to shave by – powder dry – plenty in the locker. Wishing you favourable gales,

I remain,

Your old friend and rough and tough

GRANDFATHER

Dilke and his grandson understood one another perfectly. 'My Dear Grandpapa,' signalled Charles, 'the Admiral has to report for the information of his Cockney readers that he hoisted his Flag yesterday at the main peak.'

The rough and tough grandfather, who had always made up his mind about everything, had now taken a final drastic decision. He not only gave all his money to Wentworth, he came to live, permanently, under his son's roof at 76, Sloane Street. For the next eleven years, wrote Charles, Wentworth 'consulted his father – dependent on him for bread – in every act of his life'. Wentworth's attitude to Dilke was beyond hope of change.

*   *   *

In 1854 Dilke took his grandson round south-east England. That autumn they crossed the Channel. The following year, when Wentworth was one of the English Commissioners for the Paris International Exhibition, the family settled in the French capital from April to August. They acquired, Charles recalled, a sound knowledge of its antiquities 'by rambling about it with my grandfather, who, however, soon got sick of Paris and went home to his books'.

Back in Sloane Street, the bibliophile wrote gaily to Numero 3:

> I hope a stray sunbeam or two has been seen at Paris. If not I will get cook to bottle a few and will send them over. We *eat* them here with what are called summer cabbages. Perhaps you will prefer them with *petits pois*.[12]
>
> My dear dear Charleyboy [he added], – though we are widely separated just now, yet the same sun shines on us both, and the same stars light us to bed, so that morning and evening I am reminded of you, and in the daytime you are not forgotten.

Dilke's devotion was incessant: when Numero 3 was on holiday, he sent him salmon and apricots; and 'my dear Boy', he inquired from Sloane Street,

139

CHARLES WENTWORTH DILKE

... does Bedhampton stand where it did, with its little streams
running here and there and everywhere, its little picturesque Church,
nestling like a bird's nest in its own little wood – and the rookery as
of old – and the Mills and their ceaseless music? I rejoice to know that
the same kind good people are there, on the hill and under the hill,
and therefore I know that you are happy ...[13]

In 1857 he took the boy to Oxford and Cambridge, Ely, Peterborough
and Norwich; they travelled together all over South Wales, discussing
historical memories and architectural details. They talked politics as equals:

Hope your news of the French troops landing in Genoa is pre-
mature [wrote Dilke on April 25th, 1859]. War, however, seems
inevitable; but I hope on, hope ever. I should be sorry to see the
Austrians triumph over the Sardinians, for then they would fasten
the chains on Italy tighter than ever. Yet I cannot hope that the worst
man in Europe, the Emperor of the French, should triumph.

'My grandfather', remembered Charles, 'was a conservative republican
in old age, a radical republican in youth, but a republican through life,
and ... my young ideas were my grandfather's ideas.'
In 1860, when the old man was seventy-one and had grown 'somewhat
infirm', Charles began to travel with his father; but wherever he was,
Dilke was with him in spirit, directing all he did. No gossip was too trivial
for 'the Grand' to send him: early in 1861 he reported:

On Friday I accompanied the young philosopher [Ashton Dilke]
to Faraday's Lecture. That was a day for weather – rain, hail, sleet,
snow. To tell the truth, old and young were, I believe, *equally*
instructed and amused ... As your father and grandmother dined
yesterday with Mr Proctor I hoped to collect something, but in vain –
all I can learn is that ... the new Editor of the Quarterly was there,
and *not* very *effective*. This proves nothing. What may be his ability
I know not – but this I do know that all studious men are judged
unfairly if judged by any social standard ...[14]

It was hard for outsiders to judge Dilke, for he remained retiring. But
nothing stopped the flow of his letters to his grandson:

My dear Charles

I have not, for some time, been able to write by candlelight, and now I cannot read by daylight – no not even the newspapers. I have resolved therefore to try the *combined* power, and am writing, at one o'clock, close to the window, with my lamp on my right hand – and truly we have a fine specimen of a town November day ...[15]

The letter was sent to Cambridge where, in 1862, Numero 3 was a freshman at Trinity Hall. 'T.H. for ever,' cried Dilke, 'and no foxhunting!'[16] Cambridge now became his passion.

20

THE GRAND

BY all who were fortunate enough to enjoy the acquaintance of Mr
Dilke,' *The Hampshire Chronicle* would record on his death, 'his
moral worth and rigid integrity were held in the greatest respect and
esteem.'[1] Such testimonies – and they are many – make his relations with
his own son appear all the more pathetic.

Wentworth had developed slowly, he had not developed according to
his father's rigid plans, but, civilized and versatile, exceptionally capable,
he now epitomized worldly success. He had inherited Dilke's love of
gardening, and, with Joseph Paxton and Professor Lindley, he had founded
The Gardener's Chronicle; his work for the Royal Horticultural Society had
not only revived the Society, it had strengthened his friendship with the
Royal Family. In December 1861, within a week of the Prince Consort's
death, Lord Granville wrote: 'You will be touched at hearing that the
poor Queen spontaneously enquired after you, and told me that she knew
how much you would feel the loss.'[2] On January 2nd, 1862, a baronetcy
was conferred on him. The Radical and republican Dilke had advised
him to decline it; and when he accepted, Dilke registered only qualified
approval:

> My dear Will [this to his brother in Chichester],
> ... I am naturally pleased at a public recognition of my boy's
> services in furtherance of a good cause, a cause of more than national
> importance, for it is the cause of humanity, the cause of human pro-
> gress. Beyond this the deponent sayeth not. My son's fortune is not
> strong enough to enable his children to carry such a burden with
> ease; and as to the waifs and strays which it may help them to, I
> would rather see them fight their good fight unshackled.[3]

* * *

Sir Wentworth was received at Windsor and Buckingham Palace. Dilke's
thoughts were fixed immovably on Numero 3 at Cambridge, 'though not

142

being a Cambridge man,' he wrote, at the end of his grandson's first term, 'I am at times a little puzzled. Thus I know not whether I ought to congratulate *you* personally on Troyte's double bump ... What a bore I shall be after the 13th. with my endless enquiries!'[4]

It seemed that every letter from Cambridge demanded congratulations. Two days later came the results of the college examination: 'Hurrah! hurrah! my dear grandson!' cried Dilke. 'Ninety-seven out of a hundred – eleven above the second 'man' – is a position that would satisfy a whole family of loving friends, even if they were all grandfathers.'[5] Numero 3 immediately recorded a fresh success. Dilke's cup was overflowing:

Bravo! Bravo! my dear Charles. Bravo!

Your letter, last night, was equally a surprise and a pleasure. I had supposed that all opportunity for distinguishing yourself were over for this Term. It were too the greater surprise, because ... I did not expect to find you strong in Algebra ... It is daily devotion to our great object that ensures success.

Hurrah for tomorrow – says

Your loving Grandfather[6]

Happily, now, in Sloane Street, the builder of Wentworth Place rejoiced in the brave new world revealed to him:

I belong to a past age, and shall never overtake these Railway times ...

What grand fellows you Cambridge men are! All my life every thing came *up* or was sent *up* to the great Metropolis – and when I read of your taking books *up*, your father was obliged to enlighten my simplicity, by explaining that language itself has changed since my time and that with a Cantab *up* means *down*.[7]

*   *   *

Forty years ago, and more, Keats had 'fallen foul of Politics' with his neighbour at Wentworth Place: Dilke, he had told his brother, 'whom you know to be a Godwin perfectibil[it]y Man, pleases himself with the idea that America will be the country to take up the human intellect where england leaves off – I differ there with him greatly.' Charles did not differ: in politics, as in everything else, he entirely accepted Dilke's inflexible views:

I never formed an opinion upon political questions until the breaking-out of the American Civil War when I was eighteen. I then sided strongly with the Union ... Even in this question, however, I only followed my grandfather's lead, although, for the first time, in this case, intelligently. So far indeed as character can be moulded in childhood, mine was fashioned by my grandfather Dilke.

Under his grandfather's guidance, to deserve his grandfather's praise, Numero 3 developed every gift and interest. 'I am as pleased with your letter', wrote Dilke, 'as an old dog-fancier when a terrier-pup catches his first rat – it is something to see my boy hunt out and hunt down that old humbug Oratory.' All the successes of Trinity Hall brought rejoicing to Sloane Street:

> My dear Charles,
>   I had but a bad night and am not very well today, so that my voice will not be strong enough to startle the echoes of the old Hall; but I must give a cheer for Romer, though it be like a sucking dove, and will drink his health, and wish success to our Senior Wrangler ...[8]

Dilke's toast was answered: 'Bob' Romer triumphed again in mathematics; and 'T.H. may rejoice over Romer, the exceptional man of a hundred years', decided The Grand.[9]

He himself rejoiced in the grandson brought up on his own principles. Dilke had been an editor of awe-inspiring distinction, a businessman of recognized acumen, a scholar of certain standing; but Numero 3 was to be his supreme achievement. Charles had finally ruined his relations with Wentworth, he had brought out his familiar ruthlessness; but he had also given him cause to show all the understanding acquired in a busy lifetime. The advice that Dilke sent him now reveals the wise, affectionate friend of Keats, the adviser of the Keats circle, at his most mature, and at his best:

> ... You must never for a moment forget that without devotion *to a higher purpose*, all else is valueless; and that for one who fails from want of sympathy a hundred are wrecked from too much ...
>   After all and above all remember that the highest honors of the University require only a certain amount of knowledge of a few given subjects, but that the *honors of life* require a great deal more, and among them, and first among them, the power of clearly develop-

SIR WENTWORTH DILKE
From the painting
by Arthur Hughes

SIR CHARLES DILKE
From the painting
by George Frederick Watts

JOHN TAYLOR
From a lost portrait
probably by William Hilton

RICHARD MONCKTON MILNES,
LORD HOUGHTON,
IN LATER LIFE
From a photograph

ing, literary and real, the knowledge you possess. The best training is *systematically* to do something in which *you are interested* – a subject self-imposed – and always to *do your best in a given time*. You will be surprised when you read the lives of our great men, to find how many of them had, almost in childhood, taken up the resolution to be great, and how early they struggled to develope themselves …

I am afraid that my preaching or prosing is somewhat incoherent and disjointed, but my head is not strong enough to grasp the whole subject. I console myself in the hope that what is wanting in the teacher may be compensated for in the pupil … that I have a dear and good grandson who is ever *in my thoughts* as in my heart.

Do not mistake any thing here said. I am content with the past, and look hopefully to the future. I should of course be pleased to see in my grandson the promise of a great man, because it would extend the moral influence of a good one – Therefore I say 'raise your standard' – but I am more than satisfied with the certainty I feel of a good one, and grateful …

Believe me ever

Your affectionate

Grand[10]

*   *   *

In June 1863, when Trinity Hall sent an eight to Henley, the old man watched his grandson row in the Grand Challenge Cup. The experience must have been both elating and depressing, for Dilke was now seventy-three, and though he had been the strong one of the family, his health was failing. 'I have suddenly made up my mind to run away from the Doctors', he told Numero 3 on July 5th. 'I am much better – it is a beautiful day, and I feel that fresh air and the quiet of Alice Holt would do me good!'[11]

Alice Holt was the country house near Farnham which the family had rented from the Crown the previous year. It was in Hampshire, a county which Dilke greatly loved. Alice Holt was, as Charles recorded, 'our chief shooting place'; and if The Grand, who had shot with Keats nearly half a century ago, had less Nimrod, now, in his disposition, if he was compelled to exert himself less, he could still delight in nature. At Alice Holt, as Charles pointed out, 'an almost unbroken stretch of between 2,000 and 3,000 acres of forest formed as great an attraction to my nature-loving grandfather as to my sporting father'; and here, on November 1st, the garden-lover of Wentworth Place found himself 'grubbing on, clearing out drains and laying down new ones, cutting down old trees and planting new ones, thinning and clearing, and, of course, making bad worse and the walks impassable. However, I console myself that some of you will have the benefit of it.'[12]

He was educating his grandson, too, in conversation: 'Never saw my Grandfather more brilliant than on the 23rd September 1863. Dr Doran and myself with him after dinner. Talked about John Forster, Chorley, T. K. Hervey, Sir Harris Nicholas, Monckton Milnes ...'[13] And Dilke taught Numero 3, with a certain cynicism, of the ways of the world. Talking of Thackeray's *Esmond*, he wrote a tantalizing letter from Alice Holt:

> Beatrice is, I am sorry to say, drawn with great truth – true to a bad nature. I know one woman who might have sat for the portrait – who saw at a glance the weak point in man's character – *vanity* of his vanities – and could mould him to her will, and did so – and this is a case about which the world has some interest, though it knows nothing of the mystery and never will. Talk of women's vanities, why men are ten times as vain; and the woman who finds out the weak point, and is content to use and abuse her power, may lead them as asses are led.[14]

*   *   *

The year 1864 began with fresh Cambridge delights: Charles was re-elected Vice-President of the Union. Early in February he entered for a walking race, without training, and beat the University champion. At the news of this unexpected triumph, The Grand simply threatened to compete himself.

Three days later he wrote more soberly: 'I wish you had sent me a Cambridge paper which contained an account of your Olympic games ... I reserve the right of reading everything that relates to you and your concerns.' The request was touching. Dilke was now threatened with blindness.

*   *   *

On Friday at your father's request, I saw Dr Beaumon about my eyes. He saw me twice on that day. He said on the first occasion that the pupil of one eye was so shrunk that he must excite it by bella donna before he could look into it. This done, he, at a second interview, shook his head – and said that nothing could be done, and that the only chance for me, was to refrain altogether from reading – that if I did so for a month I might call again and he should then, perhaps, be able to say whether it was worth while to try further. He evidently did not think it would be, and that the probabilities are, if I live much longer I shall be qualified for a Cambridge Professor, or ... rank with the 'prophets old'. Be the issue what it may, I shall endeavour to bear up cheerfully – I have not the presumption to say like a philosopher, but like a man ...

I was out in the open air five or six hours yesterday, and walked I think five or six miles in a circle, round the paddock and round and round again.[15]

But such forced intellectual idleness was more than the former editor of *The Athenaeum*, the manager of *The Daily News*, the founder of *Notes and Queries*, could bear; and a week later he added:

Notwithstanding Dr Beaumon's injunction, I reserve to myself a right to read as much as I wish of the Athenaeum – of N & Q – and of the political summary in the Gard. Chronicle. The last Quarterly I read before his orders were issued.[16]

He continued to resent inactivity, bitterly: 'I have ordered that newspapers are not to be sent here, so you must excuse it if, when we meet, I am a little in arrear of the course of life.' He continued, also, 'hands in Pockets making observations', to watch over his garden:

We have had a strange night here [he wrote on February 17th]: rain the first half, and snow the second. My peas were going on beautifully, and yesterday Purse and myself agreed that they were beyond danger, and therefore *uncovered* them. Now they are covered with snow. I hope there was not too much frost, and if so they may be safe still – but it is a nervous time both for peas and old gardeners.[17]

*   *   *

On February 29th, a fortnight after his triumph in the walking race, Charles announced that he had won the English Essay Prize for an essay on Sir Robert Walpole. The Grand refused to let him rest on his academic laurels, and continued, wisely, to remind him that Cambridge was preparation for life. On April 7th he sent Charles a letter that strongly, and rather sadly, recalled a letter addressed to his son some forty years ago:

> I have no thought or wish that you should turn out one of these learned Thebans. But Greek contains the poetry, the philosophy, the history of the ancient, and, as I believe, the key to the modern world of thought, intelligence, and progress. There then we are beyond the narrow limits of scholarship, and in the wide domain of the educated gentleman. It is not for itself therefore that I wish you to be master of Greek – not for mere scholarship – but that you may be master of the light and life of the old world, and so see clearer through the haze of the modern ... I submit therefore that you should make a point of reading one hour or one half-hour a day and *every* day some Greek author and of *understanding* him thoroughly. Begin with whom you please – but once resolved go steadily and knowingly right on to the end. I know that ... this may seem to be difficult, perhaps impossible; but resolution finds time and overcomes all difficulties.[18]

Charles naturally enough demurred, but The Grand refused to be shaken: 'I shall not say another word on the great Greek question,' he added, 'but as to the "insuperable difficulties in the way of immediate action", remember that "insuperables" are sometimes temperamental.'[19]

He himself remained indomitable. Failing sight and general lassitude did not stop him now from catching a train to Cambridge:

> My very dear Charles,
> It is decided, I believe, that I am to be inflicted on you tomorrow – and that your father and grandmother will not appear until Sunday ... This solitary grandeur of my appearance among the youngsters rather troubles me; and I write therefore to beg of you ... always to remember that I am never dull *because I am alone*. You say in your letter of this morning that you have ordered dinner for to-morrow at four, and *will* order a Fly. Dinner I cannot dispense with, though very little will do – but if the Fly be not actually agreed for, it were better to leave me to the chance of health, strength, and weather. A sight of you and of life and young enthusiasm may put a sort of galvanic life into me; but it may not cure the rheumatism, of which I have had some ugly reminders since I have been in town ...

I shall come by [the] twelve [o'clock] train from King's Cross, and proceed by omnibus from the Station to the Parade.

The Grand arrived for 'Soup and Lamb, ... next door but one to St Mary's Church';[20] and, on the bank at 'Grassy', he watched the second night of the May Races, when Trinity Hall, with Charles rowing at No. 3, went head of the river. The May Races were hardly over before the college law examination began, and 'our noble fellow has again won the prize', Dilke announced to Wentworth on June 3rd. 'What a blessing that boy has been to my old age! May God reward him!' Charles seemed intent on fulfilling the hopes that Wentworth had disappointed. In the Henley Regatta that year, he rowed again for the Grand Challenge Cup, and for the Ladies' Plate; and 'my movements may be absolutely regulated by your wishes or convenience', wrote the devoted Dilke as Henley Week progressed. 'If you desire to pay a visit to the Holt, I have there the chance of a quicker recovery, if I am to go on well; whereas if there be more inducements to visit London, why here I have the benefit of the doctors should I not make progress. The pleasure and the advantages being *equal* to me, you have only to decide.'

Charles spent a few days in London before he returned to Cambridge, to correspond with The Grand on the next year's essay competition. The theme was the art of government. On July 14th Dilke sent a criticism of his grandson's scheme. Reflectively he added:

Your late letters have awakened strange memories. When I was about your age I was deep in the same studies which your Essay now imposes on you. I had unfortunately no previous training – no guide – few books, and only such as the reading of to-day suggested for to-morrow, and limited means enabled me to get hold of. I had to grope my way in the dark. Then came the business and the duties of life, and I was ever after obliged to read for the profit of the hour ...

The best government, as it appears to me, is that which best represents the wishes and feelings of the governed ... In this way the British Constitution has shown itself good beyond all the hopes of my early life. Then there seemed no probability of escape, earlier or later, from violent revolution; yet the just will of the people peacefully triumphed in the Reform Bill, and in fortitude, and all our legislation and all our financial measures have for years tended in the same direction.

This is another of my old prosings – another proof that love and good will and good wishes remain when power to serve is gone.[21]

* * *

His own power to serve had almost gone. Wentworth, writing to Charles in June, had given 'but a bad account'[22] of him; and in July he mentioned the will that The Grand had made. 'In reference to y^r last letter,' answered Charles, 'may it be many y^{rs} before that man's will comes to be proved, for there are not many like him.'[23] On July 22nd, in a letter to his grandson, Dilke returned yet again to the days when Keats had called him a Godwin-methodist: 'I was about your age when I read Godwin ... The book made a powerful impression on me, and certainly made me a *self-responsible* moral man.' Six days later, for the last time, he wrote from Alice Holt:

My very dear Grandson,
    Your letters give me very great pleasure, not because they are kind and considerate, of which I had evidence enough long since, not because they flatter the vanity of the old man by asking his opinion, which few now regard, but because I see in them the gradual development of your own mind ...
                                    God bless you!
                            As ever, your affectionate Grand

* * *

Within a week, he was gravely ill, and on August 5th Wentworth wrote in anxiety to Cambridge: 'Previously to his attack I had asked Dixon and his wife to come to-morrow and we have a cricket match unfortunately ... John Snook too I think from a letter is coming to the Wakefields ...'[24] 'Mr Sandford has seen him again,' he added next day, 'and he is sadly afraid if he shakes off this attack that he will be a more confirmed invalid than he was ... I have stopped the Dixons and Wakefields by telegraph.'[25] 'I w^d come down to you,' answered Charles on August 8th, 'but that I fear my presence w^d frighten my grandfather about himself and make him worse. I *can* have nothing to say but that I shall not be long in coming down if you telegraph for me.'[26] In the moment of emotion, he signed himself: 'Y^r Affect. Grandson.'

THE GRAND

A few hours later he was summoned from Cambridge.

* * *

I received a telegram from my father at noon: 'You had better come here' [he recorded in his diary]. I left by the 1.30 train, and reached Alice Holt at half-past six. My Father met me on the lawn: he was crying bitterly, and said – 'He lives only to see you.' I went upstairs and sat down by the sofa, on which lay The Grand, looking haggard, but still a noble wreck. I took his hand, and he began to talk of very trivial matters – of Cambridge everyday life – his favourite theme of old. He seemed to be testing his strength, for at last he said: 'I shall be able to talk to-morrow; I may last some weeks; but were it not for the pang that all of you would feel, I should prefer that it should end at once. I have had a good time of it.'

He had been saying all that morning: 'Is that a carriage I hear?' or 'I shall live to see him.'

Tuesday. – When I went in to him, he sent away the others, and told me to look for an envelope and a key. I failed to find it, and fetched Morris, who after a careful search found the key, but no envelope. We had both passed over my last letter (August 6th), which lay on the table. He made us both leave the room, but recalled me directly, and when I entered had banknotes in his hand, which he must have taken from the envelope of my letter ... He said: 'I cannot live, I fear, to your birthday – I want to make you a present – I think I have heard you say you should like a stop-watch – I have made careful inquiries as to the price – and have saved – I believe – sufficient.' He then gave me notes, and the key of a desk in London, in the secret drawer of which I should find the remaining money. He then gave me the disposition of his papers and manuscripts, directing that what I did not want should go to the British Museum. He then said: 'I have nothing more to say but that you have fulfilled – my every hope – beyond all measure – and – I am deeply – grateful.'

He died in my presence on Wednesday, 10th, at half-past one, in perfect peace.

* * *

On August 16th Dilke was buried beside Maria in the family vault at Kensal Green. At his own request, there was no obituary in The Athenaeum;

but John Francis recalled that he had been 'much beloved by a large circle ... He was genial and warm-hearted, and a most faithful friend ...' Charles Wentworth Dilke, wrote Francis, 'will ever be remembered as the faithful and just critic, the earnest seeker after truth'.

The same tribute was paid, with distinction, in a letter of condolence that Keats would have signed. 'You know how heartily I admired and respected him,' Dickens wrote to Sir Wentworth, 'and what interest I derived from the association I was so fortunate as to have with that sound head and staunch true heart. Never on this earth shall I fight my fight by the side of a more reliable and faithful man.'[27]

*   *   *

After his grandfather's death, Charles set out alone on a walking tour in Devon. At first he hardly understood his bereavement; but his sense of loss was 'greater with every year that followed'. In 1866 he began a long poem on the death of 'my one great friend in all the world': it opened with a distinctly prosaic but illuminating picture of himself and The Grand at Alice Holt. But writing did not rid him of memory: years later he 'dreamt of him one night as having come back to me ... as I had last known him, and in my dream we threw ourselves into one another's arms with even greater warmth of love than we had ever shown ... within his lifetime'.

On May 10th, 1869, at the age of fifty-nine, while he was English Commissioner at a horticultural exhibition, Sir Wentworth Dilke died suddenly at the Hôtel de France, St Petersburg. His death caused 'much regret', said *The Times*, 'among a large circle of friends'.[28] The obituary extolled his association with 'the literary labours of his father, whom he largely aided by his cultivated tastes, his wide range of information, [and] sound judgment'. It recalled his distinguished services to the Great Exhibition, and emphasized that 'the resuscitation of the Royal Horticultural Society of London has been in a very great measure due to his exertions as one of the most active of its vice-presidents'. It observed that his baronetcy had been given 'in recognition of the Prince Consort's personal regard for him'. It recorded that he had been a Member of Parliament and Chairman of the Society of Arts.

Numero 3 recorded his father's death with small emotion:

In May I was suddenly telegraphed to from St Petersburg to the effect that my father was dying, and, although I started immediately, he was embalmed, and temporarily buried, before I reached that city. In my journey I shared a railway carriage with Baron Jomini, the son of the great field-marshal ... [My Father] was pronouncing the name of my mother when he died, which touched me and my brother much, for he had never made a show of loving her, and had always spoken much more of his father's love for him.

... He had no very intimate friends, although he knew every-body ...[29]

Grudgingly Sir Charles recorded that his father had invented the modern system of sighting for rifles, that the botanists had named an order of passionflowers *passifloracea Dilkea*. Briefly he described his father's second funeral, in London, attended by Louis Lindon, 'the husband of Keats' love'. Sir Wentworth was buried at Kensal Green. His mother-in-law, Mrs Chatfield, took complete management of 76, Sloane Street, and Alice Holt 'was at once given up'.

Sir Charles had gained little from his father. He had inherited The Grand's republicanism, his rigid sense of purpose, his dogmatism, his passion for work, his egotism, his interest in literature. He had inherited, too, as was only natural, a proprietary devotion to the poet who had lived at Wentworth Place. Of Keats, wrote his biographer, the new baronet was 'immeasurably fond'.

BOOK THREE

THE EVERLASTING SPELL

21

THE GROWTH OF LEGEND

In the half-century that had passed since Keats had died, his legend had grown with his reputation. Indeed, even while he was spending his final summer with Leigh Hunt in Kentish Town, legend had taken root; and Mary Russell Mitford had decided: 'Poor John Keats is dying of the *Quarterly Review*.' Months before Keats died, his assassins had been chosen; and when at last the news of his death reached literary circles, Byron wrote to Shelley: 'I am very sorry to hear what you say of Keats. Is it *actually* true? I did not think criticism had been so killing.'

Dilke would dismiss the opinion as 'wholly ridiculous'; Hessey, the poet's publisher, had written years ago that Keats had been untouched by the *Quarterly* ; Fanny Brawne had not seen him brooding over the reviews; Keats himself had insisted that self-criticism gave him pain beyond comparison with anything that *Blackwood's* or the *Quarterly* could inflict. However, the public demanded villains, and Shelley had attacked them. 'You may announce for publication a poem entitled "Adonais" ', he wrote to Ollier, his publisher. 'It is a lament on the death of poor Keats, with some interposed stabs on the assassins of his peace and of his fame. ... I could wish that you enquired as to the degree in which, as I am assured, the brutal attack in the *Quarterly Review* excited the disease by which he perished.' The account arrived from Hunt's friend, John Gisborne, who had been given it by that mendacious gossip, Robert Finch. By June 16th, Shelley had received 'the heart-rending account of the closing scene of the great genius whom envy and ingratitude scourged out of the world'. *Adonais* was printed in July, and Byron dashed off a stanza to John Murray:

> 'Who kill'd John Keats?'
> 'I,' says the Quarterly,
> So Savage and Tartarly;
> 'Twas one of my feats.' ...

'You Review people', added Byron, 'have no more right to kill than any other footpads. However, he who would die of an article in a Review would probably have died of something else equally trivial.' *The Literary Gazette* soon suggested that Keats had hastened his death by leaving off cravats.

The legend of the weak, unworldly poet was established. For years the tale of frail inadequacy was spread, even by his most devout admirers. The robust letters of Keats himself were still stored away by their recipients; he was not able, yet, to speak out loud and bold. So William Hone, in his *Every-Day Book for 1827*, insisted that 'virulent and unmerited attacks ... overwhelmed his spirits'; and in that 'sad tweedling book', as Dilke called it, *Lord Byron and Some of his Contemporaries*, Leigh Hunt lent authority to nonsense, and declared 'the hunters had struck him'. It seemed that Hunt was so obsessed by Keats in his final illness that he had forgotten him in health; and, that year, in *The Olio*, Iluscenor took Hunt's cue: 'If literature had its array of martyrs, his name would not be forgotten in its calends.' In June 1829, *Blackwood's* itself burst into verse:

> Oh! he was great in Cockney Land, the monarch of his kind,
> 'Tis said he died of phthysic by the ignorant and blind;
> 'Twas *we* assassinated him – oh! regicidal deed;
> And he has left *Endymion* for those who choose to read.

Those who chose, in 1840, to read Mary Shelley's *Essays, Letters from Abroad*, discovered the twisted comments of Colonel Finch. Perhaps he had gathered a detail or two from the voluble landlady at 26, Piazza di Spagna – strangely enough, he had once lodged there himself; most probably he had heightened Severn's egotistic, hysterical recollections. The poet's passions, insisted Finch,

> were always violent, and his sensibility most keen. It is extraordinary that, proportionally as his strength of body declined, these acquired fresh vigour; and his temper at length became so outrageously violent, as to injure himself, and annoy every one around him ... He was accompanied by a friend of mine, Mr Severn, a young painter who left all, and sacrificed every prospect, to accompany and watch over his friend Keats. For many weeks previous to his death, he would see no one but Mr Severn, who had almost risked his own life, by unwearied attendance upon his friend, who rendered his situation doubly unpleasant by the violence of his passions exhibited even towards him, so much, that he might be judged insane.

Fanny Brawne, now Mrs Lindon, was so shocked by the publication, and by Severn's failure to contradict it, that she broke nineteen years' silence, and gave a written statement to Thomas Medwin, who was busy preparing his Life of Shelley. In 1847, with information 'from a most authentic source', Medwin gave a true likeness of Keats. He also dismissed the effect of the *Quarterly* as 'a mere unit, and not the last in the glass'.

* * *

In the delicate allusions of Brown, Fanny Brawne herself had already entered history. In 1837, G. C. Cunningham's *Lives of Great Englishmen* had included Keats and indicated 'some perplexities of a nature too delicate, though unfounded, to be mentioned here'. In 1843 the *Life of Gerald Griffin* had appeared, with his reminiscences of the Brawnes at Wentworth Place, and in 1844, in *Imagination and Fancy*, Hunt had touched the heart of *St Agnes' Eve*: Keats, he said, is 'as much in love with his heroine as his hero is ... He, doubtless, wrote as he felt, for he was also deeply in love'. In 1845, Severn had urged Monckton Milnes to publish the 'real cause' of Keats's death: 'I mean the poor fellows anguish at the first symptoms of consumption when he was about to be married to a most lovely & accomplished girl, which anguish never ceased ... This Lady was a Miss Brawn, she was possessed of considerable property in addition to her beauty & youth and was devotedly attached to Keats & his fame.'

Milnes suppressed the name, and confused Fanny Brawne with Jane Cox, the Reynolds's cousin: the meteoric, East Indian 'Charmian' to whom Keats had once been attracted. But he recognized that, in 1818, Keats had been inspired 'with the passion that only ceased with his existence'. And of this passion which had to be, for the moment, a nameless passion, Milnes wrote with tact and notable understanding:

> The strong power conquered the physical man, and made the very intensity of his passion, in a certain sense, accessory to his death: he might have lived longer if he had lived less. But this should be no matter of self-reproach to the object of his love, for the same may be said of the very exercise of the poetic faculty, and of all that made him what he was. It is enough that she has preserved his memory with a sacred honour, and it is no vain assumption, that to have inspired and sustained the one passion of this noble being has been a source

of grave delight and earnest thankfulness, through the changes and chances of her earthly pilgrimage.

* * *

'Implicitly do I rely on your judgment', Brown had written, 'as a friend to his fame.' Brown's devoted task had been completed. The faith that he had put in Monckton Milnes, seven years ago, had been excellently justified. *The Life, Letters, and Literary Remains of John Keats* appeared in the summer of 1848, and marked the beginning of serious Keats studies. For the first time the poet's circle were publicly drawn together. For the first time Brown and Dilke appeared among the moving spirits of his life. For the first time, in his letters, Keats himself could speak: magnificent and delicate, human and robust. 'I think I shall be among the English Poets after my death', he had told George in the autumn after *Endymion*. 'The attempt to crush me in the Quarterly has only brought me more into notice, and it is a common expression among book-men, "I wonder the Quarterly should cut its own throat".' With the help of Milnes, he himself had scotched the legend of the critics. And, as he had modestly predicted, he was among the poets.

Until now, he had been poet of the lettered and elect; now, for the first time, radiantly, he was revealed to the public. *Chambers's Edinburgh Journal* observed that from the tomb of Keats 'there has come a light to which the eyes of rising genius are turned from the ends of the earth. Keats is one of the great teachers of the new world, and of new spirits in the old'. 'Killed by a savage article in a review!' cried *Sharpe's London Magazine*:

> Look in the face of this man, and believe it if you can. Is that a weak, irritable, vanity-devoured boy? Are those the eyes likely to be filled with tears? Or that the mouth to quiver with emotion because an ignorant reviewer said he was no poet? Heaven help the poor dear public! To think that it has gone about believing such nonsense these many years!

Late in 1849 *The Times* bestowed official benediction:

> It is the spirit of Keats that hovers over the best of our national poesy, and inspires the poetic genius – such as it is – of our unpoetic age. Had he lived, he would eventually have towered above his con-

temporaries; dying before he was twenty-six, he took his place at once amongst the examples whom he so passionately loved.[1]

*   *   *

Admiration had become the almost unbroken rule. It remained, of course, the admiration of a Pre-Raphaelite image. Keats had not been killed by the critics, but he was still 'poor Keats'. He had still died young:

> So you have been with Severn, and have heard
> The tongue that spoke to Keats the last farewell,
> His on whose breast our darling's dear head fell,
> When his great life sank from his latest word ...[2]

Class-consciousness seemed as important as lachrymose sentiment. Hunt, with the most devout intentions, still propagated old misunderstandings; and in his *Autobiography*, which appeared in 1850, he still lamented that Keats was 'a little too sensitive on the score of his origin'. That year the American writer, Henry T. Tuckerman, decided in his *Thoughts on the Poets*: 'The cherished aim of Keats was doubtless to retrieve his social condition by the force of his genius.' As for *The English Woman's Domestic Magazine*, it thought *Endymion* a remarkable achievement for the son of a man 'employed in the establishment of a large livery-stable proprietor'. It was fortunate that the poet's father, 'a person of excellent natural sense, and entirely free from vulgarity, became the son-in-law of his master'.

With the cult of this lower-class phenomenon, there went, as time progressed, a cult of the whole Keats circle:

> High honour to those whom the God on earth knew,
> Cowden Clarke, Leigh Hunt, Severn, – the fine faithful few ...

cried a worshipper in 1852. When J. H. Reynolds died that year, *The Athenaeum* recalled that Hunt had once discussed him in the same article as Keats. 'It is no small honour *now* to have been thus associated.'[3] Alas, with the growing devotion there went a growing confusion. Keats forgeries were exposed in *The Athenaeum*; and in 1853, in *Salad for the Solitary*, 'an Epicure' rashly claimed to print the last lines 'ever penned by that gifted young poet ... Many pieces have purported to be his last production, but these now transcribed are the last that ever emanated from his pen'. Milnes himself still confused Jane Cox with Fanny Brawne; and James Russell Lowell, introducing an American edition of Keats, repeated the traditional error:

It was his body that needed to have its equilibrium restored, the waste of his nervous energy that must be repaired by deep draughts of the overflowing life and drowsy tropical force of an abundant and healthily-poised womanhood ... This glimpse of her, with her leopardess beauty, crossing the room and drawing men after her magnetically, is all we have. She seems to have been still living in 1848, and as Mr Milnes tells us, kept the memory of the poet sacred. 'She is an East Indian,' Keats says, 'and ought to be her grandfather's heir.' Her name we do not know.

It would soon be known; and an eager American publisher, on a visit to Rome, was among the first to hear it. In the spring of 1860 James T. Fields and his wife called on Severn, and Mrs Fields reported: 'He showed us a letter, the last Keats ever wrote, in which he says his pain at parting from Miss Brawne, whom he was about to marry, would cause death to hasten upon him.'

Severn himself had now lost touch with Fanny Brawne; in 1863, he only knew of 'two personal friends of the poet to be now living': Cowden Clarke and Taylor. Within a year, Taylor was dead, and Dilke had followed him. In 1865, Fanny Brawne died, almost unrecorded, in Pimlico; and in the simple grave in Brompton Cemetery was buried the maligned and dignified woman who had inspired the poet most and understood him best.

Keats now found his inevitable champion in the grandson indoctrinated by Dilke of Wentworth Place.

22

SIR CHARLES *v.* FANNY BRAWNE

NUMERO 3 had inherited *The Athenaeum* and *Notes and Queries*, and he used them both to advantage. On October 26th, 1872, *The Athenaeum* printed a letter from 'An Admirer of Keats'; he gave the poet's unpublished notes on Milton, and the original sonnet *To Sleep*, and inquired what had become of Keats's Shakespeare. Sir Charles knew perfectly well who owned it: Fanny Brawne had mentioned it in a letter to Mrs Dilke, years ago, and the letter was in his possession. But the query had its purpose: on the next page of the magazine appeared the pregnant statement: 'We have to mention the death of Mr Louis Lindon, an old friend of the Keats family.' Sir Charles had expressed his diplomatic interest in a relic which might now appear on the market.

On November 16th he duly published Keats's notes on Shakespeare, and added that his folio 'is, by the great kindness of its owner, now in my hands. It belongs to the daughter of the lady to whom Keats gave it, and to whom he gave also his Spenser which cannot for the moment be found. The possessor of the Shakespeare has also some most interesting letters about Keats'. The Spenser, which Keats had marked for Fanny Brawne in his last summer at Kentish Town, had been lost in Germany; but Fanny Brawne's son, Herbert Lindon, sold Sir Charles the Shakespeare and some letters. These included (for Numero 3 was determined to stop publication) the letters Keats had written to his mother.

In his two periodicals, Dilke's grandson continued to stimulate and satisfy inquiries after the poet. On May 31st, 1873, he contradicted the legend that Keats had undermined his health by drink: 'This statement was naturally annoying and painful to the surviving friends of the poet, among whom are the Cowden Clarkes, the Olliers, and that attached friend and affectionate attendant of his death-bed, Mr Severn ... The author of *Endymion* died of simple consumption – a malady which was in the family.' The mention of the Olliers sent An Admirer of Keats to 'the great mass of George Keats' letters' in his possession; and the following week he printed the Olliers' letter to George.

* * *

It was in 1875 that Sir Charles made his chief contribution to Keats studies. In *The Papers of a Critic* he printed not only his grandfather's findings on Pope and Junius, but a memoir of Dilke which did the poet grave disservice for sixty years.

Since the memoir was a work of piety, Dilke was presented as an exemplary father. 'The relations between Mr Dilke and his son', wrote Numero 3, 'were throughout life as affectionate as those between Mr Dilke and his father.' The hypocrisy might be forgiven; it was less forgivable that Sir Charles chose to distort the truth about Fanny Brawne. 'Mr Dilke's grandson', he wrote, 'has still in his possession a great number of Keats's letters ... In addition, however, to the letters which appear in Lord Houghton's Life of Keats, there are a good many of a more intimate character still, of and about the poet, from which extracts may be made.'[1]

Sir Charles had bought the letters to prevent their publication; he now quoted one himself. But while The Grand and Maria had understood and admired Fanny Brawne, while Wentworth had shown his sympathy by employing her husband at the Great Exhibition, Numero 3 irrevocably detested her. Did he see her as a calculating flirt who had failed to appreciate Keats or to love him? Did he consider, like Fanny Llanos, that she should have stayed in perpetual mourning and spinsterhood? Did he see her sale of the Severn miniature as a sign of profiteering rather than hardship? Whatever the reason, he made up his mind as fixedly as Dilke had done in the days of George Keats; and the senior legalist at Cambridge now became the prosecuting counsel. In his memoir of his grandfather, he carefully published Jane Reynolds's waspish comment – for Jane had been attracted to Keats – on the 'most unhappy connection'. Keats, added Sir Charles, 'gave in to a passion which killed him as surely as ever any man was killed by love; and even ten years after his death, when the first memoir was proposed, the woman he had loved had so little belief in his poetic reputation that she wrote to Mr Dilke: "The kindest act would be to let him rest for ever in the obscurity to which unhappy circumstances have condemned him." ' The phrase had, in fact, been taken from the draft letter to Brown, in which Fanny Brawne had given him unrestricted permission to publish Keats's poetry. Cut from its context, it bred the legend of a vapid flirt that persisted into the coming century.

Determined to convert the poet's official biographer, Sir Charles sent some 'elegant extracts' from the love-letters to Richard Monckton Milnes. Lord Houghton (as he had now become) kept his old opinions, but the following year – still confusing her with Charmian – he made the first public mention of Fanny Brawne. Keats, he wrote, introducing a new edition of the poems, 'had met at Mr Dilke's a Miss Brawn [*sic*], a lady of East Indian parentage, and with a prospect of some fortune ... He congratulated himself that "she was not a woman to fall in love with a poem, and be given away by a novel".' The unidentified phrase came from one of the letters.

Sir Charles had only bought the right not to publish the correspondence. He had broken his agreement. If the letters could be quoted, why should they not be published in their entirety? By the end of the year, Herbert Lindon had asked Sir Charles to return them: legally they still belonged to him. Sir Charles returned all but two of them. On December 29th Herbert Lindon offered the rest to Lord Houghton. The offer was refused, and he showed them to Harry Buxton Forman.

* * *

Mr Forman was an industrious and persistent civil servant. He had entered the Post Office at eighteen, and would remain in it for forty-seven years. He had worked a long time in the foreign branch of the Secretary's office, he would later be Surveyor of British Post Offices in the Mediterranean; and by the time he retired in 1907, he would be Second Secretary of the Post Office, Controller of Packet Services, and a Companion of the Most Honourable Order of the Bath.

Yet the Kelmscott Chaucer given him by his colleagues on his retirement was, perhaps, a more appropriate tribute, for if he had earned his crimson ribbon as a civil servant, he had by then done still more important work as a man of letters. In 1876 he had started to issue his eight-volume edition of Shelley. It was followed by a Shelley bibliography, and by several Shelley reprints and facsimiles edited for the Shelley Society of which he was an original member. Even Professor Dowden called him 'the chief living authority on all that relates to Shelley's writings', and, when he died on June 15th, 1917, *The Times* would lament him as an expert on Shelley rather than Keats.

However true this estimate, Mr Forman must be recognized as a Keatsian of the first importance. He edited Keats with constant care, and with a foresight so far beyond that of his age that, as late as 1917, *The Times* would deplore his publication, in 1890, of 'a little volume of new Keats matter, some of which at least had been better left in oblivion'. This little volume was, to be accurate, the reissue of the essential publication of 1878 that had reorientated the study of the poet.

*   *   *

When the Lindons discussed with Mr Forman the letters to be published, they 'fully considered what was proper for publication'; they identified Keats's description of their mother, which 'answered to the facts in every particular except that of age', and they told Mr Forman of 'one or two personal traits'. On July 6th, 1877, Mr Forman sent a first discreet inquiry to Keats's ageing sister in Madrid; and on July 25th she answered that she was 'quite convinced' that Charmian was 'not Miss Brawne, she not being an East Indian, nor having a Grandfather living at that time'. This was the beginning of a long and courtly correspondence,[2] in which the nature of the letters was never revealed. The publication demanded secrecy, and only Severn was let into the secret. 'Your letter is a joy to me,' he told Mr Forman on September 26th, '– that you have received 37 letters of Keats to Fanny Brawne astonishes me with delight for they must be even superior to Keats's poetry & will be a boon to the world quite unlooked for. I will maintain your secret & now I proceed to answer all your questions.'

Throughout the autumn of 1877, the letters flew to and fro between the aged artist in Scala Dante and Mr Forman in Marlborough Hill, St John's Wood, discussing the site of Elm Cottage, the Bright Star Sonnet, and the appearance of Wentworth Place; and, aided by Mr Forman's diagram, Severn tried to reconstruct the house as he had known it some sixty years ago. 'My memory has been fairly taxed,' he admitted to his sister, 'and has just come up to the mark, the work is dedicated to me and so 'twas my duty to aid all I could on this account, added to which my regard for the Poet and my joy at these 37 letters which I am told are of a beauty beyond his poems ... I expect you'll see Keats new work in the papers for Mr Buxton Forman tells me there has never been anything like it.'

On February 2nd, 1878, the press announced the *Letters of John Keats to Fanny Brawne*.

*   *   *

Severn read them 'with great pain'. Sir Charles chose to see the publication as a confidence trick, and as sacrilege. On February 16th, with a fury worthy of *Blackwood's*, *The Athenaeum* denounced Mr Forman, the Lindons, and, of course, Fanny Brawne:

It will be remembered that Miss Brawne, ten years after Keats's death ... had so little faith in his poetic reputation that she wrote to Mr Dilke: 'The kindest act would be to let him rest for ever in the obscurity to which circumstances have condemned him.' 'The whirligig of Time', however, 'brings in his revenges.' Mr Forman tells us that when the world had decided that Keats was *not* to be left in that obscurity, she said more than once that the letters ... should be carefully guarded, *'as they would some day be considered of value'*! And now her representatives seem to have decided that the 'some day' has come ... If the publication is the greatest impeachment of a woman's sense of womanly delicacy to be found in the history of literature, Mr Forman's extraordinary preface is no less notable as a sign of the degradation to which the bookmaker has sunk ...

My dear Dilke [wrote Lord Houghton],

Since the *Athenaeum* fixed my place in poetical literature between Rogers and Eliza Cook, I have naturally not read that journal, but I have been shown a capital flagellation of those unfilial wine-merchants ... I thought I had even gone too far in my 'elegant extracts' – with which you furnished me. I have, alas! no poetical amours to be recorded, out of which my family can make anything handsome.

The letter ended with an invitation to lunch and 'talk Keats'. The unfilial wine-merchants – Fanny's husband, to be precise, had worked for Ruinart – had brought the two admirers of Keats together.

While the letters passed between Lord Houghton, at Fryston, and Sir Charles, in Sloane Street, *Notes and Queries* reviewed the book, and cast a curious light on Victorian criticism: a criticism dictated by sentimentality, coquetry, and the prudish evasion of unpleasant truth:

This dainty little book, creditable to the microscopic industry of its editor, contains an Introduction of lxvii pages and 128 pages of love letters addressed by John Keats to his sweetheart, Mistress Fanny Brawne ... We, and all men have here before us for judgment the sacred and confidential utterances of a dying poet's only love – utterances which add nothing to our knowledge of the poet's character and life ... Yes, they do one thing ... they show us the bitter workings of illness and physical decay upon his spirit and his heart. And surely it is not well for those who love his poetry to see him thus; the painful impression ... will be with them when they turn again to *Endymion*, or *Lamia*, or the sonnets.[3]

Sir Charles not only condemned the publication in print, he deplored it privately to the poet's sister; and Fanny Llanos wrote: 'I am greatly vexed that letters of such a nature should have been placed before the public. The letters must have been lent to Mr Forman by Miss Lindon, a want of delicacy which surprises me, and which I should not have expected from her.'[4] Sir Charles could not waste such ammunition. On March 23rd, *The Athenaeum* announced: 'MADAME LLANOS, the sister of John Keats, has written to her friends in England expressing strong disapproval of the publication.'

Mr Forman's years in the civil service had taught him to combine resolution with diplomacy. He now sent the hurt, indignant old lady a copy of the book, with a letter that must have shown exemplary tact. On May 6th Fanny Llanos assured him that he was more than forgiven:

To be frank with you, I must own that my first impression on hearing of the Letters was most painful, and in the heat of the moment, I thus expressed myself to Sir Charles Dilke; but without the slightest idea of my opinion being made public.

In my letter to you I made no observation upon the publication, for I had then had time for reflection, that as the Letters did not belong to me, the owner of them was at liberty to publish them, under the condition of their being true and faithful copies, which I plainly see that they are.

My enthusiasm and adoration of my dear brother are as strong in me at this moment, as when the blood of youth flowed in my veins. Is it strange, then, that knowing his excessive sensitiveness, I should shrink that the idea that his most sacred feelings should be conned over by persons indifferent to his merit?

Have the kindness to answer this, and let me know if I have lost your esteem by my hastiness.

If this should unfortunately be the case, I can assure you I shall be most deeply grieved.[5]

Mr Forman answered with all his official courtesy, with all his personal powers of persuasion:

I counselled and took part in the publication of those to me sacred letters on full consideration, and with the knowledge that I should have many people hotly against me ... Those who have thought less about the matter than it has been my duty and my necessity to do, have not understood that this question of publishing your brother's letters was not one as between speech and silence, but as between perfect speech and imperfect speech; and in deciding for perfect speech I regarded the matter not only from posterity's point of view. I asked myself – 'If Keats had to choose between total oblivion and giving his whole story to posterity, which would he have chosen?' And I could not bring myself to answer but that he would *not* have chosen oblivion. Then I looked at all we had been told about him, and I saw only half the story, inaccurate in many particulars, and *not* – a thousand times *not* – portraying the man's soul as it was. These letters, to my mind, set him right with posterity; and thus it came to be, to me, a sacred duty to take all the risk of personal opprobrium that might attach to counselling and abetting their publication. The only thing I have to regret is that you ... have been put to pain, even though, as I hope, that has passed by; for I cannot affect to be in any way disturbed by the vulgar outcry of pressmen here or in America, who care no more in reality for your brother's works and his dear memory than they do for the sacred and eternal truths ... whereof his love was one.[6]

There would be no doubt, henceforward, of Madame Llanos's moral support, or of her personal friendship. On May 14th she sent her 'warmest gratitude ... May heaven reward you for your affection towards the memory of my poor brother!'

Meanwhile 'the vulgar outcry of pressmen' continued on both sides of the Atlantic. In April, reviewing the American edition, *Scribner's* took a lead from Sir Charles and dismissed Fanny Brawne. 'Her only two recorded utterances regarding the poet are, first, that "the kindest act would be to let him rest for ever in the obscurity to which unhappy circumstances have condemned him", and second, that his letters should be carefully guarded, "as they would some day be considered of value", a prediction at last fully verified by her dutiful and thrifty offspring.' That Fanny Brawne might have considered literary values rather than commercial worth did not, it seems, occur to the *Scribner's* critic: he decided that Keats's 'mistake was fatal with regard to this woman, and his approaching death a merciful release'. At home, the *Spectator* insisted that the letters should have been burnt, and that if Fanny Brawne had foreseen their publication, she had only betrayed 'how imperfectly she understood, or how little she respected, Keats's horror of any revelation of the kind.'[7] The comments were repeated in *The Contemporary Review*, though one thing, said the *Review*,

> is exceedingly obvious, though perhaps not always remembered – love-letters cannot tell their story truly unless we are made welcome to the part which both the lovers took in the correspondence. Nor even then can we pluck out the heart of the mystery ... Of the lady we gather nothing, except what is confirmed by the silhouette portrait of her, – namely, that she had a strong will, a full share of self-reliance, and a good understanding prone to specialities of pursuit.[8]

Mr Forman, undisturbed, visited Wentworth Place with William Dilke, The Grand's aged brother. He made mental notes for future editions.

23

AGAINST OBLIVION

On March 15th, 1878, when she had deplored Mr Forman's publication, Fanny Llanos had added a request; for 'I have', she told Sir Charles, 'no doubt of your willingness to serve the only sister of John Keats.' The last Civil War had reduced her income, her daughter Isabel had just been left a widow with six young children, and she and Valentine were obliged to give them a home and education. Half a century ago, The Grand had wrung Fanny Llanos's inheritance from Abbey; now she asked Numero 3 to secure her a Civil List pension as 'a small token of reward to her brother's memory ... I find no man more qualified to aid me', she explained, 'than the grandson of our family friend, not only on account of his high literary acquirements and sympathies, but of the elevated political and social position he occupies among the most influential men of England.'[1]

The compliment was far from empty. The watching shade of The Grand must have delighted, now, in the results of his teaching. Sir Charles's book, *Greater Britain*, had done much to encourage a reformed imperialism; and since his belief in the supremacy of the English race was not incompatible with radical views, he had carried Dilke's politics to extremes and become a notorious republican. Disraeli declared that the Liberal Member for Chelsea was the most powerful younger man he had known.

The Liberals were out of office, and Sir Charles advised Fanny Llanos to approach Lord Houghton; but *The Athenaeum* duly suggested that the Prime Minister should grant a pension 'to the sister of the great poet whose fame as an English classic is so securely established'. Early in 1879 Lord Beaconsfield sent £150 from the Royal Bounty Fund to Lord Houghton for 'Mrs Llanos, the sister of Keats'.

The sum was little enough for her needs, and Mr Forman determined to enlarge it. In May *The Graphic* noted that

an endeavour is being made to treat this grant as the nucleus of an adequate fund ... Subscriptions will be received, and promptly acknowledged, by Mr R. Garnett, Superintendent of the Reading Room, British Museum, W.C.; by Mr W. M. Rossetti, of 56, Euston Square, N.W.: and by Mr H. Buxton Forman, of 28, Marlborough Hill, St John's Wood, N.W.

From a rather more distinguished address, The Travellers' Club, Pall Mall, Lord Houghton wrote in his execrable hand:

Cher Dilke. *Voilà l'histoire.*
... Forman is a well-meaning man, but his publication of the 'Letters' is the measure of his delicacy and discretion. He wrote to me about this subscription, and I took no notice of it – nor shall I ... It seemed to me a wrong manner of doing a right thing.[2]

The public subscription was a tactless tribute; but late in 1880 Mr Forman closed the fund. The Liberals had returned to power, and, acting on his information, Lord Houghton and Sir Charles – then Under-Secretary of State for Foreign Affairs – used their influence. Mr Gladstone, an early admirer of Keats, asked the Queen to grant a pension, and happily reversed his predecessor's decision. Mr Forman and Sir Charles became joint trustees.

* * *

The whirligig of time brings strange revenges, and Sir Charles's partnership with Mr Forman was not the least of them. It was some forty years since Brown had etched his portrait of Robert Wydel, and the Dilkes and the Browns were again in touch. Early in 1879, Carlino, now Major Brown, a Member of the House of Representatives, and Civil Commissioner at Taranaki, sent Sir Charles the copy of Bacon's *Advancement of Learning*, which had been given to Keats by his brother George; he also dispatched Keats's Beaumont and Fletcher, and 'a mass of family papers which contain references to the poet. The Beaumont and Fletcher', announced Sir Charles, 'has the under-scorings which Keats made in all the books he read. The Bacon is full of manuscript notes, which are, however, the work of the poet's schooldays, and altogether without literary value.'[3] The Grand must have turned in his scholar's grave.

Yet if Brown had been the first active Keatsian, and Monckton Milnes the second, Sir Charles might have challenged Mr Forman for third place.

Slowly but inexorably, as death or financial straits released more Keatsiana for the market, he drew it in to Sloane Street. In April 1876 Walter Severn, the artist's son, sold him a letter from Keats for £5 (alas, a year later he found that 'a letter sold lately for £23. 5. od.'). In 1877 Sir Charles corresponded with Severn himself, 'from whom I bought, among other things, a letter to Brown, being the last that Keats wrote'. He was anxious to identify Severn's original miniature, and early in 1879 a letter in an extremely shaky hand arrived from Rome:

Dear Sir Charles,
... What you ask is difficult without my seeing the various miniatures you have and so I beg the great favour of you, to trust them to a friend's hand and I will carefully and faithfully return them
The one I presented to Miss Brawne was the only one I ever painted of Keats except a small duplicate in oils done for Mr Moxon and of the many copies I know nothing, but I can understand it will be interesting to know the actual one from my hand. It *was engraved in Lord Houghton's life* and was thought to be a striking resemblance by your excellent grandfather, who told me on my last seeing him that 'he often took down the volume to see Keats' ...
The miniatures could be packed together and I have a friend Mrs Lindon returning to Rome in three weeks who would convey them
I may mention here that I have the MSS. of the 'Eve of St Agnes' and I am willing to dispose of it
Yours truly
JOSEPH SEVERN[4]

It was Fanny Brawne's daughter-in-law, Mrs Edmund Lindon, who, by some dramatic chance, had become Severn's close friend in his latter days: 'this Lady', he told his sister, 'most kindly takes me out in her fine carriage and is very attentive'. But Severn could hardly have sent a worse suggestion to Sloane Street. Since Herbert Lindon had recalled and published the love-letters, Sir Charles considered the family untouchable. 'My relations with the Lindons', he wrote, in the manuscript of his memoirs,

were not such as to lead me to willingly trust the miniature to any member of the family, and, as old Severn was very old and so poor that he was himself selling such Keats relics as he had, the chances are that, if they had not disappeared before they reached him, they would have made their way into a pawn shop or to an American collector. I consulted Lord Houghton who replied 'I should certainly make some excuse for not sending the portrait ... Nor shall I give up my copyright of my writings to Mr Forman – but I don't see how I will prevent him *using* my material. I have a certain respect for the man's scholastic earnestness in these slipshod days. He is what Carlyle calls "of the genus blockhead," ... but still useful.'[5]

There was little time for more requests to be made from Rome. On August 3rd there died the old man whom William Howitt had seen at his easel, looking 'like Coleridge in the decline of life: the somewhat corpulent tendency, the black velvet waistcoat, a certain similarity of features, and the head slightly thrown back in talking'. 'Of all I have done with brush or pen, as artist or man', Severn had said not long before his death, 'scarce anything will long outlast me; yet through my beloved Keats I shall be remembered.'

The prediction was realized. Severn's letters remain the only account of Keats's death; Severn's miniature, his posthumous recollection of the poet at Wentworth Place, and, above all, his sketch of the dying poet, make the best visual comment on Keats's life. Shelley had dedicated *Adonais* to Severn, Monckton Milnes had sent him the first copy of his work, Mr Forman had inscribed his edition of the love-letters 'to Joseph Severn, Rome'. 'I owe almost everything to Keats,' Severn had told William Haslam, 'my best friends as well as my artistic prosperity, – my general happiness as well as my best inspirations . . . I thank God I am so happy as to live to see his growing fame. It will be my lasting honour to be bound up with him.' To the end of his days he was committing the poet's likeness to canvas, on his deathbed he was planning a picture of 'Keats lying calm in death'. In Rome, in the Protestant Cemetery, he was laid by his friend.

* * *

Other reminiscent, aged friends of Keats still lingered on: among them the 'Mr W.D.' of the letters, the aged commissary who had read Shakespeare under Charles Brown's guidance, and built a house next door to Wentworth Place. 'There are many places like Chichester greatly alter'd', Matthew Snook had lamented; 'many of the best houses here unoccupied; little visiting, few dinner parties, no *Whist* ...'[6] Here, in the city where

Keats had attended 'old Dowager card parties', William Dilke had long ago retired; and here, on January 31st, 1880, Sir Charles arrived to visit him.

Great-uncle William's only son, Captain William Wentworth Dilke of the 77th, had died of cholera in the Crimean War, his daughter Emma had been 'dismissed from the house';[7] he himself remained indomitable. 'On the Sunday afternoon,' wrote Sir Charles, 'William Dilke walked in Goodwood Park with me, at a great pace for a man of eighty-four. He told me of his interview with Lord Castlereagh in 1815, [and] of his interview with Sir Charles Stuart (our envoy to Portugal), at Lisbon in 1812, when he, William Dilke, had at the direction of the chief clerk of the Foreign Office, taken out a diamond snuff-box sent from Brazil by the King of Portugal to a Mr Cassamajor employed under Stuart.'[8] There was something of The Grand about his veteran brother, and Numero 3 would in time wear on his keys 'my great-uncle Dilke's Peninsular medal marked with his battles'.

Great-uncle William would leave other titles to remembrance. It was he who had painted the name Wentworth Place on the house in which Keats had lived. He visited it, just before he died in 1885, with the poet's latest biographer, Sidney Colvin. He still recalled Keats in Chichester in 1819. He was buried in the cathedral cloisters in the city where Keats had written 'a little Poem call'd "St Agnes Eve" '.

24

THE DEVASTATING FIRE

WHILE the poet's friends faded gently away, while the critics continued to praise him, and to make him reflect all their prejudices, Mr Forman, undeterred, was busily preparing a library edition of Keats. The work could hardly be complete without the help of Dilke's grandson, and Mr Forman approached him. The editor who had received such castigation in *The Athenaeum* must have needed a certain audacity to do so. Years later he recalled his visit to Numero 3 in a grandiloquent and appropriate style. 'We were,' wrote Mr Forman, mildly,

> mutually aware of a divergence of view on the question of the Fanny Brawne letters, and particularly on the personality of the poet's *innamorata*. Nevertheless, when I had laid before him the details of my project and method, he decided, with that astonishing promptitude for which he afterwards became noted, to [give] me unrestrained access to all his material ... From this friendly and helpful attitude he never swerved.[1]

*   *   *

As Mr Forman crossed the threshold of the house in Sloane Street, he entered a Keatsian dream. In the vestibule hung a drawing of Keats, and an antique Roman fresco bought by Dilke at the Strawberry House sale. In the Blue Room were Severn's copy of his miniature, and a medallion of the poet, 'engraved from one of the lives'; a china punch-bowl gleamed enticingly on a dragon stand which had graced the house of Mr Wydel. Each step of the stairs reminded the visitor of the Dilke genealogy: here was a painting of Byng's Fleet at Naples, with Sir Thomas Dilkes second in command; here was little Anne Fisher, born in the year of the Armada, the future Lady Dilke of Maxstoke Castle. Here – for the Keatsian again took over – were thirteen water-colours by Hood, the husband of Jane Reynolds. In the front drawing-room was the Ludwig Cranach, *Charles the Bold, Duke of Burgundy and his brother*: 'a splendid specimen of work in gold', which Dilke had bought the year after Keats's death; here, too, was

Dilke's hand-painted copy of Blake's *Songs of Innocence*. The German mugs on the chimney-piece had belonged to Fanny Brawne, the ginger-jars by the window to old Mr Dilke of Chichester. As for the builder of Wentworth Place, his formidable presence loomed everywhere. Mr Forman came face to face with Arthur Hughes's portrait of Dilke, with the daguerreotype of the old man, his son and grandsons. In the new sitting-room he found a likeness of the grave editor by Sidney Inwood Jones, Lady Morgan's niece, and the miniature of that potentate by Wilkin. In Sir Charles's room, a mask of The Grand hung above the door, like the household deity it was.

And in this little crowded holy of holies, this Aladdin's cave, where dispatch-boxes recalled the distinction of the master of the house, the relics were almost too numerous to mention. Here, under glass, was Keats's tracing of a Grecian urn, done when he was writing his Ode. Here were a mask of Keats himself, a miniature of 'merry Mrs D.', old Mr Dilke's pocket-book, and an immortal snuff-box ('I wish [Dilke] would come this minute, for I want a pinch of snuff very much just now'). In the Keats boxes, so Sir Charles would record in his inventory, were

> his hair cut off after death. His Ovid with pencil verses. His notebook when a medical student. His own copy of *Endymion*, with all his sonnets and minor writings in his own hand at the end. Two love-letters. His Shakespeare, with the first draft of two poems. His Milton, with the first draft of one poem and many m.s. notes. His pocket book with Leigh Hunt's autograph and his own, and the first draft of a sonnet. His Beaumont and Fletcher. My grandfather's annotated copy of Lord Houghton's life of Keats.[2]

There were, too, 'a large quantity of letters relating to my grandfather sent me by the American nephews and grandnephews of Keats'.

It is abundantly clear that – whatever he believed – Mr Forman was not given 'unrestrained access to all the material'. It would be illuminating to know what Sir Charles withheld from him. Were the 'two love-letters' he would record in 1885 the two he had kept back from Herbert Lindon? If they were unpublished, would Mr Forman, of all people, have failed to print them? It seems impossible that Mr Forman, with his 'scholastic earnestness', would have rejected any Keatsiana of value; but Sir Charles, who detested Fanny Brawne, who knew that Brown had quarrelled with The Grand, who, all his life, admired Dilke of

Wentworth Place with uncritical and absolute devotion, had his private reasons for choosing what to show.

However, Mr Forman moved in a daze in this scholar's paradise; and 'the interview in the Sloane Street house remains so vividly impressed on my mind', he recalled some twenty years later,

> that I cannot refrain from recounting it. The books and papers ...
> were spread out on a table; and we went over them one by one.
> Concerning one after another he put the question – 'Will you have
> this away?' Whenever the answer was – 'No; it will not be necessary,'
> the book or document remained upon the table. Whenever I replied –
> 'Yes, if you please,' he turned half round and threw the book, paper
> or papers on the carpet ... The heap thus unceremoniously accumu-
> lated was at length more bulky than I could conveniently carry away,
> and included items no less remarkable than the 1808 reprint of the
> folio Shakespeare of 1623, written in by Keats, and the priceless little
> Milton with the poet's manuscript notes given him by his friend
> Dilke's wife ... When the heap of treasures was complete, the owner
> rang for his manservant and delivered the simple injunction: 'Call a
> cab for Mr Buxton Forman, and put those things in it.' They were
> not even packed up; and ... when I raised the question of fire-
> insurance, he said, 'They must take their chance with your own
> things.'

The Grand would have shuddered at this princely carelessness; Mr Forman admired it. He hastened back to his desk to enlist the devoted help of Madame Llanos; and a stream of personal details about the poet and his circle flowed to Marlborough Hill from Madrid:

> I well remember [wrote Fanny Llanos], when living with our dear,
> kind grandmother, our pleasure in keeping little fish, (called min-
> nows I think) and his love of birds, especially a favo[uri]te Tom Tit.
> I still retain the same fancy, and have always in my room a gold-
> finch and linnet, whose sweet wild notes, remind one of the green
> fields of dear England, all spangled with buttercups and daisies, and
> the sweet hedgerows smelling of May and Wild Roses ...

> Can you say whether Keats called Margaret Brawne by the pet-
> name of 'Toots' [inquired Mr Forman on April 30th, 1883]?

Do you know who enjoyed the nick-name of Millamant; and whether 'the Bishop' was the name of a dog, or someone's nick-name? Was 'Elm Cottage' the house at which Mrs Brawne resided between her residence at Brown's and Dilke's houses?

I do not of course expect you to remember one quarter of these things, if indeed you ever knew about them ... Two days ago, I made the acquaintance of Miss Charlotte Reynolds, who gave me some valuable information and assistance ...

Mr Abbey [came the answer] would not allow [me] to form any acquaintance beyond his own circle of friends. Much against his inclination I became acquainted with the Dilke's and the Brawne's, and a slight knowledge of the Reynolds ... Before going to live at Wentworth Place, Mrs Brawne resided at West End, Hampstead, but I don't know the name of the Cottage ...[3]

That year, in four volumes, there appeared *The Poetical Works and other Writings of John Keats, now first brought together, including Poems and numerous Letters not before published.* The Athenaeum observed somewhat smugly: 'A variorum edition of Keats of quite remarkable interest.' *Macmillan's Magazine* declared that 'from this mass of material one section only could have been well spared: it is that which contains the letters to Fanny Brawne. Mr Forman ... is apparently impenitent.'

* * *

It was to Mr Forman's credit that he remained impenitent: that he could be as firm as a Dilke. The poet's *inamorata* was still a cause of bitter contention; and the reissue of the love-letters started a correspondence between Sir Charles and the ever-diligent editor. Numero 3 still maintained his inflexible hatred of Fanny Brawne; and on June 2nd, 1890, determined to convert Mr Forman, he revealed that he had withheld a quantity of Fanny Brawne's correspondence. As incriminating evidence, he quoted from the letter in which she had offered Dilke the miniature. Mr Forman's answer was sadly revealing:

Dear Sir Charles Dilke,
    Accept my thanks for the trouble you have taken in writing to me about the reissue of Keats's Letters to Fanny Brawne ...

My view of what I had to do in this matter goes beyond the aggre-
gation of bare facts. I think one's first duty in doing that kind of work
is to get at the characters of the set of people concerned. Of the character of Fanny Brawne, both as girl and as wife and mother, I formed
a definite conception, from such documents and statements as were
accessible to me; and I endeavoured to touch the character in that it
might be viewed in juxtaposition with the letters and taken in mitiga-
tion of passages which seemed to me to be the result of disease and
misconception. I am not obstinately bent on keeping that conception;
but as far as I have gone with fresh evidence, my view remains un-
changed; and I think this revised introduction to the Letters expresses
that view adequately, without making the lady out a saint or even a
heroine. The passage you have been kind enough to send me at the
close of your letter of the 2nd instant fits in with my conception of
her character; but I cannot say what I might get to think if I saw the
letters you mention in their entirety. At present, I am doing nothing
fresh about Keats; but if, for example, I had to write his life, I should
feel compelled to ask for a sight of those letters, in order to give
myself a chance of revising the fundamental conception of her
character ...

Perhaps I ought to say *how* the episode of Mr Lindon and the portrait fits my idea of Mrs Lindon's character: it certainly confirms the
view that she was reserved, self-contained, and reticent; and those
qualities do not, I think, go so often with shallowness of feeling as
with the reverse ...

Believe me to be
Very truly yours
H. BUXTON FORMAN[4]

✳ ✳ ✳

It seems inexplicable that Mr Forman did not demand, then and there,
to see the letters. It was an extraordinary lapse of judgment. But Sir Charles
did not press the point. An eccentric American, Fred Holland Day, had
already gained an auspicious *entrée* to Sloane Street. He had been invited
to lunch, proved himself a social success, and returned more than once to
photograph 'the Keats things'. He sent copies of photographs to Sir
Charles, and Sir Charles sent him tracings of signatures on letters and in
books. In 1891 he arranged for Day to photograph pictures.

It was not Mr Forman, but Fred Holland Day who photographed the now fragmentary letter in which Fanny Lindon had offered Dilke the miniature. He also recorded the letter to Maria, deploring Finch's account of Keats.[5]

*   *   *

Of all the Keats circle, there is no doubt that, in worldly terms, Dilke had been the most successful; and his interest in *The Athenaeum* and in *Notes and Queries*, duly inherited by Numero 3, added a regular and substantial income to that which Sir Charles received in his political capacities. On Dilke's financial security – and, too, on Brown's – Wentworth Place had been built; with Dilke's financial sense the monetary problems of the Keats family had at last been solved. Now, in the third generation, it was Dilke's business acumen that helped his grandson to acquire the manuscripts and relics which the hard-pressed Lindons and Severns were forced to sell. The presence of Dilke, that formidable man of affairs, helped to shape not only the poet's life but his posthumous reputation.

Numero 3 inherited a keen sense of family: among his papers he preserved a business letter of his father's 'wh. I bought back from a sale, as I dislike such things being sold'.[6] In his father's writing-desk he kept not only the key to his safe, but 'a Keats triplicate, Father duplicate and Great Uncle W. Dilke duplicate'. His grandfather's photograph he kept at one of his country houses in case of fire at 76, Sloane Street.[7] But, like many of his contemporaries, Sir Charles allowed his prudery to outweigh his sense of permanent values.

Some of his prudery may be explained by his own private life; for the grandson whom Dilke had groomed for greatness, who would probably have led the Liberals in the House of Commons, whose 'extraordinary authority' had made him a Privy Councillor and Under-Secretary of State for Foreign Affairs, and might have made him one of the great foreign ministers of Europe, had been ruined, irretrievably, by domestic scandal. In 1885 he had been cited as co-respondent by Donald Crawford, the Member for Lanark. Mrs Crawford was the sister-in-law of Sir Charles's overshadowed brother, who had died, two years earlier, in Algiers. Nemesis had a crude sense of justice.

The case against Sir Charles was dismissed, Mrs Pattison – to whom he was privately engaged – had married him. But the career The Grand had longed for, the dazzling career for which Numero 3 was almost certainly destined, was now impossible. 'I should of course be pleased to see in my grandson the promise of a great man, because it would extend the moral influence of a good one': The Grand's aspirations had finally and ironically been denied him.

The natural reticence which led Sir Charles to deplore publicity, to riddle his papers with holes, could only have been intensified by the Crawford case. His tendency to destroy private papers grew stronger than ever. Posterity might learn an immense amount about Dilke of Wentworth Place from the material that he discarded; but he could not bear, now, to remember The Grand's proud confidence in him. 'I have', he wrote, 'destroyed hundreds of letters of my dear grandfather's about me in 1851 –2 and –3 which made me – if possible – love and worship his memory for all his goodness and his nobleness of heart – more at this lapse of time than even I did before.'[8] In 1855, when he was in Paris, with The Grand, he had kept a diary: but 'my diary was worthless, and I have burnt it'. 'In every page of the destroyed notebook of [1863] I c^d', he wrote, 'see the influence of my grandfather.'[9] Much illuminating material had vanished for ever, before, in 1905, he committed his diaries to the flames; and among it, beyond any possible doubt, was some correspondence in Keats's hand.

The late Mr Harry K. Hudson, who was his private secretary from 1887 to 1911, told Holland Day in December 1890 that Sir Charles knew nothing 'ab^t the quotation sent by his grandmother to Fanny Brawne, and the original letter from Keats is not extant'. In 1951 Mr Hudson wrote, more precisely: 'I remember seeing Sir Charles put some of Keats's letters in the fire, as he thought they were not things that should be seen by anyone.' Perhaps these included the 'two love-letters' mentioned in the inventory in 1885: were these the lost love-letters of May and September 1820? And what of the three missing letters to the Dilkes, or the journal letters to George Keats?

There are some sixty letters mentioned in Keats's correspondence which have yet to be found. One may guess with confidence which Sir Charles would have burnt; and the letters to Brown, the letters to Fanny Brawne, the final letter to Dilke from the *Maria Crowther*, must have been among the most significant that Keats wrote. The letters that Mr Forman mentioned on June 4th, 1890, were probably those mentioned in *The Papers of a Critic*: the letters that Fanny Lindon had sent from Spain in the early years of her marriage. Among the papers, 'calculated by the bushel', there would also have been her other letters to Dilke, her trustee, and to Maria Dilke, her great friend, a correspondence that covered some thirty years. These letters – which Mr Forman apparently never saw – are unknown today. So are a mass of letters from old Mr Dilke of Chichester, with whom Keats and Brown stayed early in 1819 (the manuscript of Sir Charles's memoirs quotes two of 1817 and 1820).[10] Where, too, is the 'large quantity of letters relating to my grandfather sent me by the American nephews and grand-nephews of Keats'?

Sir Charles had satisfied his personal prejudices. He had ensured his poet some privacy. Many permanent misconceptions of Keats and his circle, many permanent failures in our understanding, many glorious contributions to English literature, must be traced to that devastating fire.

THE EVERLASTING SPELL

Here lies one that passion slew!
Mourn him, flowerets, charged with dew;
Mourn him, doves with murmurous moan;
Streamlets, weep on mossy stone ...

So Maxwell Gray wrote, in 1891, in a poem on Keats's grave.[1] Since *The Papers of a Critic* had made their appearance, since the love-letters of Keats had burst on the world, the public had decided on a new scapegoat. Keats had not been killed by criticism, he must therefore have died of love, and love was only fatal when it was unrequited. But while the Victorians did not doubt that 'poor Keats' had been killed by passion, they preferred not to know too much about it; and when, that year, Sidney Colvin, the most distinguished among the new Keatsians, edited the poet's correspondence, even he, with astonishing disregard for scholarship, chose to ignore the facts. *The Literary World*, reviewing his edition, quite agreed that 'it was as well to omit the letters to Miss Brawne',[2] while *The Church Quarterly Review* considered that he should be 'thanked and congratulated' for the omission.[3]

The *Life and Letters of Joseph Severn*, in 1892, raised another monument to stupidity. In his preface, William Sharp referred to the mass of Brown's correspondence which he had studied; and, he had decided, 'there is much in his letters that would no longer be of interest, somewhat that is of too personal or private a nature to be disengaged from the gossip of a bygone day, and occasionally passages in that broader humour which has ceased to please; but in the main they are the letters of a gentleman ...' *The Athenaeum*, reviewing the book, noted that Dilke 'had also large masses of documents in his possession. But these questions', observed the journal, pregnantly, 'should never have been revived.'[4] However, while the ashes in his study fire were still warm, Sir Charles 'received from Major Charles Brown another valued present, the second volume of the 1813 edition of Burton's Anatomy, which belonged to Keats and contains many notes by him'.[5] This was probably the book that Carlino had meant to keep for Charles Keats Brown, his son; it was the last Keatsiana in his possession.

*　　*　　*

While documents were burnt and suppressed, while legend grew apace, a vehement septuagenarian burst from obscurity. Rosa Perrins, of Forest Hill, was the daughter of George Ramsay Rodd, a Hampstead surgeon who had attended Keats. The family had been close friends of the Brawnes. And when, in an article on 'Keats's Heroines', Katherine Tynan dismissed Fanny Brawne as 'a commonplace girl', Mrs Perrins rushed to the rescue. On August 11th she assured *The Literary World*:

> ... It is not true! Miss Brawne was my mother's great friend, and I knew her well up to the time I was almost fifteen, when she left England. She was a very striking, dignified woman; fair, very pale, with bright, dark eyes, and light brown hair; very clever, and most brilliant in society. I remember my mother saying she was a most lovely girl, but that she lost all her beautiful colour in an illness she had after her engagement with Keats was broken off – 'that mad boy Keats', – as they spoke of him then.

*　　*　　*

Keats had known that he would be among the English poets after his death; but in the last decades of his century he had earned a cult that would both have touched and angered him: touched, because it was professed so widely, felt so sincerely; angered, because it permitted all the snobbery and stupidity of which the Victorians were capable. Keats, it seemed, had not conformed to the Rugby ideal, and Dr Arnold's son could not forgive it: 'Character and self-control,' concluded Matthew Arnold, 'the *virtus verusque labor* so necessary for every kind of greatness, and for the great artist, too, indispensable, appear to be wanting to the Keats of the *Letters to Fanny Brawne* ... One is tempted to say that Keats's love-letter is the love-letter of a surgeon's apprentice. It has in its relaxed self-abandonment something underbred and ignoble, as of a youth ill brought up.'

It was indeed astonishing what errors of understanding, what vulgarity and deliberate falsification were now perpetrated in Keats's name. But Severn lay in the shadow of Caius Cestius, and many of his letters remained unpublished; Fanny Brawne lay in Brompton Cemetery, and her letters

185

to the Dilkes had probably been burnt, while her letters to Fanny Keats had been 'borrowed' from the Llanos family by the gleeful Holland Day, who was secreting them in Massachusetts. It was simple for William Graham, in *The New Review*, to fabricate an interview with Severn:

'There was certainly no possibility of further life in this world,' said Severn, the poet's old comrade. 'I did not know it then, but I know it now. The recent publication of the letters to Fanny Brawne puts a complexion on the case I never realized before ... That man died of love, if ever man died of love ...'
'Did Keats never allude to this cankerworm in any way to you?' I asked.
'Not a word ...' And the old man, resting his chin upon his hand, gazed out of the window into the depths of that blue Italian sky ...[6]

Yet perhaps the fictitious conversation had its uses. Severn dismissed Fanny Brawne as 'flighty and flirting'. On May 4th, when the conversation reappeared in *The Literary World* an outraged Mrs Perrins seized her pen:

Dear Mr Editor, –
Poor Fanny Brawne! 'Flighty and flirting': what a dreadful thing it is to be beloved by a genius! It seems as if people thought they could add to *his* merits by detracting from *hers*. I do not believe she was flighty, or she would not have become the clever, brilliant woman I remember; as to flirting I can't say, but Thackeray says, in the heading to one of her stories:

> That other girls besides princesses
> Like to flirt, the author guesses.

But as Mr Severn knew her so well, did *he* flirt with her? I am sure she was very much attached to Keats, as she had an illness when the engagement was broken off that nearly cost her her life. Most people said (my mother amongst the rest, who was her great friend) that Mrs Brawne was quite right to wish to put an end to it, as Keats was not able to keep a wife (even geniuses can't live on love and poetry); and his health was so bad he was not likely to return from Rome.

THE EVERLASTING SPELL

A few weeks later the vigilant old lady reappeared in *The Hampstead and Highgate Express*, and issued a reassuring bulletin: 'She would be sorry for lovers of Keats to think that the lady of his choice was anything but a refined and cultured gentlewoman. In every way she was well fitted to mate with him.'⁷

*   *   *

'Sir Charles Dilke would be pleased to show the Severn portraits of Keats to anyone interested, at 76, Sloane street, on Thursday, the 31st inst. from two to 3.30 p.m.' The announcement appeared in *The Morning Post* in October 1895, on the centenary of Keats's birth. The *Standard* reporter visited Sloane Street, and left indoctrinated: 'The unreserved publication of those letters is a gross instance of that pandering to public curiosity which TENNYSON has so rightly stigmatized.'

Curiosity remained, and admiration grew. 'If one English poet', said Robert Bridges, 'might be recalled today from the dead to continue the work which he left unfinished on earth, it is probable that the crown of his country's desire would be set on John Keats.' A bust of Keats had been unveiled in Hampstead Parish Church; a memorial tablet was set on Wentworth Place. Some admirers endowed a Keats Bed at Guy's Hospital, which the poet had walked in his brief medical career. Others printed his poems on Japanese vellum, 'the illustrations coloured by hand by Miss Cardew, sumptuously bound in full green morocco super extra, richly tooled in gilt, and inlaid with blue and purple pansies'. Others, still, it must be confessed, showed commercial understanding: in March 1897 Sotheby's auctioned the manuscripts of *Endymion* and *Lamia*, 'the property of a relative of Mr John Taylor'. The prices paid were 'almost startling: the MS. of *Endymion* at £695, works out at nearly £4 per page of MS., but the price paid for the *Lamia* was far higher ... The twenty-six leaves realized £305, or nearly £12 per MS. page'. Twelve months later, the manuscripts were offered for sale at £1,500.

As for Mr Forman, pursuing the uninterrupted tenor of his way, he issued a sixth edition of the poems. 'One knows well enough', snapped a critic, 'that there are certain persons professing a taste for literature who would far rather gossip about Fanny Brawne and Harriet than read the poetry of Shelley or Keats, but it is a pity that such trivial tastes are encouraged in an otherwise excellent edition.' Mr Forman remained the butt of the critics – the camera now recorded a white-bearded, melancholy prophet; but he continued into the twentieth century, re-editing Keats

187

and repeating his belief in Fanny Brawne. In 1901 he wrote firmly: 'I am not among those who think otherwise than kindly and respectfully of her. I fully believe she was warmly attached to Keats and mourned his loss long and bitterly ... She was a woman of considerable character and attainments.'

Other editors remained less understanding. In 1903 Laurence Binyon made the quite extraordinary statement that Keats's passion 'brought no new element into his work'; in 1904, Richard Le Gallienne took up the old refrain, and cried: 'O! why was the Bright Star sonnet not written to Cleopatra – or at least a Charmian!' In 1906, in the twelfth reprint of Lord Houghton's Aldine edition, Fanny Brawne and Charmian were still confused.

Soon there would be no one to correct the errors. On June 1st, 1907, Fanny's daughter, Margaret, died at Lausanne. On October 6th, 1909, her last surviving child, Herbert Brawne-Lindon – who had long since taken her name – died at Folkestone. On January 26th, 1911, Sir Charles Dilke died at 76, Sloane Street, a few months before the long lease of the house expired.

But the love of Keats, that 'strange personal Interest' that his publisher had known, the 'spell' that Fanny Brawne had recognized, remained for ever. A hundred years after he had died, men searched in New Zealand for a grave which had been lost to sight in the Maori Wars; and, hacking down the matted scrub on Marsland Hill, in the shadow of Mount Taranaki, a world and more away from Wentworth Place, they struck the stone with the epitaph: 'Charles Brown. Friend of Keats.'

The words might faithfully be inscribed on the tombs of Hunt and Woodhouse, of Dilke and Taylor, Monckton Milnes, Buxton Forman. They might, with irony, yet with truth, be an epitaph for Dilke's grandson. They mark the grave of John Hamilton Reynolds in the Isle of Wight, and they mark the grave of Severn, in Rome. They hold a world-wide, everlasting spell.

APPENDICES

APPENDIX I

Charles Brown, C. W. Dilke, and Keats's Financial Position

from the original letters at Keats House

I

DILKE TO BROWN

31 *July* 1824

Upon my conscience, Brown, I believe I am one of the most kind, considerate, affectionate, pleasant, sociable, unsociable fellows that 'lard the lean earth'. – I have not had your letter six hours, but, though perplexed with more than my usual no-occupation, here I am having a chat with you. – I believe there is something in good spirits, & warmheartedness, more infectious than plague, pestilence, methodism, or humbug, & your letters have the spot upon them so that one half of my amiability is to be set off to your account. – I know not that you are a 'good letter writer', or any other thing that is *good*; but somehow you contrive to put one in a good humour, & the first feeling, after the second reading, is to do one's best to thank you. – However I must not this month or two run on after my old, idle, desultory *self*-talk – Fortune, Brown & Circumstance, have thrust horrors upon me in the way of business, & I must be dull as becomes one on such occasions ... What will you say, or how open your eyes & fix your attention, when I tell you I have had a letter from Geo Keats. – Aye, and just such a letter, mind I have nibbled my pen, as in 'my strange obstinacy' I always maintained he would write, when he wrote at all. – It is three sides of foolscap, from one end to the other, with the exception of some half dozen lines of common decent civility, an explanation of *all* transactions between himself & his Brother. – I have not the letter to refer to, having sent it to his Sister at her request; but the main facts I can give you; & I feel bound to do so in justice to a man, who certainly treated me negligently and slightingly, & therefore whom I feel bound *not* to neglect,

191

as a *self* satisfaction & assurance that I did not deserve it; whose character
we should all be willing to uphold in respect of his Brother's memory, &
to that just pride and independence which having led him into the wilds
of America, has put it out of his power to protect it himself. – In the first
place, for I must begin with the beginning, he acknowledges to have
received letters from yourself & Mr Haslam, & excuses his not having
answered them from the insurmountable aversion he felt to offer exculpa-
tion or explanation when he had been so cruelly prejudged, & to men who
domineered & dictated after that fashion, when they had no right to do
either. – He more than once attempted it but found it impossible – As I
am giving *his* defence, you will have the goodness *so* to understand it. – He
finds it still impossible to sit down without reply; and as certain specific
charges have reached him through a relation of Mr Taylor's at Cin-
cinnati, he has at length thrown his defence into my hands & request[s] me
to give all possible publicity to it. – have the goodness therefore to convey
the spirit of what follows to Mr Hunt & any other likely to have heard of
the charge, which, as he understand[s] it assumes its most tangible shape in
form 'that he on his second return to America took with him £700 of his
Brother's money'. – Now he is not content with denying this, but he
enters with most *minute particulars*, quite conclusive in my judgement & of
others that have read them to *prove* that it was impossible. – John's whole
property, *at the first*, was £1500. – He then proves, by sums and dates etc
& all of which I really cannot give, that *more* than £1000 was expended by
& for John before he was of age. – That it was nearly one year & ten
months, or two years, after before Geo *first* went to America – That
as John was not more than ordinarily *near* at that time, it was not over-
rating his expences to say, every thing included, his expences could not
have been less than £200 per ann. That in conversation with his Brother,
he at that time informed him he had lent about £170. – & therefore without going into minute details, it is clear that when Geo first went to
America John had not *one shilling*, nay, he was already indebted to Geo;
and notwithstanding this Geo left him £300 *in hand*. – How Geo was
enabled to do this, he explains thus. John Premium, Hospital expences,
etc. etc. & his living for four years nearly before he was of age, owing to
his quarrel with the surgeon & leaving him he shews cost John this
amount; whereas Geo was taken into Mr Abby's without expence, lived
with him, & at the end of the time had expended a mere trifle more than
the interest of his money, & Mr Abby made him a present for his services
of nearly £100 – That the funds having risen his money sold for more than

£1600, and though within three months of being of age he left England, he did not in consequence of his advances to & for John carry with him £1100 – Up then to this time his Brother is very considerably his debtor. – But from the charge specifying £700 he presumes it has relation to his second visit, this being the exact sum he carried back with him. – Whatever monies John had after he left arose from Tom's estate, & with very trifling exceptions, could arise from no other. – Now Tom's estate, after paying his debts, funeral expences, etc etc amounted in a gross sum to £1100. – On this his sister had a previous & separate claim for £100. – On Geo's arrival he found John *had* received £100 & had remitted £100 to him in America. – Then, after the sister's portion was abstracted their [*sic*] remained £540, he thinks exactly to divide. – From this they each took £100 more, & the half of the remaining being £170 he borrowed of John – being all he ever did or ever *could have borrowed*, if it is to be called borrowing when his Brother was indebted to him more than £400 at that very time. – How he came to take this he explains by those necessities & engagements to complete which he was obliged at a great expence & all hazards to return to England; & then to borrow & scrape money in every direction. – That he does not offer this as an apology for not having remitted money to his Brother – that would be conduct without excuse or impossible to excuse by any balancing of accounts, had it been in his power – but that it was absolutely out of his power as, to use his own forcible words, if he had suffered shipwreck on his return. – That this charge can have originated directly from any thing said by his Brother he cannot believe, for his Brother knew little or nothing of his own affairs – & was so depressed, that Geo felt it to be impossible to tell him the facts, that he had but £170 in the world beyond what he had in his pocket, some £60 or 70 when he left him, & this £170 not his own. – That though his Brother never could have believed that the whole £700 was his own peculiar, he might, & Geo thinks he led him to believe that it was the proceeds of Tom's estate, although it can be proved that they had but £540 to *divide* when Geo landed in England. – That if it had arisen from any thing vaguely and indirectly said by his Brother, it has originated in those vague & general terms, which, with the kindest possible intention he had himself always used when speaking to his Brother; for such was the dreadful depression of his spirits at times, when speaking alone to his Brother, that he always feared the most dreadful consequences should he ever ascertain the exact situation of his affairs. He therefore always purposely left his Brother in uncertainty intending & hoping, under pretence,

APPENDIX I

for a time, of balancing Accts, to remit sufficient for his maintenance, & he
has only to hope that having shewn the positive fallacy of the cruel charge
against him, those whom it may satisfy, will do him the justice to believe
that he would have remitted the first & the very first moment it was in his
power – & he now intends, whenever circumstances will permit him to
discharge all debts due by his Brother, & in furtherance of this object has
given Bills to Taylor; – I have very great pleasure in concluding this long
explanation, which if it be not perfectly satisfactory must arise from my
imperfect telling, but if I had the letter I really could not go into more
detail. – Thus I take leave of business, but it is too late in the sheet to add
anything, but that we are all reasonably well. John Snook about whom
you inquire was attacked in J … etc. etc. [omission?] Richards called on me
a few days since after an absence of months, & Mancur was with me last
night. – All well …

Yours truly

C. W. DILKE

2

BROWN TO DILKE

Near Florence. 6th Septr 1824

My dear Dilke,

Much as I desired to answer the letter I received from you on 19th.
August, and that immediately, I was compelled to defer it till to-day.
I had undertaken a task, which as it was of great importance to the party
for whom I undertook it, I mentally swore I would neither read nor write
any thing else till it was fairly finished, and it turned out to be far more
tedious and laborious than I had expected; and yesterday I washed my
hands of it. This, I believe, is the first excuse of the kind I have had
occasion to make; I have now lost you for 17 days, but had I done otherwise, I should have neglected a more serious duty. What you have written
about Geo. Keats has in some measure given me pleasure, as I hope that
what appears still doubtful may be cleared up. No one would rejoice more
than myself to find him guiltless of the charge against him; and when I
can rejoice on that score, I will make him all the amends in my power.
At present every thing rests on his own assertion not only in opposition

to his brother's but to Mr Abbey's. Nor can I see, even if his assertion is correct, that he has any reason to complain of a charge being made against him, which by his own account he has taken every pains to establish. He purposely caused his brother to believe it, and through him his friends, as J K's consequent destitution compelled him to divulge the cause. His reason for this deception is so strange and uncommon, that it is barely credible; at least upon his last leaving England, when the reason could not, on the same grounds, have existed; still it is possible, from sheer want of common sense and common forethought. Now I will proceed downwards with your letter, not allowing a single fact you have stated unreplied to. He says I wrote to him like one who domineered and dictated; I deny it; my letter was very short, dry, and cold, not even accusing him, unless by implication; – what Mr Haslam wrote I know not. It was always my belief, till I spoke with Mr Abbey, that he took with him £640, or thereabouts, from his brother John. During the autumn previous to G's return from America, J. went frequently to his guardian endeavouring to procure £500 of his own money to lend to Mr Haydon; he then told me that after that loan he should have about £200 remaining. This could not be effected on account of a trustee being in Holland at the time, and the idea of the loan was relinquished, from that and other causes. So persuaded was J. that he had £700, that he used to enter with me on the calculations respecting laying that sum out in ground rents, and I could not believe otherwise. Afterwards he had, at his brother's request, George reminding him of an offer he had made to lend him money, lent all he had except £60 to him; so he told me expressly, thinking his 'brother did not act rightly in leaving him so', – these were his words. He spoke in the same manner to another person (whose name I need not mention), and who informed me the sum was £700, according to John's words. Some short time after I went, at his desire, to Taylor & Hessey, to ask for a loan till Geo should remit back some of his money, he authorizing me to tell T & H of his brother having borrowed all his money; they declined advancing money, and therefore I borrowed some from Skynner for his purpose. Under these circumstances, I say, I could not have believed otherwise than I did. The charge, therefore, contrary to G's supposition, did 'originate directly from his brother', not from any thing 'vaguely & indistinctly' said, but frequently, and positively, and with complaints against *him*, and for this there is other testimony than my own. In the spring of 1822 I called on Mr Abbey in Pancras Lane, when I asked him the am^t lent by John to George, upon the latter's second voyage to America; he answered 'about £350 to £400, – he could not tell precisely without reference to his books, – something like that amount'. When I said I understood it was about £640, he said 'that was a mistake, – it could not be so much.' On my regretting it was ever lent to him, his reply was – 'and so do I regret it; I told John at the time not to lend it, and said all I could to prevent his doing so.' Thus it appeared John had overrated his funds, likely enough in one so unused to any thing like money affairs; but it took nothing from the charge against George, in a moral point of view, whether it was £640 or £350. George says his brother expended £1,000 by the time he left the profession of surgery; while Mr Abbey expatiated to me on the folly of his having left it, after he [h]ad spent £700 on it. You can inquire of Mr Abbey on both these points [s]o contradictory to George's statements; and though it is certain Mr Abbey spoke to me, it is possible he spoke in both cases under an error, for George might have allowed him to believe he was borrowing £350, which may be disproved by the Accounts; or Mr Abbey might have spoken in forgetfulness of a fact; and it is very possible he talked of £700 when he ought to have said £1000. George say[s] he owed nothing to John for expences previously to the former's coming of age; this may have been the case, but John understood otherwise, for when walking in the Highlands, he told me George did owe him money on that account, and had repaid him, he knew not how much, as George in settling every thing before he left London, gave him no written account, and asked me if I thought he ought not to have given one. I am aware that John had debts owing to him of about £170, and he told me part of them were loans made by George, – but that he agreed to take them on his own shoulders, that George might have more to carry to America, and at George's request. This seems opposite to George's assertion of having left John £300 at that time; but John was likely to be in error, and it appears from George's account, it was his intention to deceive him on this point, not wishing it known he gave £300 of his own money. I cannot (I find) enter into the account of Tom's estate, as, through some slip of the pen which confuses it, you deduct £300 from £1100 and make £540 only remaining. Nor is it necessary; I have mentioned enough to show I could not have believed and said otherwise; and that if George is guiltless, he I contend took the best means to show himself guilty. I cannot say, nor can Hunt, from your letter, that George at present is exculpated; it is far from satisfactory, and Hunt thought so, without being acquainted with the circumstances I have related from my own and other's knowledge. Mr Abbey may settle it quickly, and I shall be most happy to hear I have been in the wrong, though I shall never reproach myself for speaking on the strong grounds I went upon ...

3

BROWN TO DILKE

[*Letter postmarked May 15th, 1826. Beginning of letter torn off.*]

... Severn will certainly be in Rome; I wrote to him [torn] fishing for you, and that I had hopes, and he has answered me in a sentence of joy on the occasion. Whether you are in three or four, or possibly in two, the expence of travelling *post* will be much the same as crawling on in a 'voiture', – rather less indeed in *amount*, only you will be a less time on the road, and therefore not *kept* so long for your money. You must hire a carriage at Calais, or you must buy one (as I did) and sell it again at half price or as you can. I'll give you facts. Six months ago our banker, Mr Johnstone, went with *three* other persons from Florence to Paris; the carriage was his own, so no expence was on that [letter torn] The £50 is not due from you till next November, nor can I possibly want it before. Pay it to Mancur, and he will either give you a receipt, or return the bill which I left with Skynner. Pay him also the money from Keats. I never heard of his having any hopes from Chancery. The return of this money is as if I had *found* it, for I never much calculated on it, and latterly not at all, notwithstanding what you wrote about Geo Keats. By good luck I have not destroyed the account between me and poor John Keats. The balance in my favour, on 22^d Decr 1819, was £6. 4. 1, agreed to by his initials. After that time, the account is as follows:

1819	Decr. 22 – Balance – – –	£6.	4.	1			
1820	Jan. 1	Examiners	2.	10.	10		
		Half Wine and Spirits' bill		5.	9.	6	
	8	Boot-makers bill	3.	6.	6		
	March	Dr Bree	4.	4.	0		
		Coach hire		3.	0		
	22	Board 3 months	15.	–.	–.		
	May 4	Sundries		6.	6.		
One week's rent in advance at Kentish Town					1.	1.	0

[May] 6 Board 1½ months	7.	10.	0
Loan	50.	–.	–.
Half Wine and Spirits' bill	5.	18.	0.
1821 [*sic*] March 6. Mr Rodd's bill	13.	11.	–

	115.	4.	5.
Less received of J.K. 6ᵗʰ Febʸ	40	–	–
1820			

	75.	4.	5.
	Balance due –		

You may mention that he and I always had a running account together. The above is an exact copy, with this exception, – I have omitted to charge interest on the £50 loan, though it is entered in the account, because it was interest I had actually *paid* to Skynner for that identical sum which I had borrowed from him to lend to Keats, before I set off on my second trip to the Highlands. But as it is unpleasant to my feelings to mention any thing about interest, especially as if that is once begun upon it would raise the amt. to nearly £100, I would rather omit it altogether. I never saw Miss Keats, – for which her guardian is answerable, – yet though I never saw her, my congratulations on her marriage, and my wishes for her welfare and happiness are not the less hearty ; – have the goodness to tell her so.

[*The rest of the letter – possibly just the signature – is missing.*]

4

BROWN TO DILKE

Florence. 17 December 1829

My dear Dilke,

In answer to your favour of 31st. July 1824, or rather in second answer, for the first I sent on 6ᵗʰ Septʳ 1824, I beg to leave to inform you, – but first I must wish you a merry Christmas and a happy new year, the usual beef, ham, turkey, plum pudding, mince pies, and a bowl of punch of

my own making; – ditto to wife, – ditto to Wentworth, and ditto to all I
know; – Carlino tells me he wished to say all that, but he is too late. Now
for my second answer to your favour of 31st. July 1824. No, I can't come
to that yet; for I've a story to tell first. (I think, if I had studied it, I could
not have commenced my letter with a more astounding interest; – but let
that rest.) A few days ago, I received a letter from Galignani in Paris,
asking me for Keats's autograph, and telling me they were on the eve of
publishing his works. I had heard of this, wished to communicate with
them, and was told the volume was published, – so, with regret, I remained silent. It appears, however, I was in time. I have answered them
in a manner to make them wish for my pen, and Keats's MSS, – now,
perhaps, too late to enter into an arrangement with them. Be that as it
may, (your father's favourite expression,) I am resolved, seeing that Keats
is better valued, to write his life. I can find time for it and Trelawny's
work together, – with a spice of fugging, to which I have not the slightest
objection. In doing this I shall want the letter from George to you, of
which you gave me a loose account in the said letter of 31st. July 1824, – or
a copy of George's, – and that as soon as convenient. Fact is, your account
of the business was, as I thought at the time, though I was willing to take
the best side, lame in the extreme. I think his may be a better story, and
therefore wish to see it. Besides, upon taking it into my head it is time to
write Keats's life, I recd a packet of letters, in which I found a few things
against your statement, (if statement it may be called,) and a letter from
Abbey, addressed to Keats, upbraiding him for having given or lent, (no
matter which,) all his money to George. Then again, I have one of Abbey's
Accts. Current with Keats, wherein there are two or three matters which
I cannot reconcile with what, you say, George asserts. There are also,
taking them in their general tenour, documents much against George.
You will guess from this that I do not think George has been calumniated,
unknowingly, by Keats, and afterwards by me, in repetition. You will give
me credit for wishing to see things in their best view, if I can. Then, be
not fearful that I will make a cruel use of the letter from George; quite the
contrary; all that I want is authority for stating that Keats's generosity to
Tom when under age, and to George after 21, diminished his fortune, or
rather finished it, – or something to that effect, – I mean that it shall not
be a stigma on George, – you understand me of course. Now, taking the
uncharitable side, in answer to George's saying he ever avoided mentioning to Keats his poverty, – I have proofs to the contrary; and proofs of
George's extravagance, in a letter from Keats to him, and to Abbey. I

know that Keats himself never was extravagant; that he well was aware of the value of money; that he could well understand an account, – though latterly (though I would not permit it) he wished to avoid examining any; that he, as he told me, impoverished himself by lending money to George before he was of age, and that George repaid him in the lump, without an account, which Keats believed he kept, and therefore Keats did not; and moreover that this sum, paid on George's first going to America, was not to Keats, or to my mind, satisfactory. All this is between ourselves. I only want George's own statement, word for word, – not, as you see, for any harsh purpose.

If, in any letters from Keats to you, there should be some passages worth recording, (for his entire letters, unless on very particular occasions, ought not to be printed,) let me have them, – with the *dates* of the letters, – for the dates are of importance to me.

Do you remember advising me never to mention Keats's origin to Hunt? I never did. He learnt it, I suppose, from Clarke, a little while before he wrote the account of Keats. Think what a use he has made of that information; – 'his origin was of the humblest description; he was born at a livery stables in Moorfields &c.' Now I can state all that affair, without telling a lie, in a more decent manner. Thank heaven, there is damned bad grammar in Hunt's indecency! As the world goes, (though you and I would not have cared if Keats had been the hangman's bastard,) such bald and untrue words may have a bad effect, – for they are untrue, as far as *humblest* is concerned, and even as far as *a* livery stables is concerned; he, Hunt, ought to have known better, because, though it is true a God was born in a manger, his admirers, or worship[p]ers, or priests would rather he had been born in a palace. I hate Hunt's account of him, though every sentence, I verily believe, was intended to his honour and fame; but what does that matter when he manages to make him a whining, puling boy? The truth is, Hunt seems to be so much impressed by his illness, that he forgets he was ever in good health. How odd, – Hunt must make some vile mistake.

[*Lower half of page torn off.*]

5

BROWN TO DILKE

Florence. 20 January 1830

MEM. I give you warning this is the most unpleasant letter I ever sent you! – to my feelings.

My dear Dilke,

Many thanks for your early reply to my letter; and I should have felt doubly thankful if you had found George's letter, and sent it, or a copy. I am, at present, at a standstill: – though not on your account, as your information respecting that letter will merely influence one paragraph; for others are tardy. Yet, if you can find, and will send the mass (which you mention) of facts, documents, and writings, I shall esteem it a high favour. My motive for writing Keats' life is that he may not continue to be represented as he was not; possibly I ought to add another motive, – that of revenge against Gifford and Lockhart, – aye, and Jeffrey. I did intend to sell it, but from what you have said, it is likely I may refuse to touch a penny of its profits, if any there should be. Your letter, relating to George's defence, is strange indeed; when I first received it, willing to believe the best, I either did not strictly examine it, or I acquiesced to broad assertions, another and a better reason is, I did not know I had it in my power to refute it. Now I put it under a keen scrutiny, backed by staunch documents, and have no hesitation in declaring that if that is his defence, and if you believe in it, you have been grossly imposed on. You will not allow John (to speak in their Christian names) to have had capacity to judge or know any thing of money affairs; therefore you contend his evidence goes for nothing. I recollect, when balancing an account of my brother James's property, he looked over me, and pointed out an error, of such a nature as required a merchant's eye. When I expressed my surprise at this knowledge of his, he said something to this purpose, – 'I detest my own accounts, because they are bad; but I have learnt accounts, and, when mine are worth looking into, I shall be a good accomptant.' The reason for his having signed Abbey's balances wrongly was his entire faith in Abbey's honesty, of which he has often spoken to me, together with his averseness to canvass his small means. He knew enough of Accounts to see (what you assure me of) that George was not capable of being a man of business, – which I have under his own hand. However, I shall not have to press John's knowledge on this point much into the service. You say I have not authority for stating that John's generosity to George finished his fortune. No? Have I not John's positive and often repeated word to that effect? And have I not their guardian's information, both verbally and written? These authorities, with the world, would be deemed sufficient evidence. But, you contend, the one's evidence is unavailing from his ignorance, and the other's from his character, – though it is difficult to imagine what purpose could be answered by a deception of this nature. In addition to these authorities I have mark you! that of George himself, as contained, by powerful implication, in his own defence, as given by you. The defence sets out with declaring that, at the time George first went to America, (June 1818) John was indebted to George, had not one shilling, and received £300 from George. Upon this setting out the greater part of the defence rests. Let us examine it. 1st. *John was indebted to George.* In another part of the defence this debt is made out to be more than £100. Did it never strike you how improbable it was that George, considered the most expensive of the brothers, especially in dress, could have maintained his capital entire, lived on the interest (£60, I believe) and out of that small sum, and the £100 he says he earned from Abbey, lent more than £100 to John? Without canvassing this improbability, for there is no occasion for it, I compel George to accuse himself of a vile falsehood. Here is a passage from a letter written by him to John, on 18th. March 1818: – 'I am about paying your's and Tom's bills, of which I shall keep regular accounts; and, for the sake of justice and a future proper understanding, I intend calculating the probable amount *Tom and I are indebted to you*; (not underlined in the original; I have done so, merely to draw your attention to the words.) 'Something of this kind must be done, or, at the end of two or three years, we shall all be at sixes and sevens.' This is positive proof. When a man is convicted of falsehood at starting, his defence, by most persons, would be thrown aside; particularly on a point where he could not be mistaken; and they would [act] rightly, for, it will be seen, as might be expected, every part of his defence rests on falsehood. 2nd. *John had not one shilling,* – that is, in June 1818. Now I have before me Abbey Cock & Co's Acct. Current with John. This is undeniable, indisputable evidence, because they acknowledge themselves debtors to him on 4 June 1818 for £500. Had it been in their favour, you would be at liberty to question it, but not when against themselves. On that day there was due to them from John no more than £31. 9. 2., for tea, chocolate, and cocoa, furnished to him George and Tom at various dates, during the previous three years. George paid all his tradesmen's bills at that time; so did John, as I recollect he told me, – besides, I knew him to be quite free from debts, when he lived with me, up to that period. For this purpose, it seems, John drew out £140, – part of which, possibly, went to pay Tom's bills. There therefore remained belonging to him, clear of all debts, £336. 16. 11, taking into account the balance of interest in his favour of £8. 6. 1. This sum, at the least, was his at that time, instead of not having one shilling! I say at the least, because the round sum of £500 does not look like the last of property; it implies there were yet some gleanings. But enough, – I have proved that George, for a second time, is guilty of falsehood in his defence. 3rd. *John received £300 from George* before he first went to America. Here I am the principal evidence. Immediately after our leaving George at Manchester, that is, on our first day's walk towards the Lakes, John told me that George had repaid the monies, furnished to him, when under age with – (I am nearly certain) – £70 or £80; – but I am certain I am not ten pounds wrong. This John did not believe was sufficient, and regretted that George had not kept, as he had expected, a regular account. John told me further, how unlucky it was for him to be the eldest of the two brothers, who could not live on their incomes; and mentioned that he had expended a good deal for Tom in his illness, taking him to Margate (before we knew them,) and afterwards to Teignmouth; add to which, there was George's and Tom's pleasure jaunt to Paris, the trip to Lyons, and the money lost at the 'rouge et noir' table in the Palais Royal, – how much, I forget, but far too much for their circumstances. John did not mention all this *against* his brothers; he loved them too well; he mentioned it as a fact, speaking all the while affectionately of them. He complained of his elder brothership, not of them. All this was in confidence, and I have never spoken of it till now that it is become necessary. I was undoubtedly of opinion that George had not fairly repaid him, and I never liked George afterwards. For, besides the above, I learnt that George had been extravagant; it was Abbey's alleged plea for dismissing him from his counting house; and I have a letter from John to Abbey, never sent, (possibly from its being torn,) wherein John hopes that Abbey will consider George cured of 'his carelessness and extravagant propensities'. Now, it is impossible that John could have related this on our walk to me within two or three days after having received £300 from him; and it is equally impossible that I should have dreamed it. We talked over it for miles, and it has never been off my mind. Then again, where were the £300? Not in Abbey's hands, or they would stand in the account; they could not be included in the £500, because no merchant or man of business whatsoever lumps two sums, received from different sources, in one; the £70 or £80, I think, John told me he had left in the hands of Tom, which is probable. Were the £300 locked up in a box at home? – no, for it appears John continued to draw on Abbey for his expences. But what ought to set this question to rest is that George had need of all the money he could scrape together for his American scheme, and John had £336 at least, say two years' provision; so there was no immediate necessity for making this handsome present; there would be time enough after George had established himself and was thriving; in the mean while the money was of importance to George, and not to John. The story refutes itself at every turn. For the third time I accuse George of falsehood, and believe that those who read this will own he is convicted of it. Thus, all his defence, resting on his being John's creditor for more than £400, becomes shameless; and John, in all likelihood, was, even at that time, his creditor. I will now examine into a few other bold assertions of his; and you must not be weary of me; but as I am weary of charging him with falsehood, I now leave that to you. 4th. He says that, on his return to America, he arrived with exactly £700. Then, forgetting his arithmetic, in his haste to depreciate Tom's estate and prove that he, a creditor for more than £400, only borrowed of John £170, he makes it out that he could not possibly have left London with more than £440, – unless indeed some kind friend there made him a present of £260, and paid his passage! 5th. You make him say Tom's estate, after paying the Doctor's bill, and the funeral expences, was reduced to about £1,100, but you meant, as I see by the after sums, £1,200. Tom's fortune was equal to George's, which was about £1,600, and the stocks had not fallen. So, Sawrey's bill, (a moderate one, though I forget the amount,) and the Undertaker's, (under £28,) amounted to about £400! 6th. George says he left £100 with John, when he went, for the second time, to America. John, after taking leave of him in town, came to me at Hampstead, pulled a packet of notes from his pocket, placed them in my hand, and told me that was all George had left him. I counted them instantly; they amounted to £40. He and I then sat down to calculate how much he owed, and we found it to be about £60; so he was left by George about £20 in debt. – 7th. George says that, on his return from America, he found that John had used £100 of Tom's estate,

John told me he had not touched a penny of it, and that George took it all, except the £40. John was certainly in the right, as I can pretty well prove. It was in 1819. On 2 and 3 April of that year he drew £106. 7. 7. out of Abbey's hands, as per Acct. Current, being the remains of the £500 and interest. A considerable portion of that sum (£106. 7. 7.) went, as I know, to pay bills; with the remainder he went to the Isle of Wight. There I joined him; we then went to Winchester, where he received £40, a loan returned from a friend. We lived as economically as we comfortably could; and, as I said, he was, at the end of the year, about £60 in debt. Now, how could he have spent £100 in addition to those sums? Indeed I am sure he never had it, – he could not.

I have done with his defence. Minor delinquencies I omit. My refuting it has filled me with disgust. I hate him more than ever, and feel tempted to put these documents to a vindictive use. Once or twice I was on the point of throwing this paper in the fire; but I wished to prove the knave a knave; and I am anxious to disprove any idea that may be entertained of my having either rashly or wantonly spoken against him. If you imagine there are any who hold such an opinion of me, let them see this letter; but I beg the favour of you to *show it to Miss Brawne & Mancur*, the two to whom I have most spoken against George. I own myself mistaken when I said that George had taken from his brother, according to my calculations, some-where about £700; the mistake arose from my not asking John whether the sum he named was money or stock, – (it turns out to have been stock,) – from my not being aware of a prior and separate claim on the part of the sister on Tom's estate for £100, and from my having under-stood that John, to the last, when George took all, had still a balance in Abbey's hands of a small amount; – then it would have amounted to about £700. But whether that sum or half the sum, the crime was the same, – leaving his brother worse than destitute, – in debt. I now calculate the sum he took was full £425, without taking into account that Tom's estate was indebted to John for the money he had advanced to Tom: so that probably it would amount to £600, – for Tom cost him a great deal. – but it is useless to explain the calculation. I'd rather write a second letter on other subjects, which I will, as an envelope for this.

Your's most truly,

CHAS. BROWN

6

BROWN TO DILKE

Florence. 31 *March* 1830

My dear Dilke,

You have wounded me to the quick. I could not have believed that any one I am acquainted with, far less you, would treat me, both in matter and manner, with such injustice. To make these words good, I must use many more.

When you sent me George's defence, you told me it was quite conclusive, in your judgment, and in that of others that had read it, to prove the 'positive fallacy of the charge against him'. You, and certainly most of the others that had read it, knew that I had promulgated this cruel charge. Add to which, in that defence the impossibility of my having heard such a charge from John Keats was urged as far as the nature of the subject would admit. I therefore stood convicted, by you and others, of having made a cruel charge against a man, of the fallacy of which you and those others were convinced, while possibly, some suspected I never had grounds for making it. You requested me to convey the spirit of the defence to Mr Hunt and any other likely to have heard of the charge. I could not believe in it, but, having no evidence in contradiction, I was compelled to accede, and make the defence, fully and faithfully, known to Mr Hunt, and four others in Italy, of which I took care to inform you. Though my case was a hard one, and though the defence rested on nothing but mere assertion, I was convinced of the goodness of your motives.

After wearing this stain on my character for more than five years, documents come into my hands by which I am enabled to prove that, root and branch, every tittle of George's defence is false. I do so, saying it is a most unpleasant and disgusting office to me, but necessary, and send the letter to you, requesting you will show it to Mancur and Miss Brawne, and to any others who may have entertained thoughts prejudicial to my character, as one guilty of having spoken indiscreetly against another. What is your answer? You say it is 'unintelligible' (assuming that I had given no reason for it, though it stared you in the face,) that I should 'inflict' an unpleasant letter on you, 'unasked for, unnecessary', stirring up your 'gall and bitterness with facts and figures'. This implies I had no right to send you such a letter: – I had. You made yourself an agent between George's character and mine; you forwarded his defence to me; I had a right to forward my defence to you in return, and more, – you were bound to act in the same manner, at my request, towards me, as I was bound, at your request, to act towards you. Instead of this, you say not one word of your agreeing to state to those, who were convinced of the fallacy of my cruel charge, the grounds of my defence. You content yourself with telling me you will show my letter to Mancur, when you see him, letting me know, on another page, that you have not seen him these six months, and that you suppose it out of all possibility that he should call on you. Now I request you will send it to him by the post, or back again to me. In respect to your not showing it to Miss Brawne, your reason is good, provided neither you, nor your wife, gave George's defence to her, or offered it, or spoke of it to her, – otherwise you are unjust. When George's character was to be made fair, backed by more assertions, it did not appear that mine ever entered into your head, – all that was tenderness for him; when mine was to be made fair, backed by incontrovertible documents, nothing but George's character is spoken of, – all is anger at me. You set yourself up as umpire, – act uprightly! George's faults, dates, and figures, without a document, were all in all sufficient, convincing to all; mine, with documents, are 'ingenious, quite conclusive to those who do not know they are erroneous, – to me', (you go on) 'they only prove how ingeniously a man may satisfy himself that error is truth, and confirm an old opinion, not of mine, but of most people's, that to build up an error *solidly*, there is nothing like facts, dates, and figures.' Why did you not apply this old opinion to George's defence? Considering you had been convinced by his unbacked facts, dates, and figures, would it not have been more to the purpose to pluck out the soul from any one of mine? You cannot do so, without doubting my word, which would be less offensive than disregarding it, because I can easily send you attested copies of these documents. How easy is it to speak positively! – how difficult, when that positiveness is called in question, by positive facts, dates, and figures, to do otherwise than sneer! You care not, you say, one farthing what I believe of George; – or if you did, what then? – but you ought to be careful that the world, – our world, – believes nothing against me without reason. The hope you express, never once noticing my character, that you may hear nothing further on this subject, by no means strengthens my faith in your perfect knowledge of George's immaculateness. You have it in your power, you aver, to prove every thing in his favour, – do it then, and I will bow to him, honour him, make him every amends in my power. I shall be rejoiced to find, by conclusive evidence, that my Keats's brother did not behave as I believe he did, that he did not borrow money without an acknowledgment, and then declare himself a creditor, – and that my Keats was not so weak and shallow as to accuse a brother of what he never committed; for this knowledge I would willingly sacrifice that part of my character, which you allow to be attacked, – I would confess myself indiscreet, defaming, – heinous, if any one insisted on the epithet; but it is enormous to expect that I should forfeit one iota of my good name in order to uphold that of the swindler of my friend. Instead of telling me you care not what I believe of George, you might have said, I care not for you. Yet, even then, I should have answered, – Care for me or not, care for your own honour; you, the active party in declaring me guilty of having made a cruel charge against another, are bound to examine, carefully examine into every particle of evidence which I may produce in my favour. You have, virtually, accused me of defaming George; this you have done, publicly as you could, short of printing; be rational enough to examine if the accusation you have made is, or is not grounded on a mistake.

You seem to think I ought to rest content with your bare assertion against me. It is, however, impossible to put faith in your infallibility on this subject; for which I will give you a few reasons. I was never aware of your being skilful in matters of account; and, judging from some self-convicting errors of account in George's defence, whether unperceived by you, or committed in your version of it, you are not skilful.

Your late knowledge of the Keatses' affairs in Chancery does not necessarily imply, as you assume, that you are well acquainted with all their affairs of twelve years standing; nor do I perceive how John's, George's, and my want of that Chancery-knowledge should have prevented either of us from understanding other matters; nor why, because an explanation to George of those Chancery affairs occupied sixteen foolscaps, he could not clearly acknowledge himself his brother's debtor in one explicit and entire sentence, which you miscall 'broken Sentences'. George's assertions in his defence did not pretend to rest on any thing but his intimate acquaintance with his own and his brother's affairs, which passed with you unquestioned; but, when a paper is discovered wherein he has condemned himself by striking at the root of that defence, you declare he knew little more than nothing of his affairs, which is not sufficiently consistent for an infallible man. Then again, your memory is not good; I have more than once told you that John's information to me of his brother's having taken from him all his money, without an acknowledgment, was clear, distinct, and often repeated, and you call it 'the ambiguous givings out of John'. For these reasons I cannot appeal to you as an oracle, to which you have but one claim, that I know of, – enigmatical positiveness. Add to which I cannot recollect you ever gave up any one of your positive opinions; so that, if my memory serves me well, I ought not blindly to yield to any one of them, knowing you, like many men, to have been positive on the wrong side.

Now I come to the [*half sheet torn away, back of top half continues*] sheer rudeness, and, terming it so, I am content. But I call, seriously, on you to make your words 'most cruel severity' – good, or to explain how you had been inadvertently led into error. Trusting you will either do the one or the other, I remain,

Your's truly,

CHAS. BROWN

With thanks for your consent to lend me £50, I have already arranged the business otherwise.

O   209

CHARLES BROWN'S PUBLICATION OF KEATS'S POEMS (1838) IN *THE PLYMOUTH AND DEVONPORT WEEKLY JOURNAL*

In May 1838 Dilke assured Brown that there was no objection to his publishing all Keats's poems; the following duly appeared in *The Plymouth and Devonport Weekly Journal* with the note 'From the unpublished Poems of John Keats'.

19 July.   *Sonnet. – To the Nile.*
6 September.   *Sonnet, written on the Summit of Ben Nivis* [*sic*].
13 September. *Ailsa Rock: In height 940 feet from the Sea, Near the Ayrshire Coast.* [This had in fact appeared in Hunt's *Literary Pocket-Book*, 1819.]
20 September. *Fingal's Cave in Staffa. – Fragment.*
27 September. *Sonnet.* [Given here for variants.]

Bright star! would I were steadfast as thou art!
    Not in lone splendour hung amid the night,
Not watching, with eternal lids apart,
    Like nature's devout sleepless eremite,
The morning-waters at their priestlike task
    Of pure ablution round earth's human shores;
Or, gazing on the new soft fallen mask
    Of snow upon the mountains and the moors: –
No; – yet still steadfast, still unchangeable,
    Cheek-pillow'd on my fair love's ripening breast,
To touch, for ever, its warm sink and swell,
    Awake, for ever, in a sweet unrest,
To hear, to feel her tender taken breath,
Half passionless, and so swoon on to death.

4 October.   *Sonnet.* ['The day is gone ...']

APPENDIX II

11 October.   *Sonnet. – To Sleep.*
18 October.   *The Faery Bird's Song.* ['Shed no tear!']
25 October.   *Faery Dirge.*
 8 November.   *Sonnet. On Sitting down to read King Lear Once Again.*
15 November.   *Lines on Seeing a Lock of Miltons's [sic] Hair.*
22 November.   *MEG MERRILIES. A Ballad, written for the amuse-
               ment of his young sister.*

On November 29th appeared the note: 'ERRATUM. – Journal,
Nov. 15. – In the "Ode", by John Keats, after the fifth line, "For ever
and for ever!" the following line was omitted:

            "Oh, what a mad endeavour".'

On July 4th, 1839, in a leading article which discussed the opponents of
progress, the writer observed:

Our modern poet KEATS, under his death-stroke, to wile away the
hours of sickness, was frequently reading his favourite SPENSER. Upon
one of these occasions, he wrote an extra-concluding stanza to the
Canto. We give it not only on account of its intrinsic merit; but
hitherto, it has remained unpublished; and *it is the last stanza, of any
kind, that he wrote before his lamented death.* Till then, he never wrote a
line of political tendency; yet it may be said, he died with his pen
weilded [sic] in the cause of Reform.

            In after time, a sage of mickle lore,
            Yclept Typographus, the Giant took,
            And did refit his limbs as heretofore;
            And made him read in many a learned book
            And into many a lively legend look;
            Thereby in goodly themes so training him,
            That all his brutishness he quite forsook;
            When meeting Artegall and Talus grim,
        The one he struck stone-blind, the other's eyes wox dim.

If Typographus thought fit to disable the Justice and Law of the
sixteenth century by blindness, he has certainly succeeded in opening
the eyes of millions. Many thanks to Typographus!

APPENDIX II

On December 5th, 1839, the *Journal* published an unsigned

SONNET, ON THE DEATH OF THE POET KEATS

And thou art dead? Thou very sweetest bird
That ever made a moonlight forest ring!
Its wild unearthly music mellowing!
Shall thy rich notes no more, no more be heard?
Never. Thy beautiful romantic themes,
That made it mental heaven to hear thee sing,
Lapping the enchanted soul in golden dreams,
Are mute! Ah! vainly did Italia fling
Her healing ray around thee – blossoming
With blushing flowers, long wedded to thy verse!
Those flowers, those sunbeams, but adorn thy hearse;
And the warm gales, that faintly rise and fall,
In music's clime – themselves so musical,
Shall chaunt the minstrel's dirge far from his father's hall.

The sonnet had appeared in *The London Magazine* in May 1821. Professor Blunden, in *Keats's Publisher*, suggests that Taylor had written it, but it is tempting to assign it to Brown.

APPENDIX III

VALENTINE LLANOS
AND *THE QUARTERLY REVIEW*

Some time in the latter part of 1825 a three-volume novel appeared in the London bookshops at the respectable price of twenty-four shillings. It bore the imprint of Henry Colburn, the fashionable publisher, and the title of *Don Esteban, or Memoirs of a Spaniard. Written by Himself.* It was a ponderous tale of adventure, a fine butt for the reviewers; and in the December issue of *The Quarterly Review* an anonymous critic duly attacked it. The criticism was no more malicious than many others of the period; it was probably less clever. But the *Quarterly* which – so they said – had snuffed out Keats with an article, happened now to attack his future brother-in-law.

Professing to doubt that *Don Esteban* was entirely the work of one author, the reviewer launched an indirect criticism:

> That a Spaniard has furnished a part of the materials of this work cannot be doubted; but 'that everything which the author relates is to be considered as simple matter of fact' ... is an assertion which no attentive reader will credit. Whatever there is of truth in these volumes has been foisted into a tale, which we are strongly inclined to attribute to some one of our English third-rate Novel writers ...
>
> We are indeed at a loss to explain how Don Esteban's English partner ... could expect that the most thoughtless watering-place reader in England would take the novel which he has provided for part and parcel of a matter-of-fact history ...

*   *   *

The *Quarterly* did not sow its seed on barren ground. Henry Colburn was renowned for publicizing his authors, and he had planned to bring out another book by the Spaniard. As for the novelist, Don Valentine Maria Llanos y Gutierrez, he proved himself a man of wit and accomplishment. There soon appeared on Gifford's desk a 32-page pamphlet:

APPENDIX III

LETTER

FROM

A SPANIARD

(THE AUTHOR OF DON ESTEBAN)

TO

THE EDITOR OF

THE QUARTERLY REVIEW

LONDON:

HENRY COLBURN, NEW BURLINGTON STREET.

1826.

The tone was vigorous and confident; the opening paragraph, written by the brother-in-law of Keats, is not without significance:

SIR:

As the judgment and impartiality by which your Review is guided, are now almost proverbial ... you will not feel surprised if I dispense here with those eulogiums to which either yourself, as the Editor of that Journal, or its learned contributors, may be entitled. Yet, I cannot refrain from observing, *en passant*, that it must be particularly gratifying to you to be thus surrounded by the very 'flower and cream' of all that is wise, learned, and original in the literary world. There is a gentleman, in particular, who must be to you an inexhaustible treasure, not only on account of his profound and varied learning in those subjects connected with English and foreign literature, morals, religion, and politics, but for the candour of his soul, the simplicity of his style, his acuteness of observation, his judiciousness, and unaffected modesty – I mean the critic who has had the goodness to review *Don Esteban*.

Point by point Llanos refuted the grammatical and typographical 'errors' imputed to him, the 'inaccurate' details of Spanish custom. Then he took the offensive: the *Quarterly* critic, he remarked, 'this accomplished Spanish scholar ... has even laid down new rules of pronunciation ... he has actually discovered in London an old Spanish poet, whose name no one ever heard.'

*   *   *

The pamphlet caused some dismay at the *Quarterly* office, and when *Sandoval; or the Freemason. By the Author of Don Esteban*, made its appearance later in the year, the *Quarterly* critic wrote rather lamely: 'We do not feel any very strong temptations to take up seriously the gauntlet so gallantly thrown down by the champion of this Joint Stock Company ... If it were worth our while, we could weary ourselves and our readers with proofs of what we assert ...'

The last words in the vendetta remained with Colburn. In *The New Monthly Magazine* (which, conveniently, he published) there appeared a glowing review of *Sandoval*: 'Since we are on the subject of this author's works, we may as well say', concluded Colburn, suavely, 'that he has lately published a letter to the Editor of the Quarterly Review, in answer to a recent attack in that publication on his former novel, *Don Esteban*. We think the Spaniard has greatly the advantage over his reviewer, whom he clearly proves to be at once ignorant of Spanish history and literature; and even of Spanish grammar and spelling.'

Don Valentine Maria Llanos y Gutierrez was himself highly satisfied; he had been handsomely paid for both his novels, and his literary future seemed bright. He was also, by now, the husband of Fanny Keats.

FANNY BRAWNE'S DESCENDANTS

Just before Christmas, 1950, I met Miss Gertrude Hathorn, the sister-in-law of Herbert Brawne-Lindon, in Folkestone. Miss Hathorn, then in her nineties, could dimly recall how, as a girl in Lausanne, she had visited Fanny Brawne's sister; she told me, too, how Herbert Brawne-Lindon and his wife had taken her on their travels and he had danced with her in Vienna when Strauss himself was conducting. One of the family showed me the solid Victorian houses in Augusta Gardens and Trinity Gardens, where Fanny Brawne's son had lived; and as I was told how he had played croquet and taken the same four-wheeler to the station every week on the way to his board meeting in London, I began to form a picture of a character from *The Forsyte Saga*.

Herbert Valentine Brawne-Lindon, Fanny Brawne's second son, was born in Bayonne on May 22nd, 1838; he was named, I believe, after Valentine Llanos, Fanny Keats's husband, who was 'everything that a Spanish cavalier ought to be'. He was educated in Germany, and returned to England with his family in 1859. That September he entered the Store Office, Woolwich, and early in 1863, as a third-class clerk, he was appointed to the War Office. He was still a minor civil servant when, about 1868, on holiday in France, he met his future wife. Euphemia Hathorn was the daughter of Vice-Admiral (later Admiral) George Hathorn, sometime captain of the port of Folkestone; and though no Victorian admiral would let his daughter marry a penurious third-class clerk, Herbert Lindon was sufficiently encouraged to stay with the Hathorns again the following year. He retired from the War Office, and in April 1880 he joined the Imperial Continental Gas Association as chief inspector of Continental accounts. His salary was handsome; and three months later, in July 1880, he married Euphemia Hathorn at St Mary Abbots, Kensington.

A photograph taken of him at about this time shows a prepossessing man, who bears a strong likeness, in features and expression, to the Fanny Brawne we know from the miniature. Moreover, Colvin, in his *Life* of Keats, declared that Fanny Brawne belonged to the 'English hawk blonde type, with aquiline nose and retreating forehead'; and someone who worked with Herbert Lindon and described him for me, wrote spontaneously: 'I well remember his appearance – a very hawk like countenance.' In tastes and talents, too, he resembled Fanny Brawne: he was a skilled draughtsman, and he illuminated manuscripts. He enjoyed classical music, and kept a permanent box at the Viennese State Opera as long as he lived in Vienna; he played the zither and was fond of singing. The hurdy-gurdy he abominated, and it was said that his children paid one to play in Augusta Gardens just to annoy him. Like his mother, he enjoyed travel: he regularly spent his holidays in Switzerland; and, like Fanny Brawne again, he was an able linguist. Long residence in Germany had made him bilingual in English and German, and he knew other languages well. One might add that his mother, who detested 'sloppy weather', would have appreciated the double windows which guarded him against the Folkestone climate. 'H. V. Lindon, when I knew him,' writes my correspondent, 'must have been in the 60's and was then grey haired ... I seem to remember that he had a short beard and moustache and hair rather long. Medium height ... head rather pushed forward, sharp nose and piercing eyes.' The description fits the photograph that was taken in old age; but the benevolence caught by the camera, and well known in the family, was sometimes hidden under an awe-inspiring manner. Fred Holland Day came to know it, to his cost, and Herbert Lindon's nephews and junior colleagues spoke of him deferentially, forty years after his death.

In December 1887, six months after the death of his mother's sister, Margaret, the last of the Brawne family, Herbert Lindon changed his name to Brawne-Lindon. He died in Folkestone on October 6th, 1909, in his seventy-second year. He is buried there, in the Cheriton Road cemetery.

Herbert Brawne-Lindon had lived to see his son at Harrow (where Mrs Keats's ambitions had lingered in vain); and, looking at the photographs of Louis da Cunha Brawne-Lindon, Harrovian and officer in the Royal Flying Corps, we see an even stronger resemblance to Fanny Brawne. The likeness is not only facial; and I would do more than record that he was born in Brussels in 1882 and died in Tangier in 1943. He inherited his grandmother's love of travel and her Brummell interest in fashion. He left no children, but his name was perpetuated by the Yacht Club International de Tanger, of which he was Commodore. Every year, in his honour, off the North African coast – at least until 1950 – the yachts of the Fish Class raced for the Brawne-Lindon Cup. And Louis Brawne-Lindon himself was well remembered:

Il était, en 1940, un homme d'une cinquantaine d'années. Il était grand (six feet) et fort maigre. Son visage long se terminait par un menton fort pointu. Des sourcils extrêmement épais couronnaient des yeux châtains très enfoncés dans leurs orbites. Ses pommettes fort saillantes lui donnaient un aspect assez particulier. Il avait le cheveu plutôt rare … Jeune, il dût être certainement très élégant … Sa mémoire est fort respectée par tous ceux qui l'ont connu au Club puisque c'était un gentleman et un excellent juge des Régates et qui, certainement, aurait pu faire mieux dans la vie si la maladie ne l'avait pris pour cible.

The portrait was drawn for me in 1950 by the Secretary of the Yacht Club at Tangier; he added: 'C'était un vrai gentleman, et ses manières étaient distinguées.' The comment would have delighted Fanny Brawne.

APPENDIX V
KEATS'S PUBLISHERS

Some years ago, in *Keats's Publisher*, Professor Edmund Blunden paid tribute to John Taylor, of Taylor and Hessey. The partnership of Taylor and Hessey was not only a business arrangement: the Taylor papers emphasize that, for some sixty years, the two men remained devoted friends. James Augustus Hessey was a ready correspondent, and his letters to his partner make some dark places plain.

They recall that Hessey's affection embraced all Taylor's family, and that Taylor took an interest in the Hesseys. In one of the earliest letters, sent on March 15th, 1811, Hessey writes from Retford (where he is staying with Taylor's parents): 'One thing I would beg of you as a great favor, – to give an eye to my brother on Sundays, and see that he goes to Church; and keep him from going out any where else.' When Taylor was away, in turn, Hessey kept a friendly eye on him; and on May 4th we find him writing to Taylor at 'Mr Falkners Bath (or Claverton)' a letter sealed appropriately with the motto *carpe diem*:

> I had quite given you up as lost and had almost, nay had quite, ordered a new suit of Black on the occasion, when I received a Letter from Woodhouse informing me that you are really alive but so changed as scarcely to be known for the same person – your Silence is to me a convincing proof that you are very happy as I who know what Claverton Valley is should not have doubted without such proof – But you seem to have forgotten the Joke I have to carry on at Retford ... I begin to fear your Father will *smoke* us if I go on any further ... Pray do steal an hour from —— and relieve me from this Embarrassment ... I long to hear an account of your Proceedings ...

In the postscript Hessey instructs his partner to fill up the blank in the letter 'with the Substantive *common* or *proper* which best suits it'. The joke was not without foundation; on May 13th another arch letter was dispatched to Bath:

> We have reason indeed to relish the Pleasures of the Country

when, wherever we go to enjoy them we find such valuable additions in the Society of our Friends – London was and perhaps ere long will be again the Scene of very high happiness of this Nature – The lovely plant you are going to transplant to this at present uninteresting Spot – will be the commencement of a garden of sweets which we may live to see flourishing even in London. So you affect to despise of the success of your Suit – well that looks pretty and all in regular Course – but if thou dost not hope thou dost not love – but I have given you my sentiments on this Subject already ... Keep possession of your Senses – that's all ...

On June 17th Hessey sent some brisk advice to an unsuccessful suitor: 'But what right have I to read lectures on love to so old a Practitioner? ... Depend upon it, unless you set about the matter in good earnest, you are just as far from your object now, as when I first knew you.' Did Taylor, disappointed at Claverton, consider consolation in Bakewell? The thought occurs; for on June 26th Hessey sends a letter to him in Derbyshire: 'Mr Hood was here this morning – he supposes you are staying *two Honeymoons* over, to take off the *Blushes* – I have some difficulty to make the people believe you are not on a matrimonial expedition, nor am I sure you may not have some such thing in view before you return.' Taylor was destined not to marry; but he remained susceptible; and the point is made in an early but undated letter from Hessey:

I have seen nothing of Miss Gabriel nor heard anything of Fanny Marriott – what should I hear – I saw Miss Crawford, and, *between ourselves*, was somewhat puzzled to find out what had so charmed you – you should always wear your Spectacles when you go on affairs of love – it may not add much to the loveliness of your own face but it will let you into a great many beauties in that of your charmer, or at all events will shew her as she is and not as your imagination may picture her. I shall send them in the parcel for your benefit on such occasions if such occur – You did not take them to *Wiltshire* ...

It was Hessey himself who announced, on September 8th, 1813, that he had got married:

You have no doubt heard from Bath the long expected, and, I may be allowed to say, happy event took place on Monday Morning last, and I suppose you will naturally be looking for some Intelligence respecting our Movements. Be it known to you then that my valuable charge and myself have reached this place [Richmond] on our way home and that we trust to have the pleasure of seeing you to-morrow ... And now, my dear Johnny, you will I dare say take it for granted that I should say I am very happy, and you would of course consider such an assertion to be just of as much value as that of a Benedick in the first week of his new State of Being is entitled to – I shall therefore only say that my happiness by far exceeds what I had expected to enjoy, and that, you will allow, is no trifling boast – and I think may venture to add that my dear Kate is as happy as myself ...

Hessey's happiness with Kate Falkner continued, as we learn from a letter of November 17th. The letter has additional interest as it mentions two future members of the Keats circle: Richard Woodhouse, the lawyer from Bath, and William Hilton, the historical painter. The doctor may well be identified as George Darling, Taylor and Hessey's physician, who would later advise Keats to winter in Italy.

I see very little of Woodhouse [writes Hessey] as this is Term Time, and the Doctor has not been here very lately ... I do not even know of the Success Hilton has obtained and which you hint at – we drank tea there on Saturday Evening and staid several hours without hearing any thing of it ...

On December 29th, from 93, Fleet Street, Hessey gives a glimpse of the offices which the poet would often visit:

The town was when I wrote last, enveloped in the thickest fog I ever saw and it has continued so ever since with no variety but that of dense and more dense – to-day I have been obliged to have the lamp lighted in the Back Room and to have Candles at both the Desks, and they have had Candles up stairs all day long ... Good news are just arrived from Lord Wellington – he has [word illegible] Soult completely with very trifling loss of British, only 300, but of the Spaniards and Portuguese 2700 – The French loss is said to be 10,000 ...

It was a time for celebration; and on January 31st, 1814, Hessey added:

'We went a Party of Ten on the Saturday Evening to see Mr Kemble in Coriolanus – the Woodhouses ... were among the Beaux, and we had a delightful Crush to get into the Pit – all were greatly delighted.' By the summer there was more personal cause for celebration: Kate Hessey gave birth to a son, and Taylor was asked to stand godfather: 'The Boy grows famously and behaves himself very well', Hessey reported on August 20th: 'The only Misfortune is he has no Name – but we only wait for your presence to confer one upon him – You were so kind as to offer your Sanction to his assuming the Christian Name and Office before he came into the world and I as readily accepted your friendly Offer – Mrs Grant is to occupy the post of Female Sponsor.'

Taylor himself (to judge from his letters to Bakewell) was not as fit and happy as his partner. On December 17th, 1816, he reported to his father: 'Anxiety makes me sometimes not so well as I have been, but I endeavour to be as easy as I can, and though it makes me look pale and poorly when I feel disturbed at anything yet I am in reality as well as usual.' But the Hesseys continued to flourish; in the spring of 1817 they moved to 'a country lodging' at Islington where Mrs Hessey made pies from pigeons dispatched by Taylor's mother and prepared for the birth of another child. Mrs Hessey, Taylor told his mother on April 30th, 'has a swelling of the glands on the side of the neck, which Mr Darling (my Doctor) attends her for, and he has greatly reduced it by a bath of acid water which effects surprising cures. I am astonished to see what good it has done Mrs De Wint'. But Dr Darling, who could alleviate the pains of Mrs Hessey and Mrs De Wint ('bow for me very genteelly to Mrs D.,' Keats would write), could offer no cure for Taylor's depression. 'The difference between our situation[s] ought to enter his head', Taylor wrote of Hessey, on June 25th, 1817. 'He has all his joys about him, I have but few at any time.' Taylor was living over the shop at 93, Fleet Street, and the premises were too small for himself and the Hessey family (returned, it seems, from rural Islington). 'I have not yet taken lodgings, from the difficulty I find in determining what part of the Town will be best for me', he told his father on December 11th. 'I am called upon so much by Authors and others that we actually want accommodation here, for I am compelled to see everybody either in the shop or in the Drawing Room, which is very inconvenient to Mrs H.' But the problem was soon solved: on December 17th he reported home:

I have met with a lodging which Hessey and all my friends think will suit exceedingly well. It is in Piccadilly, at Needham's and Dobson's, Silversmith's, next door but one to Bond Street on the North East. I have the use of two Sitting and 2 Bedrooms, with accomodations for a servant for 100 guineas a year ... I am now on the point of going, this evening I propose sleeping there, and Hilton is come here for the sake of accompanying me to take possession.

In his domestic correspondence Taylor had already reported his chief claim to eternity: on November 17th he had noted: 'We have three books engaged, Endymion by Keats for which we are to give £100, Hazlitt's lectures on English poetry £100, and Birkbeck's Tour in America which we publish for the author. He wants £500!!! for it.' He was not entirely happy about Keats's poem; for on May 25th, 1818, writing from Bakewell, his brother James inquired: 'What are your sentiments of Endymion now that it is made a Book of – Does it please you any better than it did at the time I left London[?]'

The Taylor papers shed a little more light on the publisher and his author, and the catalogue of Taylor's library, auctioned at Sotheby's in 1865, sends a tremor down the spine of the modern bibliophile. Lot 398, *Testamentum Novum, Gr. et Lat. Notis Leusdeni*, printed in Amsterdam in 1717, was inscribed 'John Keats, from his friend John Taylor'; and this, Taylor's parting gift to the poet, went for 5s. One would give rather more than 6s. 6d. today for the two volumes of Keats's *Poetical Works*, 1858, 'interleaved' by the man who had published most of them. And Hessey's letters to his partner reveal a trifle more about Keats's publisher. 'Have you found out "fit mate" yet?' Hessey inquires from Fleet Street on September 8th, 1818. On October 15th, reporting on other members of the Keats circle, he returns to the attack:

> Woodhouse is returned from Bath, blooming like a Rose ... Reynolds has not yet written the Article on Birkbeck – his mother has been very ill – but she is now better ... Miss Dyball is to be married on Saturday and is going to Lincoln to reside – another Chance gone!

The *London Magazine* (which they acquired on April 26th, 1821) brought Taylor and Hessey a new glory. On August 22nd Taylor was forced to deplore the lethargy of a famous contributor:

> One gentleman has begun a long article and we have included it in

our present number, and his copy comes in so very slow that I cannot complete anything more for want of it. That article will be found a very curious one, it is on Opium Eating. What singular men the literary world abounds with. I sometimes doubt whether my Opium Friend be in his senses ...

On October 8th, 1822, it was Hessey's turn to complain:

I have not heard from Ayton nor from Hazlitt yet, nor from De Quincey but we shall get on very well I have no doubt so you need not cumber yourself. Allan's Tale is a very interesting one but rather long – I send it for your father's Amusement and I think it will please him. It makes me quite sorry to throw away such excellent matter on a thankless undiscerning Public that will not give us encouragement enough to pay us our expenses. Baldwin accedes to the proposal of receiving a third of the first cost for his Copyright in any of the Papers we may wish to take out of the Magazine, so that is done, and Elia is printing. I have not seen Reynolds lately. He has married a wife &c. – He means I believe to take Kings Lodgings. I have put an advertisement in the Times for a Lodging for you in the Neighbourhood of Russell or Bedford Square ...

Hessey's affection for his partner was shown by his practical help and by his sympathy. The letter of January 7th, 1823, in which he laments the death of Taylor's father, is some measure of the relationship:

I will not attempt to express to you the painful feelings with which I received the intelligence of my much valued Friend's Departure – it has so long been the habit of my life to look upon myself as a member of your family and to encourage the fraternal and filial feelings proper to such a relation that I cannot help thinking that I too have lost a father who I am sure indulged the same kindly and affectionate feelings towards me ...

And Hessey also affords an incidental glimpse of James Rice, the most elusive, endearing friend of Keats:

I am very sorry [he writes to Taylor] to call your Attention to Business so soon again, but it is time that some decided steps be taken respecting the House in Waterloo Place and I cannot stir in it till I hear from you. Woodhouse and Percival and Rice and myself have all seen Oakley & Cox – Our friends are divided as to our ground being strong on the point of the extra Rent, and that we are entitled to compensation, which Oakley says he will not give.

Hessey's letter of April 3rd makes the friendship decidedly real to us: 'We were', he writes, 'much concerned at not seeing you at our Dinner Table today, for, besides other Considerations, we had a fine Sirloin with Yorkshire Trimmings which I think you would have liked.'

In 1825 Hessey left publishing; and in 1834 Taylor recorded that 'our Friend Hessey has taken a large old school at Hampstead'. This was Johnson's School in Haverstock Terrace, and among Hessey's pupils was Arthur Elley Finch, the cousin of Fanny Brawne. In 1840 Hessey moved to Huddersfield, where his son, Francis, had been appointed Principal of the Collegiate School; and here his former partner visited him. 'I often long for the opportunity of ... an evening's gossip with you all, as it was in the olden time', Hessey wrote on February 3rd, 1842. 'You must come and pay us a visit again next Summer.' But Huddersfield was too far from London; and on January 1st, 1843, Hessey lamented:

I cannot but be struck with this remarkable fact, that you and I, who used to see and hear so much of each other, have scarcely exchanged half a dozen words during as many months. This seems strange, and not quite right, and I take the blame to myself for having appeared to forget so old and valued a friend. Not that I have done so, for ... your 'counterfeit presentment' which adorns our mantelpiece continually brings you to my mind and often to our conversation.

Taylor replied, it seems, by sending his latest contribution to literature; and

I have been hoping to read your interesting Essay on the Greek article before I wrote to thank you for it [answered Hessey, on February 11th], but my time is so thoroughly occupied ... that I fear it will be long before I have the opportunity of giving it the careful perusal that it deserves ... I live as usual in too busy a whirl of occupation to wander in the regions of invention and discovery. The delightful task of rearing the tender thought is sufficient to engross all my poor powers. But I can take a lively interest in the pleasures of my old absent friend ...

Six years later, from Kensington (for Francis had become headmaster of Kensington School), Hessey wrote (December 18th, 1849): 'We *entirely calculate* on your spending your Christmas day with us.'

Taylor and Hessey, in their mid-Victorian days, grew increasingly pious; and Hessey's letters are full of resignation and aspiration. On June 5th, 1847, arranging a visit to Oxford, he recalled:

> it will be rather more than 40 years I think since you and I went together to the same interesting place. We were young then, and beginning the world hopeful and sanguine. We are now in all probability soon to quit it, many of the early hopes disappointed, much of the sanguine temperament abated, but I hope not quite without the 'good Hope' of a better life.

On April 24th, 1858, when his daughter had just died, he wrote:

> To her the change is one of unspeakable happiness – and this feeling gives us peace and calmness – We see also clearly that, as regards this life, the dear Child had only to look forward to years of trial and sickness, for her Malady, Dr Darling tells me, 'in the present state of our knowledge, was beyond the reach of art'.

Taylor, too, had domestic problems; and on July 16th, 1859, from Manningford Bruce, Pewsey, Wiltshire, Hessey wrote touchingly:

> My dear old Friend
> I have been thinking very much of you since I left Kensington, and wishing much to hear how you had arranged the Business about which you spoke to me. I cannot but feel anxious, and wish that it were in my power to minister to your Comfort. By and by, when we are nearer to each other, I may be able at least to exchange thoughts with you, and to share some of your troubles as well as your pleasures. I hope matters are arranged satisfactorily or in the way of being so. – I do not ask for any particulars, but if you have any agreeable intelligence pray give it me in a word – I have not spoken of it to any body not stated, but I cannot help feeling uncomfortable in the suspense.

How does this tropical weather suit you? Here in the country we feel almost burnt up – even as the old joke says

> The fishes beginning to sweat
> Cried, hang it, how hot we shall be.

The 'joke' had, oddly enough, been quoted by Keats in a letter to Jane Reynolds, more than thirty years earlier.

The reminiscence was no doubt unconscious; but sometimes Hessey was reminded more strongly of the poet and his circle:

In looking over some old papers the other day [he told Taylor on January 7th, 1857] I found a Sonnet of yours, beginning

> 'When Earth half formed lay dark and still, God said
> 'Let there be light,' &c.

Do you recollect it, and have you a copy of it? I don't know whether it was ever printed in the London Mag. but I think not. I also found some pretty lines on Hilton's Picture of Nature blowing bubbles, written by Richard Woodhouse. How these sudden meetings call back old Times and old Friends!

On December 14th, 1859, he recalled them yet again:

Thank you much for ... the Newspaper account of De Quincey. I wonder who wrote it – some old Acquaintance it must have been – and it is a fine Account of him and his frailties – of which you and I are cognizant. Poor fclow! How one wants to know, when these men of note drop off, what was the *real* Character of the inward man! You saw the Athenaeum I suppose – Mr Dilke's hand seems to be concerned in it, and it is quite as good as I expected, perhaps rather better – but there is a sort of sneer throughout. And Washington Irving is gone too! an amiable clever man, who has left a memory more desirable than that of our Opium friend.

There was something pathetic about the two ageing men, facing their own physical weaknesses:

I regret much that we see so little of each other [Hessey told Taylor on March 7th, 1860] – and as you are confined to the house and I do occasionally creep out I fear I am somewhat to blame – but my powers of locomotion are so small, and are attended with so much inconvenience and uneasiness, that I hope you make allowance for me . The doctors can do nothing for me, and appear to have given me up. Perhaps when Spring comes I may recover some of my former activity, but it makes me feel strangely old when I find myself unable to move about without pain … Your servant said you were a little better – I hope you have not been unwell since I saw you …

On May 25th, 1862, Kate Hessey died; and her husband wrote:

My dear and oldest Friend

It has pleased God to remove from me my dear Wife, the faithful and affectionate Companion for 49 years of my Joys and sorrows, my Trials and Blessings – I cannot let the sad Intelligence reach you from any one but myself – No one will or can feel it more than I am sure you will. She was mercifully spared much suffering, and died peacefully in the arms of her dear son so lately returned from India – I can scarcely realize our loss yet – we are mercifully supported and resigned to His will who does all things well

God bless you my dear old friend – pray for us

Ever your most affectionate friend

J. A. HESSEY.

I hope you are better – Frank told me you were poorly when he called last week.

Slightly alarmed by progress, Hessey continued his correspondence: 'I was glad to see that article in the Times about Huxley and his Monkey theory [this on October 13th, 1862]. Certainly these *wise men* do not raise one's opinion of the Species, and might rather be supposed in their own persons to afford arguments in favor of their asserted ancestry.' But modern times had distinct advantages:

You have not sent me your New Photograph Carte de Visite which I look for with much interest [he added ten days later]. I hope it is a good one. Mr Mayall I presume has not charged a 2^d Three Guineas

APPENDIX V

for the large Photograph in lieu of the first which was certainly very
unsatisfactory.

Thank you for your Gratulations on my new Honors as a Grandfather. I am not a little proud and thankful I assure you for Frank's
Happiness.

Mayall's photograph would soon be a necessary memorial. Taylor died
on July 5th, 1864. 'We have lost a truly good and great man', Francis
Hessey wrote to John Taylor, the publisher's nephew:

I scarcely know how to communicate to my Father the sad tidings
of his removal. They were indeed like Brothers through life: and I
fear, from the precarious state of my Father's health, that in death
they will be not long divided.

There is one little memorial of him that I should like to possess: –
and one that will be valueless to any one else. It is *his spectacles*. My
eyes and his were of the same degree of shortsightedness ...

Hessey survived until April 7th, 1870. It would be pleasant to think
that his son wore the spectacles through which John Taylor had, long ago,
assessed the beauties of Bath and the unpublished works of John Keats.

NOTES

DP   = Dilke Papers, British Museum.

HP   = Hunt Papers, British Museum.

KH   = Keats House, Hampstead.

N.M.M. = *The New Monthly Magazine.*

T.L.S. = *The Times Literary Supplement.*

NOTES

CHAPTER I (pages 17–24)

[1] Mrs Osborne to R. A. Walker, January 11th, 1931. She added: 'There was a General Peter Brown in the Peninsular War who was a cousin of my grandfather.' Mrs Osborne, writing to the author on October 11th, 1951, said that Brown's mother was a Miss Davis. 'Her father (a Welshman) gave her a grandfather clock for a wedding present (my brother has it) and I have never been clear whether he was himself a clock-maker. My brother has a goblet made of a coconut set in silver: on the silver mount is the Davis crest: I think a bird with a leafy twig in its beak.'

Mrs Osborne added that Brown's brother, Henry, 'was an officer on a ship and caught fever and died in the West Indies, he was under 20 years of age. My half-sister Laura (25 years older than I am and always a very great companion of my father) said he was a midshipman, his ship after leaving the West Indies returned to Europe and took part in the Battle of Trafalgar. Henry was a pretty youth according to his portrait.' Henry's portrait, and those of Brown's parents, are now at Keats House, Hampstead.

[2] Born 1742, died 1824.

[3] Born April 15th, 1765, daughter of Benjamin Blewford.

[4] Died June 13th, 1786.

[5] See Joanna Richardson, 'Some Dilke Papers', *T.L.S.*, August 29th, 1952.

[6] *The Athenaeum*, November 17th, 1883.

[7] *Holden's Triennial Directory*, 1802–4, gives Brown, Wellbank and Petyt, Russia, ship and insurance brokers, Sun Co., Threadneedle Street.

[8] *Walter Hazlebourn*, KII.

[9] *Holden's Triennial Directory*, 1802–4, gives Mrs Jane Brown at 8, Gray's Walk, Lambeth; presumably her husband was either in an asylum or dead.

[10] In January 1816, when her son James's will was proved, she was described as the wife of Joseph Rennoit Browne.

[11] *The Examiner*, January 16th, 1814.

[12] *The Champion*, January 15th, 1814.

[13] *The Times*, October 25th, 1815. James Brown had a creole daughter, Mary, of about 13, and left her £5,000 to be paid when she came of age. Her mother, a native of Benkulen, had already died, and the girl came to England, where she often visited (perhaps even lived with) Mrs John Brown. She was, in fact, an East Indian with a small fortune; and Henry Snook and William Dilke later tried to identify her with Keats's Charmian. See Richardson, 'Some Dilke Papers', loc. cit.

[14] *Holden's Triennial Directory*, 1809–11, lists Brown, —, Esq., Well Walk, Hampstead, among the private residents. John Brown had married Jane Mavor in Hampstead on August 21st, 1806 (according to *The Gentlemen's Magazine*). He died on March 8th, 1823, at Blandford Place, Regent's Park, leaving a widow, two sons and two daughters; his death was reported in *The Times* on March 14th.

CHAPTER 2 (pages 25–33)

[1] Brown, *Life of Keats*, 1841.

[2] 'Mountain Scenery', *N.M.M.*, 1822.

[3] Fragmentary copy of a letter on notepaper headed 'Belmont Castle, by Havant,' addressed to 'Master Henry Snook, care of Mr Snook, opposite the College, Eton, Windsor.' Richardson, 'Some Dilke Papers', loc. cit.

[4] Edmund Blunden, *Keats's Publisher*, p. 56. In a letter to his father on November 17th, 1817, Taylor had written: 'We have three books engaged, Endymion by Keats for which we are to

NOTES

give £100, Hazlitt's lectures on English poetry, £100, and Birkbeck's Tour in America which we publish for the author. He wants £500!!! for it.' Taylor was not entirely happy about *Endymion*, for on May 25th, 1818, his brother James wrote to him from Bakewell: 'What are your sentiments of Endymion now that it is made a Book of – Does it please you any better than it did at the time I left London?' (Taylor Papers.)

⁵ Sir Charles Dilke, *Papers of a Critic*, I, 7–8.

⁶ 'Valentine Writing', *N.M.M.*, 1822, IV, 228–31.

⁷ *Papers of a Critic*, I, 13.

⁸ Perhaps Miss Winter was related to Matthew Winter of Somerset House, who had appeared in *Boyle's Court Guide* the previous year; since Dilke worked at the Navy Pay Office, Somerset House, there might be some reason for the acquaintance. *The Times* of June 6th, 1808, records: 'On Saturday last, Robert Brown, Esq., of Kew, to Miss Elizabeth Winter, of Somerset House.' However, the Hampstead Return of Population, 1801, includes John Winter and John Barnes; and Pigot, 1833–4, records John Winter, solicitor, at 2, Great Winchester Street; and in 1838 J. Winter, jun., solicitor, is given at the same address. The rate-book for Broad Street Ward, September 29th, 1839 – March 25th, 1840, records Barnes, Winter, & Co. at this address; and the entry is amplified in the consolidated rates as Henry Hickman Barnes, Henry Winter and Fredk. Bernard. The Secretary to the Law Society, in a letter of February 1st, 1952, says that Henry Winter, admitted Trinity 1838, ceased to practise in 1852; Henry Barnes, admitted Michaelmas 1828, practised alone from 1830–7, and was a member of Barnes & Bernard from 1837–77. The firm of Barnes was dissolved in 1909.

The *East India Register and Directory* records that in 1815 Thomas Barnes was superintendent of convicts on the West Coast establishment of Sumatra, and that in 1818 Thomas Barnes was resident at Mocomoco while the Rev. Christopher Winter was chaplain on the West Coast establishment. It seems possible that they were connected with Miss Barnes and Miss Winter and were known to Brown through his brother James, who did not leave Fort Marlborouhg, Sumatra, until May 1815. It also seems possible that Miss Barnes was connected with Thomas Barnes, the editor of *The Times*, who was known to Dilke and Leigh Hunt.

⁹ *The Athenaeum*, 1890.

¹⁰ Keats met 'Mʳ Manker' at Dilke's on January 3rd, 1819, and again at this claret feast (letter of February 14th – May 3rd, 1819). Though Mancur reappears in Brown's correspondence, he remains among the more mysterious members of the Keats circle. *Holden's Directory* for 1809–11 records 'Mr Mancur, 10, Villa row, Walworth common'; and on October 21st, 1839, Mancur wrote to Brown from 25, Great Winchester Street, offering Carlino a post with an English engineer at Aix-la-Chapelle. On November 23rd, Brown added: 'Mancur always has been too sanguine.... Mancur's proposal to take you with him to Aix la Chappelle is almost madness – of which he has shown some equivocal symptoms in his own affairs.' One wonders if the sanguine friend was the John Henry Mancur whose *Henri Quatre: or, the Days of the League*, in three volumes, appeared in 1834; his *Constance, or, the Star of the Ballet* was published in 1848. The books appeared anonymously, and the British Museum say 'there is insufficient evidence to explain how the two novels were originally catalogued as by J. H. Mancur. The ascription is, however, repeated in several reference books, one of which states that *Henri Quatre* was first published in 1833 in Philadelphia, so that it seems possible that the author was an American.' A Mary Mancur, a widow, died at 30, Queen's Crescent, Haverstock Hill, in 1867, leaving a legacy to her nephews Stephen, George and Albert Mancur of Odessa Canada West: again a North American connection.

¹¹ See Joanna Richardson, 'The Context of a Song by Keats', *The Times*, June 3rd, 1953.

CHAPTER 3 (pages 34–36)

¹ Rice was the son of James Rice, a solicitor, probably of a Gloucestershire family; James Rice senior's will (Vaughan 119) mentions a freehold estate at Ashbrook, Glos., 'formerly in the tenure of John Howse, decd.', and the transactions of the Bristol and Gloucestershire Archaeological Society (1876–) contain many references to the Howse and Rice families. (See also Joanna Richardson, 'Keats's Friend, James Rice', *T.L.S.*, May 2nd, 1952.) Rice's relative, Francis Fladgate, the 'Frank Floodgate' of Keats's letters, came of a family which continued to be linked with the Keats circle. On January 7th, 1883, Sir Charles Dilke wrote to his brother Ashton: 'I will consult Fladgate. I forget the exact form in which your will now

stands.' On January 8th he added: 'I've sounded Willie Fladgate.' (*D.P.*, Add. MSS, 43, 902, ff. 126 and 128.) In Add. MSS 43, 930, f 5, Sir Charles names Fladgate among his executors (1905).
² Mrs Osborne to F. Edgcumbe, June 30th, 1939; Carlino's birth certificate describes him 'as the son of Charles Brown and Abigail Brown (born Donaghue)'.
³ Ibid.
⁴ 'Shakespeare's Bertram', *N.M.M.*, 1822, 481–5.

CHAPTER 4 (pages 37–41)

¹ Letter of February 11th, 1820.
² Miss W. Braithwaite, writing to the author in 1952, recalled that Brown's granddaughter had drawings of Danton, Marat and Robespierre done by Brown, 'but whether originals or copies from Hogarth, I cannot tell'.
³ Richardson, 'Some Dilke Papers', loc. cit. The British Record Society, Vol. 49, Chichester wills, includes that of Jane Snook, spinster, of Broadwater, in 1791. The earliest reference in the court books of the manor of Bedhampton, Hampshire, to the Snook family occurs in 1805 when John Snook the younger of Bedhampton, miller, took up 12 acres of copyhold land. He was admitted to other lands at intervals until 1817, being described as a merchant in the various transactions. In 1870 Henry Snook of Belmont Castle, Bedhampton, Esq., was admitted to land in Bedhampton which he enfranchised two years later. From the Poll Books in the Hampshire Record Office, it seems that a family of the name was settled at Portsea in the late eighteenth century.

CHAPTER 5 (pages 42–46)

¹ *L'Estrange, Life of Mary Russell Mitford*, II, 104–5.
² On July 12th, 1820, Mrs Gisborne 'drank tea at Mr Hunt's', and 'was much pained by the sight of poor Keats under sentence of death from Dr Lambe'. A sidelight on Dr Lambe may be found in Leigh Hunt's *The Examiner*, January 23rd, 1814:
'More than sixty individuals in London have for above three years subsisted wholly on vegetables, fruits and distilled water, enjoying during that period robust health, and an exception from those maladies which, under the direction of Dr LAMBE, led to their adoption of this simple regimen. Dr LAMBE carries his abstinence still further, by abstaining from all stimulants which excite thirst, so that we are told that he does not drink a pint of any liquid in a month.'
³ DP Letter of January 9th, 1856.
⁴ William Haslam was born in 1797 or '98 and, according to Brown, was a schoolfriend of Keats. He married on October 16th, 1819, and became a father about September 1820. In November 1822 *The Gentleman's Magazine* announced among its obituaries: 'Oct. 6. At Alton, Mary, wife of Mr William Haslam, Greenwich.' In May or June 1838 Brown dined with Haslam, and his wife and daughter, Annette Augusta, 'the latter a nice girl of about sixteen'. It is not clear if Annette was the daughter of the first Mrs Haslam or the second (whose name also was Mary). *Pigot's Directory* for 1832–4 listed Haslam and Bischoff, 8, Copthall Court, City; and in 1851 Haslam owned property in Glasshouse Street from the Manor of Stebon Heath, otherwise Stepney. But his affairs did not prosper, and the will he made on March 7th, 1851, hardly suggested a wealthy man. He left 'unto my dear wife all the household furniture plate linen china printed books and household effects about my dwelling house at Roupel Road', and the sum of one hundred pounds; he left the same to each of his three executors and ordered that the remainder should be divided between his wife and daughter. *The Gentleman's Magazine* for May recorded: 'March 28. In Roupel-road, Upper Tulse-hill, aged 53, William Haslam, esq. of Copthall-court.' The supplement to *The Times* for April 2nd adds that he was 'deeply lamented and deservedly regretted'.
⁵ Sharp, *Life of Joseph Severn*, 72–3.
⁶ Ibid., 86–7.
⁷ Rollins, *The Keats Circle*, I, 230.

NOTES

CHAPTER 6 (pages 47–52)

[1] Taylor Papers. These papers also include a letter from Taylor himself to Henry C. Hutchinson, March 30th, 1845: 'I was .. extremely interested with the Inscription on Keats's Tomb, of which I had never seen the full Particulars before. Mr Monckton Milnes M.P. for Pontefract is preparing for publication a work on the Life and writings of Keats, and if he has not a copy of this Inscription I will take care to send him a Transcript of yours. I think Severn the painter caused the Tomb to be erected and the Inscription to be engraved – he is now living in London. When you return to England I should like to introduce him to you.'

James Augustus Hessey, Taylor's partner, left publishing in 1825; and in 1834 Taylor wrote: 'Our Friend Hessey has taken a large old school at Hampstead.' This was Johnson's School in Haverstock Terrace, and among Hessey's pupils was Arthur Elley Finch, the cousin of Fanny Brawne. On July 29th, 1894, Finch wrote to The Hampstead and Highgate Express: 'I was a Johnson's boy when the school was transferred to James Hessey, the father of Archdeacon Hessey, headmaster of Merchant Taylors' School. Young Hessey (the future Archdeacon), fresh from his Oxford triumphs, came to assist his father in scholastic work, and I well remember how dazzled and delighted we boys were with his brilliant scholarship and engaging manners.'

For some account of Keats's publishers, see also Appendix V.

[2] Sharp, op. cit., 111.

[3] For Dilke's tributes to Hilton, see The Athenaeum, March 31st, 1832, and January 4th, 1840.

[4] The following contributions to the N.M.M. are possibly Charles Brown's; he is known to have signed with his own initials, and with the initials 'S.Y.' I think he may have used these last initials separately; the following articles by 'Y' recall his style and way of thinking.

1821

I	644–8	'Sonnettomania'
II	117–20	'Old Books'
	165–70	'Modern Fictions'
	220–24	'Blues and Anti-Blues'
	299–302	'Cant'
	349	'Song'
	561–71	'On the Superstitions of Highlanders and Londoners'. [This article is signed 'S'. The story of the fairy 'whose name sounded like Trilby' was told to Brown by a guide as he led him 'across the braes of Loch Carron'.]
	603–8	'On Affectation in Portraiture' [Signed C.B.]

1822

IV	13–16	'The Travelling propensities and opinions of John Bull'
	47–48	'Stanzas on Some Skulls in Beauley Abbey, near Inverness'. [Signed S.Y. A few of the lines had been written by Keats; the rest were written by Brown.]
	121–125	'Physiognomy and Craniology'
	144	'Sonnet: To Sleep'
	329–333	'State of Religion in the Highlands'. [Signed S. This article included part of the 'Lines Written in the Highlands After a Visit to Burns's Country', by Keats.]
	449	'Sonnet: On Darkness'
	469	'Sonnet'
	481–485	'Shakespeare's Bertram' [Signed S.]
	490	'Sonnet' [Signed B.]
V	47–8	'Love and Folly' [Signed S.Y.]
	140–5	'Dialogues of the Dead'. No. 1.
	314	'Song. The Devil and the Nuns' [Signed C.]

1823

VIII	32–8	'Actors and Theatricals'

236

1824

X   222   'Translation of Guidiccioni's Sonnet to Italy' [Signed S.]
        517–21   'National Prejudices'

[5] *The Times*, October 26th, 1821. The initials are probably those of William Steil, who lived for some time in Brown's part of the house; but, writing to Thomas Richards on November 15th, Brown still dated his letter from Hampstead.

[6] Among the figures of the past was old Mr Lewis, who had brought 'some fruit of the nicest kind', every day, to the dying Tom Keats. He was surely the Israel Lewis living in Well Walk, Hampstead, from 1815–21. On April 22nd, 1822, the 'capital and substantial Copyhold Mansion of the late Israel Lewis esq.', was advertised in *The Times*; it had 'a handsome approach, tastefully laid out, enclosed by a wall, with a southern aspect, commanding extensive views of the hills in Kent and Surrey', and among its amenities were 'a detached kitchen garden, enclosed with lofty walls covered with fruit trees in good bearing, with greenhouse, hothouse and cold bath'. It must have been on these premises that old Mr Lewis had picked the fruit for Keats's brother.

CHAPTER 7 (pages 53–54)

[1] His obituary appeared in *Blackwood's*, October 1824, p. 390.

[2] The Brown crest was a lion rampant bearing a fleur-de-lys; Brown called it 'the cat with the artichoke'. Mrs Osborne to R. A. Walker, January 11th, 1931.

CHAPTER 8 (pages 55–70)

[1] Severn to Sarah Severn, June 27th, 1823. Severn Letters, KH. For Severn's miniatures of Carlino, see Richardson, 'Two Miniatures of Carlino', *Keats–Shelley Memorial Bulletin*, No. V, 1953.

[2] Brown to Finch from Venice, September 19th, 1823. Finch Papers, Bodleian Library. Robert Finch had already touched the Keats circle at several points. On January 28th, 1814, he recorded (MS. Finch e. 6) that he had been to Drury Lane, and seen 'the pantomime of Harlequin Harper, in which there was not much to admire': this was the pantomime given with Brown's *Narensky*. The following year (MS. Finch e. 13) he recorded his arrival in Rome where on April 28th he 'fixed [his] abode' in lodgings which would gain immortality.

I pursued my enquiries after apartments, which are not at all scarce here at present, as there are very few foreigners in Rome. I call'd on Signor Vasi, who has a magazine of books and engravings here, and is a very amiable obliging old man. I chatted with him some time, after which he directed me to his niece, Signora Angeletti, with whom I have fix'd my abode. It is No 26, Piazza di Spagna at the corner of the steps leading up to the church of Santa Trinita del Monte, and I pay 19$ a week for four rooms elegantly furnish'd. The neatness which distinguishes every thing about the Signora is truly charming; and is rare in this country. Her husband has been some years in Portugal, and has quite neglected her. She is a lively, smart, handsome little woman, and has two nice daughters, who scarcely appear younger than their mother. She has much taste for the fine arts & draws and engraves.

On April 29th, Finch added:

The coffee-houses here are very imposing, so that I shall adopt the plan of breakfasting at home; which is convenient, as a flock of goats comes to the steps of my door every morning. Cows traverse the city also to give milk. My apartments are like a small house, there being no communication, so that I am quite independent and perfectly quiet.

On May 14th he was still gratified by his lodgings. In the centre of the Piazza di Spagna

NOTES

there was, he wrote, 'a plain fountain in the form of a boat designed by Bernini, the sound of which I find peculiarly agreeable, as I study in my room, which is very near it'. When Finch left the Piazza di Spagna he corresponded with Signora Angeletti (MS. Finch d. 1), and recommended the lodgings to his friends. Some of their correspondence was given in *Piazza di Spagna*, my feature programme on the English traveller in Rome, broadcast on the BBC Third Programme on September 28th, 1953. For Gisborne's letter to Finch about Keats, May 30th, 1821, see MS. Finch d. 8.

³ Severn to Charles Severn, January 11th, 1824. Severn Letters, KH.
⁴ Severn to his father, from Rome, January 11th, 1824. Severn Letters, KH.
⁵ HP, British Museum.
⁶ Leigh Hunt, *Autobiography*, II, 149 ff.
⁷ *N.M.M.*, 1822, V, 314.
⁸ Letter to Finch from L'Ariccia, October 4th, 1824, MS. Finch d. 15.
⁹ HP. Draft letter to Henry Leigh Hunt, November 17th, 1824.
¹⁰ Draft letter, December 30th, 1824. Ibid.
¹¹ Letter of February 12th, 1825. Ibid.
¹² Second draft of Brown's letter of February 12th, 1825, to John Hunt. Ibid.
¹³ Draft to John Hunt, April 2nd, 1825. Ibid.
¹⁴ Second draft of a letter to Leigh Hunt, June 8th, 1825. Ibid.
¹⁵ Leigh Hunt to Novello, June 16th, 1825. Ibid.
¹⁶ Brown to Hunt, September 24th, 1825. Ibid.
¹⁷ Brown to Hunt, October 20th, 1825. Ibid.
¹⁸ On November 24th, 1825, Brown wrote to Hunt: 'In my letter to [Colburn] I avoid mentioning how much per sheet I am to receive – and indeed it would be of no use, as I'm yet ignorant of the precise quantity printed, ... for Mancur won't let me into that secret.' Ibid.
¹⁹ Brown to Hunt, May 29th, 1826. Ibid.
²⁰ Ibid.
²¹ Ibid.
²² Ibid.
²³ Brown to Hunt, October 29th, 1826. Ibid.
²⁴ He had left at Bartholomewtide 1826.
²⁵ Mrs Osborne told R. A. Walker on June 28th, 1930: 'My father said there should be a portrait of Charles Brown in oils, he supposed it fell to some other member of the family.'
²⁶ Brown to Finch, April 14th, 1829. Finch and his wife and Miss Cobbett were godparents to Severn's daughter later this year, MS. Finch d. 15.
²⁷ HP. Brown to Hunt, August 9th, 1829.
²⁸ Mrs Osborne to the author, December 31st, 1951.
²⁹ Mrs Osborne to the author.
³⁰ HP. Postscript to a letter to Hunt, 1829.
³¹ Ibid.
³² Brown to Hunt, September 14th, 1829. Ibid.
³³ Mrs Osborne to the author, December 31st, 1951.

CHAPTER 9 (pages 71–78)

¹ Richardson, *Fanny Brawne*, 120–2. Mrs Osborne told the author, in a letter of December 12th, 1951, 'My grandfather liked an intellectual woman. On one occasion he met a husband and wife in Rome, Genoa, or somewhere, and he admired immensely the mental endowment of the wife and considered that she was simply thrown away on her mediocre husband.'
² Letter of January 17th, 1830.
³ See Appendix I.
⁴ Ibid.
⁵ Sharp, op. cit., 160.
⁶ See Appendix I.
⁷ Ibid.
⁸ Ibid.

NOTES

[9] Finch Papers.
[10] HP. Brown to Leigh Hunt, June 1st, 1830.
[11] Manuscript of Crabb Robinson's diary, Dr Williams Library.
[12] Ibid.

CHAPTER 10 (pages 79–81)

[1] See Richardson, 'Richard Woodhouse and his Family'. *Keats-Shelley Memorial Bulletin*, No. V, 1953.
[2] 'I have selected mottoes from the only three poets who were the staunch advocates of liberty, and my contemporaries ... Brown, who was very anxious about the fame of Keats, has given many of his MSS for the purpose.' Trelawny to Mary Shelley, October 28th, 1830. *Letters*, 135–6.
[3] Mrs Osborne to the author. On June 25th, 1952, she wrote: 'The Browns certainly knew both Chas. and Mary Lamb, and I think they first met at the Hunts' ... My father said Lamb hesitated in his speech, – he didn't really stammer.' On July 14th, 1952, Mrs Osborne added: 'Here is another little Lamb story. It may belong to the Xmas pudding visit. Two or three of the Hunt boys ... and Carlino were going down to stay with Trelawny: they intended while there to explore the old disused tin mines. Hunt forbad their doing so, he considered the mines unsafe and he said "Why do you want to go?" – They said "Oh, we wanted to be able to say we had been there." Lamb said "But can't you say it without going?" ' In the same letter Mrs Osborne gave further details about the Browns' visits to England during their Italian interlude: 'Carlino went to England to stay with his grandmother. I don't know when. His English was not good: his cousins used to pinch him to hear him say 'Oh you do hurt my meat." They were playing games which involved some dressing up. I suppose Carlino put on feminine clothes for his cousins chaffed him for looking like a girl. His grandmother said "Never mind Carlino, you are like your mother and she was a very pretty woman." ... C.B. and Carlino were on board a ship at a French port, about to leave for England. Carlino had been sent to bed so it must have been late ... Politics – legitimist, republican, royalist and so on in France were very confused, and there was a rumour that a little French princeling was being smuggled out of the country. It had been heard that a small boy – fair and slight and so on – was on this boat and two officials went to make enquiries. They insisted on seeing the boy so C.B. went down and told Carlino to dress and come up on deck and he added "take your time over it". I think the officials, from further enquiries, meanwhile decided it was not the same boy, and went away before he appeared on the scene. Now, – I am quite sure that my father told me that the young princeling in question was the Duc de Bordeaux, born in the same year as my father ... I know that I found that somewhere about 1833 the Duchesse de Berri attempted – for his own protection I think – to get the boy out of the country. If you could fix that date that would give the date of CB's and Carlino's visit.'
[4] 'In your last letter you were slowly recovering from what you called an attack of apoplexy but what I should have called epilepsy. Our old friend Brown was subject to those attacks for many years – but then he was a huge feeder – which you are not; he took little exercise ...' Trelawny to Captain Roberts, September 19th, 1858. *Letters*, 215. See also Sharp, 175–6.

CHAPTER 11 (pages 83–86)

[1] KH. Brown to Carlino, July 6th, 1839.
[2] KH. Carlino's memoir of his father.
[3] 'After breakfast ... [Severn] informs us that the foolish inscription on [Keats's] tomb is to be supersedd by one more worthy of him. He denies that Ks death was hastened by the *article* in the Quart. It appears that K: was by no means poor – but was fleeced by Haydon and Leigh Hunt – Brown is to write a life of him.' (Crabb Robinson MS. diary, May 6th, 1837.) In a letter to John Taylor, from Rome, on April 2nd, 1839, George Stothert writes that Severn 'talks of writing to you about the publication of Keats's works, but I don't know what he has to propose.' (Taylor Papers.)
[4] See Appendix II.

NOTES

CHAPTER 12 (pages 87–92)

[1] August 1838, 164 ff.
[2] January 3rd, 1839.
[3] June 30th, July 7th, 14th, 1838
[4] *Walter Hazlebourn*; KH. 'There is not more than one character yet introduced which is not drawn from an individual,' Brown told Carlino on January 27th, 1839, 'though Walter Hazlebourn himself is certainly not *myself*, – but I have taken the liberty of putting him in many of my situations.' (Letter at KH.)

CHAPTER 13 (pages 93–100)

[1] KH. Letter to Carlino, September 30th, 1838.
[2] August 16th, 1838.
[3] August 1st, 1839. In a letter to Carlino on August 3rd, now at Keats House, Brown wrote: 'Last Thursday I advertised for a companion boarder and lodger; this I determined to try, though I do not expect to find an applicant to my mind. My neighbours are all a strange unliterary set – tories into the bargain.' According to a further letter of September 22nd, there was no answer to the advertisement.
[4] KH. Letter of October 8th, 1838.
[5] Ibid. Letter of October 26th, 1838.
[6] Ibid. Letter of March 15th, 1839.
[7] Ibid. Letter of July 1st, 1839.
[8] Ibid. Letter of July 6th, 1839.
[9] Ibid. Letter to William Brown, July 30th, 1839.
[10] Ibid. Letter to Carlino, February 7th, 1839. On January 27th Brown had written: 'I keep but £90 [a year] for myself, exclusive of that which I earn by writing.'
[11] Ibid. Letter of September 22nd, 1839. Mrs Osborne told the author on December 12th, 1951: 'When my grandfather died, two of his nephews tried to get hold of the little estate he left: my father was illegitimate as his father and mother were married in the R.C. church – a marriage in those days not recognized by the State. They would have had the estate if my grandfather had not made a will, but he was businesslike and had made a will leaving his estate to his son.'
[12] Letter of September 22nd, 1839.
[13] KH. Letter of October 24th, 1839.
[14] Ibid. Letter of October 29th, 1839.
[15] Ibid. Letter of November 23rd, 1839.
[16] Ibid. Letter of March 30th, 1840.
[17] Ibid. Letter of March 10th, 1840.
[18] Ibid. Letter of March 30th, 1840.
[19] Ibid. Letter of April 16th, 1840.
[21] Ibid. Letter of April 17th, 1840.
[21] *The Devonport Independent*, May 23rd, 1840.
[22] KH. Letter of May 17th, 1840. Carlino says in his memoir that he had been offered a government appointment on the strength of Brown's electioneering squibs.
[23] Letter of May 17th, 1840.

CHAPTER 14 (pages 101–105)

[1] KH. Letter of October 8th, 1838. 'I would not oppose your leaving me for N.S. Wales, should nothing else nearer home offer itself.'
[2] Mrs Osborne to the author, December 31st, 1951.
[3] *Plymouth and Devonport Weekly Journal*, January 14th, 1841.
[4] Wells, *The History of Taranaki*, 63 ff.

NOTES

[5] KH. Letter of April 13th, 1841.
[6] Notebook now at Keats House.

CHAPTER 15 (pages 107–109)

[1] KH. Letter to Capt. Liardet, R.N., and Capt. King, R.N., March 11th, 1842.
[2] Ibid. Letter to Robert Skynner, February 26th, 1842.

CHAPTER 16 (pages 113–116)

[1] Richardson, 'New Light on Mr Abbey,' *Keats-Shelley Memorial Bulletin*, No. V, 1953.
[2] *The Keats Circle*, I, 318. Letter of March 19th, 1829.
[3] *The Athenaeum*, January 1832.
[4] John Hamilton Reynolds was born at Shrewsbury on September 9th, 1794, the son of G. C. Reynolds (a master at Shrewsbury from September 1798 to June 1805) and of Charlotte Reynolds, *née* Cox. In 1803 he entered Shrewsbury School, and on March 4th, 1806, when his father returned to London, he entered St Paul's School (Churchyard). At sixteen he became a junior clerk in the Amicable Insurance Office, and on August 31st, 1822, he married Eliza Powell Drewe, of Exeter. He entered the literary world, but in November 1817, with financial aid from Rice, he began to study law. *Pigot's Directory* for 1826–9 records Rice and Reynolds, attorneys, at 42, Great Marlborough Street. In 1832, the year of Rice's death, *Pigot's* list of attorneys includes John Hamilton Reynolds, 27, Golden Square; he was still there in 1834. In 1847 he went to the Isle of Wight, but 'he does not appear to have taken any part in civic activities', wrote Mr R. J. Eldridge, of Messrs James Eldridge and Sons, on September 11th, 1952. 'On June 23rd, 1849, he took a lease from Joseph Poore of the property now known as No. 36, St James Street, Newport, St James Street having formerly been known as Nodehill. The property is now our Newport offices. The lease was for seven years from the 24th June, 1849, at £35 a year, and the original lease signed by Reynolds is with the deeds of this property. I assume that Reynolds, in addition to using certain rooms here as County Court Offices, lived on the premises until his death.'
[5] See Appendix III.

CHAPTER 17 (pages 117–130)

[1] Letter of February 12th, 1833; *The Keats Circle*, II, 7.
[2] Chorley, *Autobiography*, I, 87 ff.
[3] Mitford, op. cit., III, 14–15.
[4] DP.
[5] Broderip, *Memorials of Thomas Hood*, pp. 116, 169.
[6] *The Keats Circle*, II, 160–1.
[7] Ibid., 222.
[8] January 1st, 1831.
[9] February 15th, 1840.
[10] The article appeared on March 31st, 1832. The obituary, in 1840, gives a glimpse of two members of the Keats circle. Lamenting 'one among the few British painters who bent his efforts to sustain Historical Art', it adds that Hilton 'died on Monday, the 30th of last month, aged fifty-three, at the house of his brother-in-law, Mr De Wint, the water-colourist. His death was occasioned by the asthma, and by the strength of his affections; for he never recovered the loss of a beautiful wife some years since. Though his frame was attenuated by sickness and sorrow, he retained the lustre of genius in his eye, and its brightness on his expansive forehead, to the last.'
[11] *Browning and Barrett Letters*, II, 135.
[12] DP. Add. MSS, 43, 910, f 77.
[13] Ibid. Add. MSS, 43, 909, f 145.

NOTES

[14] *Notes and Queries*, July 15th, 1876. DP. Add. MSS, 43, 910, f 74.
[15] Ibid. Add. MSS, 43, 935.
[16] Smyth, *Sir Rowland Hill*, 29.

CHAPTER 18 (pages 131–134)

[1] *Papers of a Critic*, I, 13.
[2] Ibid., I, 18–19.
[3] Ibid., 21–3.

CHAPTER 19 (pages 135–141)

[1] Obituaries in *The Gentleman's Magazine* and *The Annual Register*.
[2] Letter of November 4th, 1853, KH.
[3] DP. Add. MSS, 43, 930.
[4] Ibid. Add. MSS, 43, 899, f 2.
[5] Ibid. Add. MSS, 43, 899, f 4.
[6] Ibid. Add. MSS, 43, 930, f 19.
[7] Ibid. Add. MSS, 43, 899, f 247.
[8] Ibid. Add. MSS, 43, 899, f 184.
[9] Ibid. Add. MSS, 43, 899, f 246.
[10] KH. Letter of November 4th, 1853.
[11] DP. Add. MSS, 43, 930, f 249.
[12] Ibid. Letter of June 29th, 1854.
[13] Ibid. Letter of January 9th, 1856.
[14] Ibid. Letter of January 3rd, 1861. Ashton Dilke became a traveller and politician and died at Algiers on March 12th, 1883.
[15] Ibid. Letter of November 6th, 1862.
[16] Ibid. Letter of November 9th, 1862.

CHAPTER 20 (pages 142–153)

[1] August 13th, 1864.
[2] DP. Add. MSS, 43, 901, f 176.
[3] Ibid. Add MSS, 43, 930, f 111/2. Letter of January 4th, 1862.
[4] DP. Letter of December 6th, 1862.
[5] Ibid. Letter of December 11th, 1862.
[6] Ibid. Letter of December 12th, 1862.
[7] DP.
[8] Ibid. Letter of January 31st, 1863.
[9] DP.
[10] Ibid.
[11] Ibid.
[12] Ibid.
[13] DP. Add. MSS, 43, 929 f 31.
[14] DP. Letter of February 17th, 1864.
[15] Letter of February 1st, 1864.
[16] Letter of February 1864.
[17] DP.
[18] DP.
[19] DP.
[20] DP. Add. MSS, 43, 900, ff 35 and 38.
[21] DP.
[22] DP. Add. MSS, 43, 900, f 40.

NOTES

[23] Ibid., f 43.
[24] Ibid., f 45.
[25] Ibid., f 46.
[26] Ibid., f 47.
[27] DP. Add. MSS, 43, 901, f 202. Letter of August 12th, 1864.
[28] May 12th, 1869.
[29] DP. Add. MSS, 43, 931, ff 14, 18.

CHAPTER 21 (pages 157–162)

[1] December 17th, 1849.
[2] W. Cox Bennett, *The Worn Wedding Ring*, 1861.
[3] November 27th, 1852.

CHAPTER 22 (pages 163–170)

[1] *The Papers of a Critic*, I, 2.
[2] Correspondence at KH.
[3] March 2nd, 1878.
[4] Letter of March 15th, 1878. DP. Add. MSS, 43, 910, f 212.
[5] Correspondence at KH.
[6] Ibid.
[7] March 30th, 1878.
[8] March 1878.

CHAPTER 23 (pages 171–175)

[1] DP. Add. MSS, 43, 910, f 212.
[2] Ibid., f 282.
[3] March 8th, 1879.
[4] DP. Letter of February 21st, 1878. Add. MSS, 43, 910, f 204.
[5] DP. Add. MSS, 43, 910, ff 199 sqq. Add. MSS, 43, 898, f 279. See also Appendix IV.
[6] KH. Letter of November 4th, 1853.
[7] DP. Add. MSS, 43, 933, ff 116/7 and 119.
[8] Add. MSS, 43, 934, ff 107/110. In Add. MSS, 43, 932, f 126, William Dilke had discussed when the outcome of Waterloo (fought on June 18th, 1815) had been known in London: 'I should say the 21st ... I was in London under orders to rejoin the army when the news arrived, so I thought it time to be off; sent my servant and horse to Ramsgate and embarked thence for Ostend ... Lord Castlereagh passed me on the road to Paris, to which I was sent forward, at a post-house near Cambray, where I had a talk with him. Rothschild's agent got the news of Waterloo from Louis XVIII, to whom the Duke sent a message, and who was at Ghent with horses ready to take him to the coast. Rothschild thus gained twenty-four hours on the official report, for the Duke only wrote his despatches on the 19th, which were delivered at St James's Square by Major Percy to Lord Castlereagh before the Regent was informed at Carlton House.'
William Dilke married Mary Silverlock, a widow, and the offices of the West Sussex County Archivist contain a settlement on their marriage, May 21st, 1825, bearing their signatures and that of Dilke of Wentworth Place. On June 2nd Dilke wrote to his father in Chichester about William's marriage and a present of £80 worth of plate which the old man had asked him to buy for his younger son.

NOTES

CHAPTER 24 (pages 176–183)

¹ Introduction to Williamson, *The Keats Letters*.
² DP. Inventory of 76 Sloane Street, 1885. Add. MSS, 49, 421, 49, 422, 49, 423.
³ Correspondence at KH. The second letter is a draft; the third was written on May 4th, 1883. Fanny Llanos's reference to the cottage at West End is interesting. Dilke noted that when Brown returned from his northern tour in 1818, Mrs Brawne 'took another house at the top of Downshire Hill'; but *The Times* recorded on March 19th, 1822:

SMALL DETACHED COTTAGE, Hampstead. – To be LET, at West-End, Hampstead, ELM COTTAGE, on a repairing Lease of 8 years, at a low rent: containing 2 sitting rooms, 2 bed-rooms, 5 small ditto, kitchen, washhouse &c., and neat garden ...

The Brawnes had been living on a farm in the hamlet of West End in 1800, when Fanny was born.
⁴ See also Richardson, *Fanny Brawne*, 166–8, 169.
⁵ See Hyder E. Rollins: 'F. H. Day and Keats's Biography,' *Harvard Library Bulletin*, Vol. IV, No. 2, Spring 1950.
⁶ DP. Add. MSS, 43, 901, f 148.
⁷ Ibid, f 173.
⁸ DP. Add. MSS, 43, 929, f 1.
⁹ Ibid, f 20.
¹⁰ DP. Add. MSS, 43, 930.

CHAPTER 25 (pages 184–188)

¹ *Westminster Chimes, and Other Poems.*
² July 24th, 1891.
³ October 1891.
⁴ April 2nd, 1892.
⁵ *The Athenaeum*, January 7th, 1893. Mrs Osborne wrote to the author about 1951 or '52: 'My grandfather did not bring a big selection of books to N.Z. The best, I suppose, were his copies of Italian classics, which were leather-bound. When we came to Auckland and were intending to go to South Africa a friend of my father's advised my mother to send the bulk of the books home to Christie's. He undertook the sending. Well, the books were sent. We retained only those written by or connected with Keats, Shelley, Lamb, Hunt, and so on. All the Italian classics went. In the course of time, after expenses had been paid and the books sold my mother received the sum of 7s. 6d. That was, I suppose, in the year 1902. I don't know if the books were sent to Christie's or to some other dealer. I don't suppose they could be traced now. Brown frequently pasted inside his books a visiting card with "Mr Charles Brown" on it in copperplate. The friend who sent the books home was Dr John Logan Campbell. He may have sent them in the name of the Campbell Ehrenfried Company.' In a letter of June 25th, 1952, Mrs Osborne added: 'When my father died, ... we had a very thorough clearing up, heaps of things were burned, – I mean papers, memos and so on.'
⁶ May 1894.
⁷ July 25th, 1894.

SELECTED BIBLIOGRAPHY

ADAMI, MARIE
  Fanny Keats (Murray, 1937)

ARNOLD, MATTHEW
  Essays in Criticism, second series (Macmillan, 1888)

BAINES, F. E.
  Records of the Manor, Parish, and Borough of Hampstead (Whittaker, 1890)

BARRATT, THOMAS J.
  The Annals of Hampstead (A. & C. Black, 1912)

BEDDOES, T. L.
  Complete Works (Fanfrolico Press, n.d.)

BLESSINGTON, COUNTESS OF
  The Idler in Italy, 2nd edition (Colburn, 1839)

BLUNDEN, EDMUND
  Keats's Publisher (Cape, 1936)

BRODERIP, MRS (ed.)
  Memorials of Thomas Hood (Moxon, 1860)

BROWNING, ROBERT
  Letters of Robert Browning and Elizabeth Barrett Browning, 1845–1846 (Smith, Elder, 1899)

CHORLEY, H. F.
  Autobiography (Bentley, 1873)

COBBETT, JAMES P.
  Journal of a Tour in Italy ([Printed for the author], 1830)

COLVIN, SIDNEY
  Keats, ('English Men of Letters', Macmillan, 1887 and 1889)
  John Keats, 3rd edition (Macmillan, 1920)

COWDEN CLARKE, C. and M.
  Recollections of Writers, 2nd edition. (Sampson Low, 1878)

DILKE, SIR C. W.
  The Papers of a Critic (Murray, 1875)

SELECTED BIBLIOGRAPHY

FIELDS, MRS J. T.
  A Shelf of Old Books (Osgood, McIlvaine, 1894)
FORMAN, H. BUXTON (ed.)
  The Works of John Keats, 1883, etc. (O.U.P.)
  The Life of Percy Bysshe Shelley, by Medwin (O.U.P., 1913)
FORMAN, M. BUXTON (ed.)
  Some Letters and Miscellanea of Charles Brown (O.U.P., 1937)
  The Letters of John Keats (O.U.P., 1942)
FORSTER, JOHN
  Walter Savage Landor (Chapman & Hall, 1895)
FRANCIS, JOHN C.
  John Francis, publisher of The Athenaeum (Bentley, 1888)
GWYNN, S., and TUCKWELL, G. M.
  The Life of the Rt. Hon. Sir Charles W. Dilke (Murray, 1917)
HAZLITT, W.
  Notes of a Journey through France and Italy (Hunt & Clarke, 1826)
HEWLETT, DOROTHY
  A Life of John Keats (Hurst & Blackett, 1950)
HEWLETT, H. G.
  Henry Fothergill Chorley (Bentley, 1873)
HOGG, T. J.
  Two Hundred and Nine Days (Hunt & Clarke, 1827)
HOWITT, MARGARET
  Mary Howitt: an Autobiography (Isbister, 1889)
HOWITT, WILLIAM
  Homes and Haunts of the Most Eminent British Poets (Bentley, 1847, and Routledge, 1863)
  The Northern Heights of London (Longmans, Green, 1869)
HUNT, LEIGH
  Foliage (Ollier, 1818)
  Lord Byron and some of his Contemporaries, 2nd edition (Colburn, 1828)
  Imagination and Fancy (Smith, Elder, 1844)
INGPEN, ROGER (ed.)
  The Autobiography of Leigh Hunt (Archibald Constable, 1903)
  The Letters of Percy Bysshe Shelley (Bell, 1914)

JENKINS, ROY
  Sir Charles Dilke. A Victorian Tragedy (Collins, 1958)

JERROLD, W. (ed.)
  The Complete Poetical Works of Thomas Hood (O.U.P., 1906)
  Thomas Hood: his Life and Times (Alston Rivers, 1907)

KEATS, JOHN
  Poetical Works with a Memoir by Richard Monckton Milnes, new
    edition (Moxon, 1854)
  Poetical Works with a Life by Jas. R. Lowell (Boston, Little, Brown,
    1854)
  Poetical Works (ed.) W. M. Rossetti (Moxon, 1872)
  Poetical Works chronologically arranged and edited, with a memoir, by
    Lord Houghton (Bell, 1876), 3rd edition (Bell, 1883)
  Poems with the annotations of Lord Houghton and a memoir by
    Jno. Gilmer Speed (N.Y., Dodd, Mead, 1883)
  Poetical Works with an introductory sketch by John Hogben (Walter
    Scott, 1885)
  Poetical Works with a memoir by James Russell Lowell (N.Y., Hurst,
    1890)
  Complete Works edited by H. Buxton Forman (Glasgow, Gowans &
    Gray, 1901)
  Poems with an introduction by Laurence Binyon (Methuen, 1903)
  Poetical Works (ed.) H. W. Garrod (O.U.P., 1939)

L'ESTRANGE, A. G. (ed.)
  The Life of Mary Russell Mitford (Bentley, 1870)

MARCHLAND, LESLIE A.
  The Athenaeum, A Mirror of Victorian Culture (Chapel Hill, University
    of North Carolina Press, 1941)

MARKHAM, VIOLET R.
  Paxton and the Bachelor Duke (Hodder & Stoughton, 1935)

MASSINGHAM, H. J.
  The Friend of Shelley: A Memoir of Edward John Trelawny (Cobden-
    Sanderson, 1930)

MILNES, RICHARD MONCKTON (LORD HOUGHTON)
  Life, Letters and Literary Remains of John Keats (Moxon, 1848)
247

SELECTED BIBLIOGRAPHY

MORGAN, LADY
   Memoirs (Allen, 1862)

MORLEY, E. J. (ed.)
   Henry Crabb Robinson on Books and their Writers (Dent, 1938)

NITCHIE, ELIZABETH
   The Reverend Colonel Finch (N.Y., Columbia University Press, 1940)

PENDERED, MARY L.
   John Martin, Painter (Hurst & Blackett, 1923)

PENROSE, A. P. D. (ed.)
   The Autobiography of Benjamin Robert Haydon (Bell, 1927)

PROCTOR, B. W.
   An Autobiographical Fragment (Bell, 1877)

RICHARDSON, JOANNA
   Fanny Brawne: a Biography (Thames & Hudson, 1952)

ROLLINS, HYDER EDWARD (ed.)
   The Keats Circle: Letters and Papers, 1816–1878 (Cambridge, Mass., Harvard University Press, 1948)

   and STEPHEN MAXWELL PARRISH
   Keats and the Bostonians (Cambridge, Mass., Harvard University Press, 1951

ROSSETTI, W. M.
   Life of John Keats ('Great Writers' ... Scott, 1887)

SEVERN, JOSEPH
   Letters to H. Buxton Forman (Oxford. Printed for private circulation, 1933)

SHARP, WILLIAM
   Life and Letters of Joseph Severn (Sampson Low, 1892)

SMYTH, ELEANOR C.
   Sir Rowland Hill (Fisher Unwin, 1907)

TRELAWNY, E. J.
   Letters, H. Buxton Forman (ed.) (O.U.P., 1910)

TUCKERMAN, HENRY T.
   Thoughts on the Poets (Slater, 1850)

SELECTED BIBLIOGRAPHY

WELLS, B.

The History of Taranaki (New Zealand, Edmonson & Avery, 1878)

WILLIAMSON, G. C.

The Keats Letters, Papers and Other Relics Forming the Dilke Bequest in the Hampstead Public Libraries (John Lane, 1914)

INDEX

251

INDEX

133, 135–6, 138, 139, 152–3; marriage, 133; and CWD, 30, 131–4, 135–6, 138, 142, 153; and Sir Charles Dilke, 152–3; death of, 152–3

Dilke, Sir Charles W. (grandson of CWD): birth, 133; childhood, 133; education, 134, 137, 141, 142–51; character, 164, 176, 178, 181–3; career, 171, 181; marriage, 181; and Sir Wentworth Dilke, 152–3; and CWD, 133–53, 162, 181–2; and Crawford case, 181; and FB, 163–70, 173, 177, 179–80, 182–3; and JK, 153, 162, 163–83; 184–5, 187; death, 188; and Harry Buxton Forman, 167, 172, 176–83

Dilke, Christopher, 13

Dilke, Ethel, Lady, 13

Dilke, Fisher, 18

Dilke, Jane (sister of CWD), 18

Dilke, Sir John, 13

Dilke, Letitia (sister of CWD): see Snook, Mrs John

Dilke, Maria (wife of CWD): appearance, 22, 122; character, 22, 114, 116, 119, 122; and JK, 27, 28, 124, 125; and FB, 115–16, 124; quoted, 28, 125; death and burial, 135, 151; mentioned, 113, 118

Dilke, Mary (Lady Wentworth Dilke): character, 135, 138; marriage, 133; and CWD, 134; death, 138

Dilke Papers, the, 13 and *passim*

Dilke, Mrs C. W. (mother of CWD), 18, 115, 133

Dilke, William (brother of CWD): birth, 18; career, 174–5, 243; and CAB, 18–19; and Sir Charles Dilke, 175; and Harry Buxton Forman, 170; marriage, 243; death, 175

Dilke, Mrs William, 243

Dillon, Lord: CAB's friendship with, 64

Dodsley's Old Plays: CWD edits, 23, 128

Don Esteban, 213–15

Donohue, Abigail: *see* Brown, Abigail

D'Orsay, Count, 64

Drewe, Eliza Powell (Mrs J. H. Reynolds), 241

Duncombe, Mrs, 133

EASTLAKE, Charles: CAB entertains, 57

Elm Cottage: site discussed, 179, 244

Endymion, 27, 105, 158, 160, 161, 187

Essays, Letters from Abroad: Robert Finch and, 55, 157; FB and, 159; JK misrepresented in, 158–9

Etty, William: CAB entertains, 56

Evans, Frederick: colleague of CWD, 127

Ewing, William: kindness to JK, 51; and FB, 51; and CAB, 51, 57

Examiner, The: financial problems of, 59–61; mentioned, 21, 63

Fairy Bird's Song, The: JK writes, 33; CAB publishes, 210

Fairy Dirge: JK writes, 33; CAB publishes, 211

Fairies' Triumph, The: CAB writes, 32–3; JK contributes to, 32–3

Finch, Arthur Elley (cousin of FB), 225

Finch Papers, the, 13 and *passim*

Finch, the Rev. Col. Robert: character, 55, 57; career, 55; CAB's friendship with, 55, 57, 67–8, 76, 77–8; wild account of JK, 55, 157, 158–9; death of, 77

Finch, Mrs Robert: 55, 57

Flitcroft, Henry, 18

Florence: CAB lives in, 55–81; CWD visits, 64–5; described, 61, 67

Folkard, Miss, 133

Forman, Harry Buxton: character, 165–6, 174; career, 165–6; and JK–FB letters, 165–166, 168–70, 188; and Sir Charles Dilke, 167, 172, 176–83; and FK, 166, 168–9, 171–172, 178–9; death, 165; quoted, 169, 176, 179–80, 188; mentioned, 187

Forman, Maurice Buxton, 13

Forster, John: fails to edit *The Daily News,* 126; collaborates with CWD, 127

Francis, John: and CWD, 128, 152

GALIGNANI: to publish JK's poems, 71

Gibson, John: CAB entertains, 57; and JK, 57, 85

Gisborne, John, 157

Gisborne, Mrs John, 43

Gladstone, W. E.: admires JK, 172

Gore, Mrs: CWD condemns her stories, 120–1

Graham, William: fabricates Severn interview, 186

Granville, Lord, 142

Gravesend, 41

Gray's Walk, Lambeth: CAB born in, 17

Great Exhibition (1851), 135–6, 152

Great Smith Street: CWD living in, 30, 38

Griffin, Gerald, 159

Guy Mannering: CAB tells JK, 26

Hampshire Chronicle, The, 142

Hampstead: described, 23, 40

Hampstead and Highgate Express, The, 187

Harlequin Harper, 20, 237

Haslam, William: discussed, 45, 235; quoted, 45

Hathorn, Euphemia: *see* Brawne-Lindon, Mrs Herbert

Hathorn, Admiral George, 216

Hathorn, Miss Gertrude, 216

Haydon, Benjamin Robert, 23

Hazlitt, William: meets CAB in Italy, 61

INDEX

INDEX

INDEX